LEGAL ENVIRONMENT, HUMAN RIGHTS RESPONSIBILITY AND DEVELOPMENT IN THE OIL INDUSTRY: THE CASE OF CAMEROON

RICHARD MBIFI

LEGAL ENVIRONMENT, HUMAN RIGHTS RESPONSIBILITY AND DEVELOPMENT IN THE OIL INDUSTRY: THE CASE OF CAMEROON

GALDA VERLAG 2024

Bibliografische Information der Deutschen Nationalbibliothek
Die Deutsche Nationalbibliothek verzeichnet diese Publikation in der Deutschen Nationalbibliografie; detaillierte bibliografische Daten sind im Internet über https://dnb.de.

ISBN 978-3-96203-362-0 (Print)
ISBN 978-3-96203-363-7 (Ebook)

DEDICATION

This study is dedicated to my children:

Emmanuel Ntangsu,

Emmanuella Menyi,

Frank Vughose-Achu,

And

Kelam Perland.

PREFACE

The primary objective of this book is to promote a favourable business climate in the oil industry in Cameroon. Cameroon is an oil producing nation and like other oil producing countries in Africa, is under a "resource curse". The citizenry does not benefit from the exploitation of this resource. From a human rights perspective, the exploitation does not take into consideration the third-generation rights of Cameroonians namely the right to development, the right to a healthy environment, to name just a couple.

The primary obligation for the protection, promotion and fulfillment of these human rights rests on the State, but non-State actors like multinational corporations, whose activities have a high potential to violate human rights, equally have an obligation to do same. This means that the State and oil multinational corporations have a collective responsibility to ensure that the activities associated with oil exploration and exploitation should be carried out in such a way that will enhance the enjoyment of the right to development and the right to a healthy environment. The government has set up a National Commission on Human Rights and Freedoms, whose National Plan of Action on Promotion and Protection of Human Rights actually addresses the issue of third generation human rights, but does not seem to implicate non- state actors in the exercise. This National Plan of Action does not seem to articulate the fact that human rights need to be the concern of business in Cameroon. The Ministry of Justice also produces an annual report on the human rights situation in Cameroon. But the focus is more on Civil and Political rights, leaving out third-generation human rights, whereas in fact, third-generation human rights are violated as a result of the activities of the extractive industry.

National and international norms exist, regulating this industry, with provisions aimed at enhancing the enjoyment of these rights. But the reality is the contrary. The question which begs an answer is: why the mismatch between the system of legal control and the reality on the ground. For example, why is it that the local communities and Cameroonians in general still live in abject misery and in environments degrading daily whereas oil exploitation is done within a legal framework which provides benchmarks for best practices. Are human rights the concern of business in Cameroon?

This study argues that the right to development and the right to a healthy environment are inalienable rights of Cameroonians. Based on the principle of Permanent Sovereignty over Natural Resources, this study argues that the petroleum oil found in Cameroon belongs to Cameroonians. Thus, its exploration and exploitation are supposed to be done with due regard for their human rights. The study, however, establishes that the inalienable human rights of Cameroonians highlighted herein above are violated by the activities of the oil industry. The study goes ahead to argue that the system put in place to monitor the activities of the oil industry is inefficient. In this connection, it argues that Cameroon has a weak judiciary system wherein the justiciability of human rights is problematic. It also argues that the legislature whose role consists of representing constituent interests, making or shaping public policy and overseeing policy implementation, is largely captured by the executive in an advancing democracy like Cameroon.

The study recommends the need for greater monitoring of the industry. This entails a vibrant and independent legislature which will propose more effective laws, and challenge oil contracts and conventions whose clauses supersede national laws. It is important to indicate that Article 45 of the Cameroon Constitution provides that duly approved or ratified treaties and international agreements shall, following their publication, override national laws, provided the other party implements the said treaty or agreement. However, agreements entered into by Cameroon and private business entities are not international agreements for the purpose of Article 45. The study equally recommends transparency in the management of the oil industry. Consequently, it recommends greater commitment to the EITI principles. The study equally argues in favour of an effective judiciary void of corruption. It concludes by pointing out that if comprehensive laws are put in place and the executive and oil companies forced to align with them, then local communities and Cameroonians in general will enjoy the right to development and live in a healthy environment.

The book is a useful source of reference for studmets of Oil and Gas Law, legal practitioners, judges and investors who actively do deal with issues related to the extractive industry in Cameroon particularly the exploitation of oil.

MBIFI Richard, Ph.D

ACKNOWLEDGEMENTS

I will first and foremost thank God the Almighty for making it possible for this work to see the light of day. May God Almighty richly bless, strengthen and replenish all those who took an interest in this work.

I want to express my most profound gratitude to my academic mentor, Professor Martha S. Tumnde née Njikam for her valuable and enriching comments throughout this work as she made me burn the mid-night candle.

A special thank you to Professor Claire Moore Dickerson (Breaux Professor of Business Law, Tulane Law School, New Orleans, USA, who was very instrumental in sharpening the outline and most of the ideas in this work. Words cannot express my inner feelings but let me say that I really appreciate the enormous sacrifices which she made in all dimensions. Indeed, she initiated and coordinated the academic sojourn which took me to the USA in the Summer of 2010. In this connection, I owe a debt of gratitude to Jane Johnston, Professor's Assistant, Tulane Law School (USA), Professor Oliver A. Houck of Tulane Law School, The Staff of Howard Tilton Library – Tulane University, Cathy Dunn (Lodging Department) of Tulane University, The Staff of the Library of the University of Wisconsin, Whitewater (USA), Professor Taku Michael of Louisiana State University (USA).

I owe a debt of gratitude to Barrister Peter M. Tumnde for his contributions and mind-searching comments which gave the work a practical dimension.

I would also like to thank friends and Colleagues with whom I have had stimulating discussions over the past years on this work. They include friends like Barrister Michael Etie Enow (New Orleans-Louisiana USA an expert in Petroleum law, with whom I had quite exciting and stimulating discussions and who also left his personal library at my disposal), Kimbeng Frankline

(Compliance Specialist, Louisiana Housing Finance Agency USA), Tran Viet Ha (Legal Expert in the Ministry of Transport of Vietnam, with whom I shared an apartment while at Tulane), and colleagues of the Englis Law Department of the Faculty of Law and Political Science – University of Dschang, Cameroon who offered suggestions to ameliorate the work, and also took off time to read the proofs. They include Professors Nah Thomas, Simon Tabe Tabe, Djieufack Roland, Mbetiji Michel, Ghogomu Dorothy, and Dr./Barrister Tantoh A. C. I owe a debt of gratitude to Professor Lambi Cornelius Mr Ngaba Donatus and Mr Abono Humphrey for reading through the proofs.

A study of this nature would not have been possible without the encouragement of the hardworking staff of the Department of English Law, University of Buea, Cameroon notably Professors Fonyam J. B, Amadou Mounkare, Ekome Emmanuel, Dr. Konneh Gaspa, and especially Professor Yanou Michael whose stimulating Course on Law and Development during my tenure in the University provided a springboard for this work.

Finally, to my wife Glory Wopong, and Children (Ntangsu, Menyi and Vughose-Achu), I say thank you for inspiring me and having to make do with my long absence from home.

TABLE OF CASES

TABLE OF STATUTES AND INTERNATIONAL INSTRUMENTS

LIST OF ABBREVIATIONS

ATCA	Alien Tort Claims Act
BLCC	Bakweri Land Claims Committee
BP	British Petroleum
BTC	Baku-Tbilisi - Ceyhan
CC	Concession Contracts
CCEIG	Commercial Companies and Economic Interest Groups
CCR	Corporate Community Relations
CDC	Cameroon Development Corporation
CEMAC	Communautaire Economique et Monetaire en Afrique Central
CEO	Chief Executive Officer
CERES	Coalition for Environmentally Responsive Economies
CESR	Center for Economic and Social Rights
CFCs	Chlorofluorocarbons
COTCO	Cameroon Oil Transportation Company
CPR	Civil and Political Rights
CSOs	Civil Society Organisations
CSR	Corporate Social Responsibility
EA	Environmental Assessment
EC	European Community
ECJ	European Court of Justice
EDF	Environmental Defence Fund
EIA	Environmental Impact Assessment
EITI	Extractive Industries Transparency Initiative
EMP	Environmental Management Plan
ESCOR	Economic and Social Council Organisation Resolution

ESR	Economic and Social Rights
EU	European Union
GA	General Assembly
GATT	General Agreement on Trade and Tarrif
GOPAC	Global Organization of Parliamentarians Against Corruption
GRI	Global Reporting Initiative
HCFCs	Hydro Fluorocarbons
HIPC	Heavily Indebted Poor Countries
HLTF	High-Level Task Force
ICCPR	International Convention on Civil and Political Rights
ICESCR	International Convention on Economic Social and Cultural Rights
ICJ	International Court of Justice
IFC	International Finance Corporation
ILM	International Legal Material
ILO	International Labour Organisation
IMF	International Monetary Fund
LIAMCO	Libyan American Oil Company
MAI	Multilateral Agreement on Investment
MNCs	Multinational Corporations
MOSOP	Movement for the Survival of Ogoni People
NDI	National Democratic Institute for International Affairs
NGOs	Non Governmental Organizations
NNPC	Nigerian National Petroleum Company
NOCs	National Oil Companies
NOW	Nonhazardous Oil field Waste
NO_x	Nitrogen Oxides
OAU	Organization of African Unity
OECD	Organization for Economic Co-operation and Development
OEWG	Open-Ended Working Group
OGEL	Oil, Gas and Environmental Law
OHADA	Organisation pour L'Harmonisation en Afrique du Droit des Affaire
P&A	Plugging and Abandonment
PSC	Production Sharing Contracts
PSNR	Permanent Sovereignty over Natural Resources
PWYP	Publish What You Pay

RENAC	Réseau National Anti Corruption
RTD	Right To Development
SADC-PF Forum	Southern Africa Development Community Parliamentary
SERAC	Social and Economic Rights Action Center
SNH	Societe Nationale des Hydrocabure
SONARA	Societe Nationale de Rafinage
SO_x	Sulphur Oxides
SPDC	Shell Petroleum Development Company
TNCs	Transnational Corporations
TOTCO	Tchad Oil Transportation Company
UA	Uniform Act
UDHR	Universal Declaration on Human Rights
UN	United Nations
UNCED	United Nations Commission on Environment and Development
UNCLOS	United Nations Convention on Law of the Sea
UNDP	United Nations Development Programme
UNEP	United Nations Environmental Programme
UNESCO	United Nations Educational, Scientific and Cultural Organisation
UNGA	United Nations General Assembly
USAID	United States Agency for International Development
VOCs	Volatile Organic Compounds
WCED	World Commission on Environment and Development
WTO	World Trade Organization

CONTENTS

1

GENERAL INTRODUCTION

1.0. Background of the Study

The concept of sustainable development has been at the base of almost all Cameroonian government's action in recent times. In principle, the government is bent on alleviating poverty so as to give her citizens the opportunity to live dignified lives. In line with this objective, the government has engaged herself in several policies aimed at attracting foreign capital which is believed[1] to be a booster to economic development. At national level, the government is making efforts to put in place a healthy environment for business.[2] At regional level, Cameroon is leaving no stone unturned. She is a member of the Central African Economic and Monetary Community (better known by its French acronym CEMAC), whose aim[3] is to eliminate barriers to trade so as to boost development in the sub-region. She is equally a member of the Organization for the Harmonisation of Business Laws in Africa (better known by its French

[1] Borris Martor, 'The OHADA Legal Harmonisation Process : The Benefits for Africa's Development', Proceedings of the OHADA Seminar held at the University of Buea, Cameroon, under the theme : The Applicability of the OHADA Treaty in Cameroon, at P 17 – 27, September 2003.

[2] Law n° 2002/004 of 19th April 2002 instituting the investment charter of Cameroon. This law contains incentives to foreign investor who wish to invest in Cameroon.

[3] See Regulation No. 17/99/CEMAC – 020-CM-03 Relating to the CEMAC investment Charter. See precisely the Preamble (The Investment Charter shall be a general framework involving all the measures aimed at ameliorating the institutional, fiscal and financial environment of enterprises so as to promote growth and diversify the economies of member states, on the basis of a better definition of the role of the state and of a harmonious development of the private sector through investments from within and outside the country.)

acronym OHADA)[4] which was created by the Port Louis Treaty.[5] The primary objective of this treaty was to provide a secured legal and judicial environment for companies to operate in.[6] This was to be done through the elaboration and adoption of simple modern and common rules adapted to their economies, by setting up appropriate judicial procedures and by encouraging arbitration for the settlement of contractual disputes.[7] In furtherance of this objective, nine Uniform Acts have been adopted till date. Prominent among them and of interest to this work, is the Uniform Act on Commercial Companies and Economic Interest Groups which governs among other things,[8] the creation, management and dissolution of private as well as public companies.

The phenomenon of Multinational Corporations (MNCs) bringing foreign capital into an emerging economy like Cameroon has resulted in Oil companies establishing and operating therein. Cameroon is endowed with the rich natural resource, namely, oil.[9] Though being the smallest producer on the African continent,[10] producing just 4% of Nigeria's production,[11] oil is the country's main source of exchange earnings and government revenue.[12]

Oil exploration which began in Cameroon in the early 1950s is carried out by both national and international companies through joint venture agreements with the state, represented by "Societe Nationale des Hydrocabures" (SNH).[13] By virtue of Law No. 99/013 of 22nd December 1999, instituting the Petroleum Code of Cameroon, oil companies are expected to choose between two types of contracts, namely, Concession Contract (CC) and Production Sharing Contracts (PSC).[14]

Oil reserves are located both offshore and onshore in three major oil producing basins, namely, Logone Birni basin in the northern part of the country, the Rio del Rey basin in the Niger Delta and the Douala/Kribi-

[4] Organisation pour L'Harmonisation en Afrique du Droit des Affaires

[5] The Treaty was signed in October 1993 and ratified in 1997.

[6] Art. 1 of the OHADA Treaty.

[7] Ibid. The rules adopted are known as Uniform Acts.

[8] It also covers to some degree sole proprietorship.

[9] She is among the eight oil producing countries of the Gulf of Guinea.

[10] Albert G. Zeufack, "Governance and Oil Revenue in Cameroon", GDN Tenth Annual Conference, 'Natural Resources and Development', February 1 – 5, 2009, Kuwait.

[11] Ibid.

[12] Ibid., Produces 87000 b/d; 55% of export revenue and 33 % of government revenue.

[13] Created in 1980, it reports directly to the President of the Republic.

[14] Art. 13 (1) of Law No. 99/013 of 22nd December 1999.

Campo basin. Cameroon witnessed an oil boom in 1979 which was, however, short-lived as she started noticing a decline soon after in 1985.[15] However, recent events in the industry are indicative of another oil boom in a not-too-distant future.[16] This will definitely lead to an increase in oil revenue for the government. This is because the government is a party to the joint ventures, through SNH.

The oil industry engages in both upstream[17] and downstream[18] activities which have socio-economic and environmental consequences on the citizenry. This means that the oil companies involved are supposed to conduct their activities taking cognizance of the human rights and environmental concerns of the local communities hosting their activities and the citizenry in general.[19]

The incorporation of socio-economic and environmental concerns in business is a long-standing issue which emanates from the concept of Corporate Social Responsibility (CSR). This concept has been defined by the World Business Council for Sustainable Development[20] in the report 'Making Good Business Sense' as:

> The continuing commitment by business to behave ethically and contribute to economic development while improving the quality of life of the work force and their families as well as that of the local community and society at large.

This definition notwithstanding, the shareholder primacy people[21] argue that a healthy business sector should try to create wealth for the benefit of all constituencies in society.[22] In other words, they claim that it is socially

---

[15] Albert G. Zeufack, supra note 10.

[16] The recent handing over of Bakassi to Cameroon after the Cameroon-Nigeria border dispute, onshore exploration by Kosmos Energy and Euroil, and event in the Gulf of Guinea.

[17] Exploration and exploitation of petroleum oil.

[18] Commercialization of petroleum oil.

[19] Iris Halpern, "Tracing the Contours of Transnational Corporation's Human Rights Obligations in the Twenty-First Century", (2008), 14 Buff. Hum. Rts L. Rev. 129.

[20] www.wbes.org, (last consulted on June 19th 2010)

[21] Milton Friedman, "The Social Responsibility of Business is to increase its Profit", N. Y. Times Magazine, September 13, 1970, cited by Claire Moore Dickerson, in Harmonizing Business Laws in Africa: OHADA Calls the Tune, (2005), Colombia Journal of Transnational Law.

[22] Ibid.

responsible for a corporation to make profit.[23] The focus of this work is on the enhancement of the socio-economic and environmental conditions of the local communities wherein oil company activities are located and the citizenry in general.

The importance of a natural resource like oil cannot be overemphasised. The industry remains till date the largest and most important world-wide.[24] The industry has continuously provided for the world's energy and industrial needs from transport to agriculture.[25] The fact that the industry touches both the rich and the poor, has made it an indispensable one in man's daily life. It provides fuel for the daily transportation of the rich and the poor alike. However, a perplexing problem facing Cameroon is that of converting valuable revenue from oil exploitation into an enhanced standard of living for the citizenry. Menacham Katz[26] considers this kind of scenario as an "oil curse", which denotes an inverse relationship with the rich natural resource, and economic development. Notwithstanding the substantial revenue generated from the resource over the years, Cameroon has remained a low-income country with relatively weak social indicators.[27] Exploration and exploitation of oil comes with the need to protect the environment. The challenges range from oil spillage which destroys land and sea environment, to gas flaring which pollutes the air. With increased onshore exploration and recently constructed Chad-Cameroon pipeline project, the connection between the people, government and the oil companies is likely to become even greater. The socio-economic and environmental impact is going to be more glaring than where exploitation is predominantly offshore. E. Royce, the Republican Chairman of the US House of Representatives Sub-committee on Africa puts the issue tellingly: "things usually work fairly well if you're out in deep water"[28]

Activities involved in oil exploitation ought to bring prosperity and the

---

[23] Ibid.

[24] Razav H, 'Financing Oil and Gas Projects in Developing Countries', http://www.worldbank.org/faudd/English/0696/article/08069.htm, (last consulted on June 19 2010).

[25] Dias A., Oil and Human Rights, http://www.gasandoil.com/ogel/samples/frearticles/articles32.htm, (last consulted on June 18 2010).

[26] Menacham Katz, Lifting the Oil Curse, Improving Petroleum Revenue Management in Sub-Saharan Africa, International Monetary Fund Publication Service, Washington DC, 2004

[27] See Zeufack, supra note 10 ; See also Michel Kounou, Petrole et Pauvrete au Sud du Sahara, Edition Cle, Yaounde, 2006

[28] Dieterich J., "The Gulf of Guinea and the Global Oil Market: Supply and Demand", (2004), Traub-Merz and Yates, No. 5,28.

elevation of the human person, with the highest consideration for the human rights of the owners of the oil. Most constitutions vest the ownership of mineral rights in the State but the State only holds such for the people as an expression of the collective will of the people. [29] Unfortunately, the reverse seems to be the case as vulnerable communities in many oil producing countries especially in emerging markets are paying a tragic price to satisfy the world's need for oil.[30] Oil where found, seems to bring a curse to the people by putting them at the losing end of an apparent conspiracy between the oil company and the host government, both of whom need the oil to satisfy other objectives.[31]

For example, in Cameroon, oil exploration in the Rio del Rey basin for close to fifty years has hardly helped promote prosperity in Ndian Division. Millions of barrels of oil have been pumped out of the area but the people have little to show for it.[32] Indeed, this region contributes about 75% of the total crude oil produced in Cameroon;[33] yet, it does not have even a single kilometre of tarred road and ironically does not have even a single filling station. The oil companies operating in this area have constantly been criticised, in relation to human rights issues. According to Paul Sieghart,[34] human rights may be said to constitute the claims made by persons on their communities. He has stressed a three-fold categorisation of human rights, based on the time at which these rights emerged on the scene. This division of human rights into three generations was first proposed by Karel Vasak, a Czech Jurist at the International Institute of Human Rights in Strasbourg. His division followed the three cardinal principles of the French Revolution: Liberty, Equality and Fraternity. We therefore have first, second and third generation human rights. First generation rights consist of Civil and Political Rights, whereas second generation rights deal with socio-cultural and economic rights. For their part,

---

[29]See Preamble of Cameroon Constitution; See also the discussion on Permanent sovereignty over Natural Resources, infra chapter three.

[30]See Oil Curse, http://www.tufts.edu,stories/091603oilcurse.htm (last consulted on June 19, 2010)

[31]For example, revenue from the Chad-Cameroon pipeline project is geared more towards the payment of Cameroon's external debt than taking care of the needs of the local populations living along the pipeline.

[32]Andrew Edimo, "Oil Production in Our Land", The Frontier Telegraph, A bi-monthly News Publication, http://www.thefrontiertelegraph.com/content/oil oil in our land.html (last accessed on February 19 2010)

[33]Ibid.

[34]International law of Human Rights, Oxford University Press, 1983.

third generation rights which are the most recent to have emerged and which are of concern to this work, stress solidarity, developmental and environmental issues.[35] Claire M. Dickerson[36] considers this as an evolution of human rights norms from individual to increasingly collective rights.

Human rights are increasingly linked to development. Consequently, development is not possible without the protection of human rights. The relationship between human rights and development occupies a prominent place in international discourse. The African Union looks at development and human rights as inseparable.[37] One way by which it links development to human rights is through the concept of sustainable development. Consequently, sustainable development has been interpreted to include human rights protection. The right to development as a human right has generated a lot of controversy.[38] While the African Union (AU) argues for the existence of this right in international law,[39] scholars like Jack Donnelly[40] and P. Alston[41] think that the right is both conceptually and practically misguided. However, others believe that the right to development is an inalienable human right which has passed into customary international law by virtue of the fact that the African Charter on Human and People's Rights recognises it (Art. 21 & 22), coupled with the fact that the right was promulgated in the Declaration on the Right to Development and reaffirmed in the Vienna Declaration and Programme of Action on RTD[42] making it part of the international human rights framework.

In a nutshell, Cameroon is an oil producing nation and like other oil producing countries in Africa, it is under a "resource curse". The citizenry

[35] These rights include the right to have roads, schools, health services, the right to live a dignified life, the right to live in peace, the right to live in a healthy environment, etc.

[36] Claire Moore Dickerson, "Cultural and Trans-Border Effects: Northern Individualism Meets Third Generation Human Rights", (2002), 54 Rutgers Law Review.

[37] Art. 22 of the African Charter on Human and People's Rights. See generally U. O. Umozurike, "The African Charter on Human and Peoples' Rights", (1983), 77 American Journal of International Law, 902.

[38] See discussion on this controversy in Chapter four infra.

[39] Supra note 37.

[40] Jack Donnelly, Universal Human Rights Theory and Practice, NY: Cornell University Press, 2004.

[41] Philip Alston, Non-state Actors and Human Rights, Oxford University Press, 2005.

[42] Art. 12

does not benefit from the exploitation of this resource. From a human rights perspective, the exploitation does not take into consideration the third-generation rights of Cameroonians, namely, the right to development, the right to a healthy environment, only to name a couple.

The primary obligation for the protection, promotion and fulfillment of these human rights rests on the state but non-state actors like multinational corporations, whose activities have a high potential to violate human rights, equally have an obligation to do same. This means that the State and oil multinational corporations have a collective responsibility to ensure that the activities associated with oil exploration and exploitation should be carried out in such a way as to enhance the enjoyment of the right to development and the right to a healthy environment. National and international legislation exists, regulating this industry, with provisions aimed at enhancing the enjoyment of these rights. But the reality is the contrary. The question which demands an answer is: why is there a mismatch between the system of legal control and the reality on the ground? For example, why is it that the local communities and Cameroonians in general still live in abject misery and in environments degrading daily, whereas oil exploitation is done within a legal framework which provides benchmarks for best practices?

This research will be guided among others, by the following questions:

- Is there regulation (domestic and international) conferring rights on Cameroonians, accruing from the extractive industry?
- What is the legal responsibility of oil multinationals and the State?
- How effective is the mechanism for enforcement/monitoring of the regulatory framework?
- Is there transparency in the management of the oil industry?

This work is based on the following hypotheses:

1. Oil exploitation has an impact on social and economic rights.
2. The rights to development and to a healthy environment are available to Cameroonians under municipal as well as international laws governing the extractive industries.

Corporate human rights violation is rife in Cameroon. In response, the government is making efforts both domestically and internationally, to promote and protect human rights. The government has set up a National

Commission on Human Rights and Freedoms, whose National Plan of Action on Promotion and Protection of Human Rights addresses the issue of third generation human rights, but does not seem to implicate non- state actors in the exercise.

The Ministry of Justice also produces an annual report on the human rights situation in Cameroon. But the focus is more on Civil and Political rights, leaving out third generation human rights. Third generation human rights are nevertheless in fact violated as a result of the activities of the extractive industry.

The main objective of this study therefore is to contribute to the understanding of human rights issues in relation to the exploitation of oil in Cameroon. The study has been prompted because of evidence to the effect that natural resource exploitation and human rights are strongly interconnected. The dominant argument or view is that natural resource exploitation should be done in a way that will enhance the enjoyment of the rights to development and to a healthy environment. The idea is to show that the respect for human rights when exploiting natural resources can go a long way to reduce poverty and raise the standard of living and create a healthy environment for development within the community from which the resources are exploited. This is consistent with the government policy of poverty reduction and development and it is also in consonance with the human right to development.

This research makes use of both the quantitative and qualitative approaches to data collection relevant to legal research. The researcher carried out a survey of the opinions of the representatives of the local communities from which oil is exploited and of the opinions of the representatives of the companies engaged in the exploitation. This gives a first-hand impression about their perception of oil exploitation and the issue of human rights.

The responses from the unstructured surveys and interviews constitute one of the primary sources of materials for the work. The study also makes use of cases, statutes, and codes of ethics, which are also primary sources of materials.

In addition, extensive use has been made of secondary sources of data on the subject. Here, reliance was placed on text books, journal articles, conference reports, newspaper reports and other documents found relevant to the work. Extensive use was equally made of electronic libraries and internet sources. Data bases like WESTLAW and LEXIS were of great assistance.

Significantly, this study touches on a socio-legal issue which is very topical, in the sense that it is a serious issue of concern in the business world. Corporate managers and shareholders are at daggers-drawn over the raison d'être of putting human rights issues or ethical behaviour in business. The traditional view is that a company is owned by shareholders, and their directors must manage the company in the interest of shareholders. However, some corporate managers and scholars are pressing the point that it makes good business sense for companies to be socially responsible.

The primary responsibility to ensure sustainable development and the respect for human rights lies on the government. The government of Cameroon has done and is doing a lot in an attempt at attracting foreign investments which is a necessary ingredient for development. The government needs to understand that left on their own, investors pursuing only their own short-term self-interests will pursue only the goal of profit maximisation and disregard the costs on society. This work therefore highlights the need to balance the objective of attracting multinationals with the need for them to behave responsibly, with the overall goal of achieving sustainable development. The government cannot be trying to achieve development by attracting multinationals, and at the same time fail to provide concrete guidelines for the conduct that will avoid the abuse of human rights, which is one of the indicators of development. It will also be in the interest of the government to put in place a mechanism to audit the responsible behaviour of these multinationals so as to avoid the kind of situation which led to the hanging of Ken Saro Wiwa in Nigeria and the consequent suspension of Nigeria from the Commonwealth of Nations. Ken Saro Wiwa was the leader of the movement for the survival of the Ogoni People (MOSOP), in Nigeria. Today, in the Ndian Division of Cameroon, we hear of the Oroko Cultural Association, whose USA chapter has intimated its intention of making its voice heard in relation to their claims for oil royalties. The manner through which they intend to "make their voices heard", has not been indicated. One can therefore not jettison the possibility of the use of violence in "making their voices heard". This research highlights a framework which will balance profitability for the oil multinationals and quality life for Cameroonians so as to avoid the "Ken Saro Wiwa" kind of situation in Cameroon with its attendant consequences. An added significance to government may be for the benefit of one of its agencies, for example, the National Commission on Human Rights and Freedoms. This agency will discover that their activities are supposed to extend to cover legal persons like MNCs and not be limited only to physical persons. Once MNC subsidiaries are incorporated in Cameroon, they acquire Cameroonian nationality and thus come within their jurisdiction. MNCs are legal persons with a high potential to disregard the human rights of physical persons. Consequently, it ought to be the responsibility of the National Commission on Human Rights and Freedoms to ensure that they do not jeopardise the rights of others. With respect to oil MNCs, it is important to indicate that corporate social responsibility concerns giving back to society a share of what companies have benefited from it.

This work throws light on the fact that it makes good business sense to give back to the society what has been taken from it. Consequently, if local communities living around the oil installation are comfortable, then the installations and personnel will be secured and vice versa. Hence, the kind of situation in the Delta region of Nigeria will not likely occur for example, in the Rio del Rey basin. Thus, compliance with their elaborated codes of conduct, as well as with other human rights legislation, will be in the overall interest of the oil multinational.

There is abundant literature on the link between human rights, corporate social responsibility and development. In the light of this existing literature, Juliette Bennett[43], discusses the role of Mutinational Corporations (MNCs) in promoting peace and avoiding conflicts. She asserts that CSR has an interest in leveraging skills and impact to promote stability in their area of operation not only because it is the right thing to do but because it makes good business sense. She also points out that traditional human rights groups are agreed that MNCs operating across borders should bear some responsibility for the effects of their operations on local environments and communities. She warns that the international business community will be blamed for conditions that lead to violent conflicts if they fail to promote greater economic inclusion and social justice in their operations. However, she remains optimistic that while corporate activity may be disruptive of local communities, it can also help provide stability by addressing the concerns of those who are neglected and excluded from the benefits of the operations. Stability as in physical stability since it will reduce the likelihood of rebellion against the offending MNC, or the government that did not protect the indigenes adequately against marauding MNCs. She goes ahead to discuss the concept of a social licence under which MNCs should work, which goes hand-in-hand with local capacity building efforts.

[43]'Multinational Corporations, Social Responsibility and Conflict', (2002), Journal of International Affairs,Vol.55,No.2, Pg 393 – 410.

Bede O. N. Nwette[44], points out that respect for human rights and sustainable development ought to be the basic tenets upon which any country rich in natural resources must base any investment in its extraction. He acknowledges that this is not the case pointing out that instead of sustainable development and human rights, investments associated with oil exploitation have rather come to be a curse to the people, depriving them of their basic rights. He assesses the role of the MNCs involved in the BTC Pipeline project as well as the host government, the IFC and other multilateral agencies with a view to ascertaining whether these roles conform to human rights and sustainable development standards. He concludes by acknowledging that human rights and sustainable development is a sore point for MNCs especially in relation to oil and pipeline development, pointing out that the steps taken by various stakeholders to depart from the pathetic stories of the past have proven not to be enough to give glaring hope for human rights and sustainable development.

Jan Wouters and Leen Chaanet[45], underscore that corporations often bring significant benefits to the state where they operate by raising the standard of living thus making a positive contribution to the development of the country. They, however, assert that these corporations may also cause human rights problems, acknowledging that the current state of international law regarding the position of MNCs is strikingly unbalanced. In this connection, they point out that international law still focuses too much on protecting the rights of corporations, but lags far behind in regulating their responsibilities. Thus, in the absence of hard laws, the tendency has been to resort to soft norms (which are legally non binding), when dealing with corporate human rights responsibility. They go further to indicate that since human rights are a core principle of the European Union (EU), it has a special responsibility to ensure that they are protected. Against this backdrop, the EU addresses the issue of corporate human rights responsibilities as part of its CSR policy.

Angela M. Bushnell[46] opens by pointing out that the process of exploiting natural resource is almost inevitably linked or interwoven with the violations of

[44]'Human Rights and the International Natural Resource Industry. MNCs and the BTC Pipeline Project : Any Hope For Human Rights and Sustainable Development?', (2004), OGEL, VOL. 2, Issue 4.

[45]'Corporate Human Rights Responsibility: A European Perspective', (2008), Nw U. J of Int'l Human Rights.

[46]'The Emerging Custom of Human Rights – Based Development: A Model Agreement for Successful Exploitation Lake Albert's Oil Reserves.' (2009), Nw U. J of Int'l Human Rights, 327.

the human rights of the local populations. She catalogues the possible human rights violations that can occur with the development of a natural resource like oil, and discusses the growing pattern and practice of using human rights–based planning in international development agreements, concluding that this could help to prevent the violations of the recognised human rights of local populations. She further underscores the fact that human rights–based development is an emerging custom, because it is a common practice adopted by different states in similar situations. According to her, a custom in international law is established by a pattern of state practice that implies general consent to a binding principle of international law.

International custom is a recognized source of international law.[47] Customary international law is "the practices or customs of states, undertaken based on a sense of legal obligation."[48] Customary international law can be recognized when there is evidence of extensive and uniform practice of the rule and it must appear that the practice comes from a sense of legal obligation (*opinio juris*).[49] In practice, complete uniformity is not required; substantial uniformity is sufficient.[50] It is generally required that the conduct is consistent with the customary rule and that inconsistencies with the rule are treated as a breach of the rule, not as recognition of a new rule.[51] Uniform practice can further be shown through State legislation and court decisions, as well as statements by government officials, among other things.[52] *Opinio juris* may be established using, inter alia, policy statements and press releases, international and national judicial decisions, and resolutions and declarations by the United Nations. When a significant number of states have accepted a treaty, it may become customary law under which even non-parties to the treaty may be bound.[53] The International Court of Justice allows treaties to be evidence of both state practice and *opinio juris*.[54] Once customary law is recognized, all

[47] David Hunter, James Salzman & Durwood Zaelke, International Environmental Law and Policy 310, (2nd ed. 2002).

[48] Koriambanya S.A. Carew, Note, "David and Goliath: Giving the Indigenous People of the Niger Delta a Smooth Pebble-Environmental Law, Human Rights and Re-Defining the Value of Life", (2002), 7 Drake J. Agric. L. 509.

[49] Ibid.

[50] Ibid.

[51] Ibid.

[52] Ibid. at p. 510

[53] Ibid.

[54] Ibid

states (and actors) are bound by it to the same degree as treaty law.[55] However, while treaty law only binds parties which consent to a treaty, customary international rules become universally binding with or without the consent of states or other actors.[56]

There is significant support for the contention that TNCs should be held liable for international environmental and human rights violations under customary international law. Uniform practice is evidenced by international instruments, including United Nations declarations, which dictate acceptable standards for TNCs, the acceptance by TNCs of voluntary codes of conduct based on international environmental and human rights law, as well as increasing state regulation of corporations in developing countries and judicial decisions in countries where TNCs are headquartered allowing legal liability for violations of international law. *Opinio juris* is demonstrated by international and national court decisions recognizing TNC liability for environmental and human rights violations and by declarations by the United Nations sanctioning conduct by TNCs in accordance with recognized international human rights and environmental standards.

Enyinna S. Nwauche[57], points out that the presence of a natural resource like oil in the lands of a minority peoples is prone to generate conflict with respect to the issue of ownership, control and benefits of the exploration and exploitation of the resource. He cautions that these conflicts touch on the human rights of these minorities in their individual and group capacity, pointing out that to resolve these conflicts, a number of measures must be put in place by the state aimed at recognising, promoting and protecting the rights of such minorities. He then examines the measures which have been employed by the Nigerian government to protect the ethnic minorities of the Niger Delta and concludes that the measures have not been effective, judging from the worsening separatist and militant agitations in the oil rich delta region.

Patterson Ogon[58], while contributing to the debate on justice for the oil

[55] Melissa Robbins, 'Powerful States, Customary Law and the Erosion of Human Rights Through Regional Enforcement', (2005), 35 Cal. W. Int'l L.J. 295.

[56] Ibid.

[57] "Ethnicity, Human Rights and Constitutionalism in Africa", ed. George M. Wachira, (2008), 6 Minn. J. Global Trade, p. 181.

[58] Oil Exploitation and Economic Justice: A community Development Perspective, Paper presented at the Political Education Seminar organized by Social Action and NUPENG on the theme "The Other Side of Petro Dollars. Climate, Poverty and Pollution". February 25, 2009, Port Harcourt.

producing communities and setting an agenda for proper development, indicates that the health and livelihood of the people of the Delta region in Nigeria have been visibly impaired by oil interest. He makes allusion to a scientific presentation by Professor Reginald Nwakoala[59], which revealed that the inhabitants of the two Delta-region states suffer from cancer of different types and other forms of neo-plastic diseases, whose causes have been traced to prolonged and undiminished exposure to crude effluents by reason of multiple oil spillages and/or environmental incidents. According to him, the peoples of the Delta region are regretting the presence of oil on their land. He illustrates this by saying that the state of social infrastructure is deplorable although the statistics and reports churned out by the oil companies addressing Corporate Social Responsibility (CSR) paint a different picture. In the same light, he also makes allusion to a pastor's prayer before a Christian congregation in Nigeria's Niger Delta:

> We pray to God on this holy morning that no petroleum oil will be discovered in our communities. Indeed Lord, let the oil underneath our houses and farms drift away from us. Lord, spare us the pains and misfortunes and diseases that petroleum oil brings to our people and to our farms and rivers. Lord protect us from further harm in the hands of those who want our properties. Amen[60].

He concludes by saying that although the peoples of the Niger delta derive no benefits from their oil, there are several international legal regimes for the protection of the forest and the land, to which Nigeria is a signatory.[61] However, the pertinent question which he poses is as to how much of these legal regimes can be used by social movements and community organizations to hold governments and corporations accountable for the unbridled destruction of the ecosystem?

---

[59] Analysis of the occurrence of cancer and other Tumours in Rivers and Bayelsa States from December 1997 – 2000, Findings and Recommendations of the Legal Advisory Panel on the investigative Hearing of the petition by the Ijaw Aborigius of Bayelsa State Against Shell Petroleum Development Company (SPDC) set up by the House of Representatives, Abuja, Nigeria, February 24, 2003, P 11-12.

[60] See www.waado.org/environment (Last accessed on July 7th 2010).

[61] They include the African convention on conservation of Nature and Natural Resources 1968, The African Charter on Human and Peoples Rights 1981, The convention for Co-operation and Development of Marine and Coastal Environments of the West and Central Africa Region 1984)

Steve Metiboba[62], shares the view that oil exploitation has no doubt enhanced socio-economic transformation in many oil prospecting and producing states. He, however, asserts that the accompanying fallouts remain tragic and disturbing in several States and the oil producing communities in Nigeria. He attempts a discussion of some of the socio-cultural factors that are often neglected in oil exploitation and which inevitably trigger a chain of socio-economic, religious and political tensions and conflicts in the oil-producing areas. He centres his discussions on the fact that oil exploitation further impoverishes the oil producing communities and destroys their ways of life. According to him, culture refers to a configuration of learned and shared patterns of behaviour and of understanding concerning the meaning and value of things, ideas, emotions and actions. Thus, when a people's socio-cultural context is not taken into due consideration during socio-economic activities such as oil prospecting and production, individuals living within those areas in which such socio-economic activities are taking place may be marginalized in their own locality. He continues to posit that a socio-cultural or socio-environmental analysis of petroleum exploitation will provide the means of identifying the effects of the project on the population, and the perception of the people in the project area with reference to their definition of socio-economic development. Consequently, socio-cultural factors could be brought to bear on petroleum exploitation by taking cognizance of the people's norms and values, having regard to man's basic means of livelihood, making provision for displaced persons, having regard for historical places of importance as well as increasing community participation in decision making. He ends up by suggesting that in order to control the incessant incidences of clashes, conflicts and disputes between oil companies and the oil-bearing communities, both the government and the oil firms should make an in-depth examination and analysis of rural communities with respect to their social system, cultural practices, and attitudinal dispositions, with a view to facilitating more profound and dynamic adjustments among the local people to the dynamics of modern technology.

Legborsi Saro Pyagbara[63], opens up by acknowledging that crude oil has had

---

[62] Socio-Cultural Issues in Oil Exploitation in Nigeria, Department of Sociology, University of Ilorin, Nigeria. Seehttp://www.unilorin.edu.ng/unilorin/publications/Dr%20metiboba%20 Article%202%20corrected.htm (Last accessed on July 7th 2010).

[63] "The Adverse impacts of oil Pollution on the Environment and Wellbeing of a local Indigenous Community: The Experience of the Ogoni People of Nigeria" International Expert Group

a profound impact on the world civilization than any single natural resource in recorded history. He points out that as oil was struck in commercial quantities in Nigeria, it also signaled the beginning of a profound transformation of Nigeria's political and economic landscape. He further stresses this point by citing the Late Chief M.O Feyide[64], who asserted that:

> All over the world, the lives of people are affected and the destiny of nations is determined by the result of oil exploitation. Oil keeps the factors of the industrialized countries working and provides the revenue which enables oil exporters to execute ambitious national and economic development plans. The march of progress would be retarded and life itself would be unbearable if the world is deprived of oil. That is why oil has become the concern of the governments, a vital ingredient of their politics and a crucial factor in the political and diplomatic strategies.

He, however, points out that these benefits to the nation are at the cost of the negative impact on people's health and property. The most worrisome aspect of oil pollution in Ogoni is the rise in occurrence of certain ailments that were previously unknown in the area. It has thus been reported that there exist a correlation between exposure to oil pollution and the development of health problems.[65] He concludes by saying that the externalities of oil extraction have resulted in profound adverse impacts on traditional lifestyles and livelihood patterns of the Ogoni community where unchecked oil exploration and exploitation have been taking place for decades.

Emeka Duruigbo[66] notes that the negative social, economic, and environmental effects of oil and gas development in Nigeria are glaring. To him, while Nigeria, as a country, has seen the effects of what economists refer to as the "resource curse,"[67] people in the oil-producing communities

---

Meeting on Indigenous Peoples and Protection of the Environment, Khabarovsk Russian Federation, August 27- 29, 2007.

[64]Chief M.O. Feyide, Oil in World Politics, Proceedings of 1986, Public Lecture at University of Lagos.

[65]O.S. Olusi, "Nigerian Oil Industry and the Environment", Proceedings of the 1981 International seminar, Lagos, Nigeria, NNPC 1981.

[66]"Managing Oil Revenue for Socio-Economic Development in Nigeria: The case for Community-Based Trust Funds", (2004), 30 N. C. J. Int'L. & Com. Reg., 121.

[67]The "resource curse" is a paradoxical situation in which there exists an inverse relationship

have experienced the adverse effects of oil production more than the rest of the country.[68] In his article, he focuses on the role that both the Nigerian government and oil corporations have played to ameliorate the plight of oil producing communities, which have more directly borne the brunt of oil and gas development than any other part of Nigeria.[69] The government's approach, he indicates, has been two-pronged: corrective, attempting to repair the damage done by oil and gas development and progressive, providing opportunities for people in these communities to share in the benefits of petroleum exploration and extraction.

In addition to governmental efforts, he points out that the oil corporations operating in Nigeria have instituted private financing initiatives to develop their host communities, embarking on a number of community assistance and development projects ranging from scholarships to the construction of roads and buildings. He reports that they have also started extending loans for micro-enterprises and support for agricultural projects, as well as involving public-private partnerships with development agencies including the United Nations Development Programme (UNDP) and the United States Agency for International Development (USAID).

He presents an appraisal of the public and private initiatives to cushion the negative effects of oil and gas production and ensure the development of these communities, and points out that although the work uses Nigeria as a framework for the discussion, its ramifications and relevance extend beyond one single country and may be beneficial to people in other resource-rich countries like Cameroon.

He centres his discussions on the social, economic and environmental

---

between endowment with natural resources and economic growth. See Richard M. Auty, Sustaining Development in Mineral Economies: The Resource Curse Thesis (1993). See also Alan Gelb, Oil Windfalls: Blessing Or Curse? (1988) (stating that for countries who export oil, it is ordinary to see an inverse relationship between oil exploration and subsequent growth and development); Menachem Katz, et al., Lifting The Oil Curse: Improving Petroleum Revenue Management in Sub-saharan Africa (International Monetary Fund 2004) (stating that macroeconomics, oil sector policies, and governance issues may be related to the inverse relationship between domestic oil production and subsequent domestic growth in African nations).

[68] Augustine A. Ikein, The Impact of Oil on a Developing Country: The Case of Nigeria 25-26 (1990).

[69] Emanuel U. Nnadozie, Oil and Socioeconomic Crisis in Nigeria, (1995) (discussing the people of Egbema in southeastern Nigeria).

impact of oil and gas development in Nigeria's oil-producing communities, focusing on the public initiatives introduced to address the negative effects of oil production. He also examines corporate approaches to community development in the oil-producing communities of Nigeria, presenting a general discussion of the various activities of the major oil-producing companies in Nigeria. He pays particular attention to the approaches adopted by Royal Dutch/Shell and ChevronTexaco, because they are two of the largest oil companies in Nigeria and also have a long presence there. Both of these factors suggest that they have had the opportunity and the capacity to either be a huge blessing to, or inflict maximum damage on, the environment and lives of people in these communities. In addition, these two companies have been at the centre of the greatest controversies concerning oil production in Nigeria. Both companies are currently the subjects of two separate lawsuits in the United States regarding their operations in Nigeria.[70] According to him, a number of factors account for the dismal performance of public and private actors in Nigeria. The most prominent factors appearing to be the corruption present at all levels of Nigerian life and the absence of a meaningful participation of the public in the formulation and implementation of these policies and projects. He examines these two factors and concludes that there is a dire need to stamp out corruption or minimize its influence, stressing that public participation, which has gained ascendancy in the international arena as an important component of sustainable development, also deserves greater attention than is presently the case in Nigeria. It is critical, he intimates, to ensure that community members have a stake in these programmes and are allowed to take their destiny in their own hands. The challenge, being to design a framework for institutional arrangements that take these factors into consideration.

Writing on Permanent Sovereignty and Peoples' Ownership of Natural Resources in International law, Emeka Duruigbo,[71] expresses regret over the

[70] Shell was sued in New York and the lawsuit is still pending. See Wiwa v. Royal/Dutch Shell, 226 F. 3d 88 (2d. Cir. 2000), cert denied, 532 U.S. 941 (2001) (holding that Nigerian émigrés' suit, brought under the Alien Tort Claims Act, alleging that Shell participated in human rights violations against them in retaliation for their political opposition to its oil exploration activities in Nigeria should not be dismissed for forum non conveniens). A lawsuit is also pending against Chevron in California. See Bowoto v. Cheveron, 312F. Supp. 2d 1229 (2004) (holding that ChevronTexaco can face trial in the U.S. for the alleged human rights abuses of its subsidiary in Nigeria).

[71] 38 Geo. Wash. Int'L. Rev. 33, 2006

fact that the most disturbing issue facing the world today is the inability of many countries to convert valuable natural resources into an enhanced standard of living for their citizens. He explains this by capturing an ugly scenario that displays the defining characteristics of many resource-rich countries, with those in political offices working hard to ensure that the rest of the population receives almost no benefit from the resources with which their countries have been abundantly endowed. The ugly scenario presents itself as follows:

> In the dilapidated Portuguese cocoa plantation houses in Agua Ize, Sao Tome, and Principe, residents gather under a rotting roof to avoid the rain. Above their heads, offering a tantalising glimpse of a world beyond the surrounding dank disrepair, an old election campaign poster hints at the country's anticipated oil boom. "It is now!" says the propaganda of the opposition Party of Democratic Convergence, pledging "better sharing of resources." Domingas da Costa Frota Pereira, an unemployed mother of three children, looks up and laughs: "They would put the money in their own pockets," she says.[72]

He points out that the contrast between real life and the original dream of placing in the hands of peoples and nations the right to the natural resources found in their territories could not be much starker. He then examines the origins of the principle of permanent sovereignty over natural resources (PSNR) in international law with the goal of using PSNR as a tool to empower and benefit people, rather than a vehicle for their immiseration or the glorification of a handful of rulers.

He goes ahead to point out that a few decades ago, the notion of permanent sovereignty over natural resources was a source of great controversy, generating highly polemical debate among international legal scholars, representatives of developed and developing countries, and multinational oil corporations.[73] Those favouring sovereignty of developing countries over their resources envisioned resources as a catalyst for economic development.[74] Yet, fifty years

[72] Michael Peel, '"Oil Curse" Stalks Africa's Newest Petro-State', Fin. Times, Jan. 27, 2005, at p. 10.

[73] Ruth Gordon, "Racing U.S. Foreign Policy", (2003), 17 Nat'l Black L.J 1, 3, See also David J. Halperin, Human Rights and Natural Resources, (1968), 9 Wm. & Mary L. Rev. 770, (discussing a state's power to exploit natural resources).

[74] See Samuel K.B. Asante, "The Concept of Stability of Contractual Relations in the

after the concept of permanent sovereignty over natural resources entered the international legal lexicon, the developing countries that pressed for this idea, or in whose interest it was championed, remain mired in economic doldrums; their predicted integration into the international economic system is far from truly materializing.[75]

He traces the subsistence of this predicament to the fact that rulers of developing countries have apparently interpreted PSNR as conferring ownership of their nations' resources on themselves (the leaders), thereby perceiving a license to corner the countries' wealth where none (no license) exists.[76] For instance, he cites the case of the deposed Iraqi ruler, Saddam Hussein, who is believed to have "personalized" a portion of Iraqi oil wealth by allegedly stashing billions of dollars in foreign banks and businesses.[77] Likewise, Nigeria's military strong man, General Sani Abacha allegedly transferred billions out of his country's treasury and deposited it in several safe havens abroad before he died in office.[78] Equatorial Guinea started

---

Transnational Investment Process, in Legal Aspects of the New International Economic Order", 234-35 (Kamal Hossain ed., 1980) (expressing the expectation that development will result from the enshrinement of the principle of permanent sovereignty over natural resources); Nico J. Schrijver, "Permanent Sovereignty over Natural Resources Versus the Common Heritage of Mankind: Complementary or Contradictory Principles of International Economic Law?", in International Law and Development 87, 87-88 (Paul de Waart et al. eds., 1988) (noting that the concept was geared toward economic development of developing countries).

75 The principle of permanent sovereignty over natural resources was expected to help usher in a new international economic order that would benefit developing countries. Subrata Roy Chowdhury, Permanent Sovereignty over Natural Resources: Substratum of the Seoul Declaration, in International Law and Development. ("The principle of permanent sovereignty over natural resources, economic activities and wealth is the substratum of the legal philosophy for the establishment of a new international economic order.").

76 See Ndiva Kofele-Kale, Patrimonicide: "The International Economic Crime of Indigenous Spoliation", (1995), 28 Vand. J. Transnat'l L. 48, 116, [hereinafter Kofele-Kale, Patrimonicide] (for those countries "that have been victims of looting on a massive scale, indigenous spoliation has become the single most important obstacle to economic development").

77 W. Michael Reisman, "Institutions and Practice for the Restoration and Maintaining Public Order", (1995), 6 Duke J. Comp. & Int'l L. 175, 183-84.

78 . Ndiva Kofele-Kale, "The Right to a Corruption-Free Society as an Individual and Collective Human Right: Elevating Official Corruption to a Crime Under International Law", (2000), 34 Int'l L. 149, 55-57 and accompanying text. See also Editorial, Hope in the Land of Dashed Hopes, N.Y. Times, Mar. 7, 2005, at p. 16 ("Given the second-highest proven oil reserves in Africa, Nigerian officials spent oil income on lavish estates in Europe instead of decent schools and water systems back home.").

exporting oil in 1996, but press accounts indicate that within only seven years of shipping oil abroad, the country's ruler, Teodoro Obiang Nguema Mbasogo, had already diverted about $300 million into a U.S. bank account directly under his control. Mbasogo enjoys a lavish lifestyle while the vast majority of his country's 500,000 people languish in economic prisons and wallow in abject poverty.[79] This may also explain why according to him Jose Eduardo dos Santos, the President of Angola, is not only that country's most powerful figure, but also its richest person, even though he has spent a large period of his adult life in one form of political office or another.[80]

He further argues that while in the past the focus was to protect resources from foreign intervention, it was today undeniable that "the wealth and natural resources of a country can be spoliated as thoroughly and efficiently by a native as by a foreigner,"[81] which calls for a higher degree of condemnation than was visited on foreign spoliators. To him, to reverse the present state of affairs would require a proper interpretation of who the rightful owners of national properties are, and articulate same in applicable instruments.[82]

In this light, he presents two major arguments. Firstly, that the right to permanent sovereignty over natural resources is vested in peoples, not states, although states retain a pivotal role in so far as government exercises the right to permanent sovereignty. Secondly, that the term "peoples" should be used to denote the owners of natural resources rather than faceless populations, which will help begin to construe governments in their proper role as temporary custodians[83] or trustees[84] of natural resources charged with managing them for the benefit of all the people in the country.

He nevertheless aposites that, contending that the resources belong to the people is one thing, ensuring that governments act as faithful trustees and

---

[79] See Andreanna M. Truelove, "Oil, Diamonds, and Sunlight : Forstering Human Rights Through Transparency in Revenue from Natural Resources", (2003), 35 Geo. J. Int'l L. 207, 221-22NN. 72-74.

[80] Nick Cohen, The Curse of Black Gold: Oil Is Bad News for a Country; Far from Bringing Prosperity, It Is the Harbinger of Poverty, Malnutrition and Oppressive Government, New Statesman, June 2, 2003.

[81] W. Michael Reisman, "Sovereignty and Human Rights in Contemporary International Law", (1990), 84 Am. J. Int'l L. 866,872.

[82] See infra chapter three.

[83] See W. Michael Reisman, "Harnessing International Law to Restrain and Recapture Indigenous Spoliation", (1989), 83 Am. J. Int'l L. 56.

[84] Kofele-Kale, Patrimonicide, supra note 76, at 97.

competent managers of these resources is an entirely different and much more difficult matter. Consequently, the work of changing the natural resource paradigm can be described as "the pursuit of answers to problems which are so complex and so politicized as to have little prospect of being resolved."[85] But he ends on a positive note by saying that even that slight prospect is enough to animate those of them who share a passion for alleviating poverty around the world.

Andreanna M. Truelove,[86] establishing a nexus between human rights corruption and transparency, begins with a well known quote from Justice Brandeis: 'Sunlight is said to be the best disinfectant; electric light the most efficient policeman'.[87] She then asserts that government corruption provides both an incentive and a means for human rights violations, and further that corruption provides an incentive for government officials to engage in human rights abuses in order to retain their access to the public coffers. Corruption she continues, provides government officials with a source of wealth and power that can be harnessed to inflict human rights abuses on anyone who attempts to stand in their way. She then points out that one of the best ways to combat such corruption is through transparency, for corruption does not grow well in sunlight. And some of the largest sources of the means and fruits of corruption are the industries that extract oil, gas, and minerals in natural resource-rich countries.

She indicates that recently, a few non-governmental organizations (NGOs) have started to bring these connections between corruption and the extractive industries (the industries that extract, produce, or mine oil, gas, or minerals) into the public eye. In 2000, the International Monetary Fund (IMF) published a report stating that transparency in oil revenue is necessary for the sound economic development of Angola.[88] In commenting on that report, Human Rights Watch added that transparency in oil revenue is a human rights issue in places like Angola, where oil revenues are used to finance civil wars in which hundreds of thousands of people die and over a million people are internally

---

[85] See Philip Alston, "Making Space for New Human Rights: The Case of the Right to Development", (1988), 1 Harv. Hum. Rts. Y.B. 3, 12.

[86] "Oil, Diamond, and Sunlight: Forstering Human Rights through Transparency in Revenues from Natural Resources", (2003), 35 Geo. J. Int'l L. 207.

[87] Louis D. Brandeis, Other Peoples Money, 92 (1914).

[88] See Public Information Notice by International Monetary Fund, Public Information Notice No. 00/62, IMF Concludes Article IV Consultation with Angola, (Aug. 10, 2000), available at http:// www.imf.org/external/np/sec/2000/pn0062.htm (last visited June 20th 2010).

displaced.[89] Still in the same light, the director of Transparency International also argues that transparency is needed to combat corruption and promote human rights.[90] He points out that since these few organizations have begun to recognize actors in the international community who are striving to improve human rights, they could accomplish a great deal by promoting transparency of revenue for extractive industries. Also, the disclosure of all economic benefits that governments and their officials gain from extractive industries, is the first step towards addressing the corruption that allows many of the world's most repressive regimes to stay in power and increases their incentives to do so.

In examining the links between human rights and corruption, and between corruption and transparency, she also examines the lessons that those seeking greater transparency can learn from current anti-corruption measures and describes some recent proposals for bringing transparency to extractive industries and the governments with which they deal. She equally proposes and describes the contours of anti-corruption transparency initiatives targeted at extractive industries and the governments with which they do business. Finally, she addresses potential obstacles to implementing initiatives for combating corruption that relates to extractive industries.

She then concludes by pointing out that the disclosure of revenue from extractive industries would be an important step towards creating an environment that respects human rights, because transparency provides tools for NGOs and citizens to hold governments accountable for the money they are receiving. The need for disclosure she notes is clear, but the means for implementing disclosure are not. She offers a few steps that could increase the disclosure of the revenue of extractive industries, calling on States and NGOs to work both unilaterally and through multilateral agreements such as the OECD to require disclosure from companies and encourage disclosure from resource-rich governments.

Stephane Cosse,[91] while discussing the issue of transparency in Cameroon's

[89] See Press Release by Human Rights Watch, The IMF and Angola: Oil and Human Rights (June 2000), available at http:// www.hrw.org/press/2000/06/ang0622.htm (last visited June 20th 2010).

[90] See Laurence Cockcroft, Working Paper, Corruption and Human Rights: A Crucial Link, Transparency International (Oct.1988), available at http:// www.transparency.org/working_papers/cockcroft/cockcroft.html (last visited June 20th 2010).

[91] Strengthening Transparency in the Oil Sector in Cameroon: Why Does It Matter?, IMF Policy Discussion Paper, African and Policy Development and Review Departments, 2006.

oil sector, begins by saying that there has been a growing recognition by governments over the last decade of the importance of transparency and strong governance for economic growth and social development, particularly in the oil-producing economies. He notes that the sharp rise in international oil prices resulting in large windfall profits for oil-producing countries has also strengthened calls from the civil society and a broader range of stakeholders for greater transparency and accountability. He makes allusion to the International Monetary Fund's *Guide on Resource Revenue Transparency*, and to the U.K.-led Extractive Industries Transparency Initiative (EITI), pointing out that they have garnered increasing international support in both oil-producing and consumer countries.[92] He highlights the aims of EITI to range from fostering voluntary cooperation between governments, private oil companies, and civil society to enhancing transparency in the oil and mining sectors. Against this background, he analyzes transparency issues in Cameroon's oil sector, showing that while substantial efforts have already been undertaken to strengthen transparency, continued and sustained action is necessary to address the remaining gaps in this area. He points out that in early 1990s, the Cameroonian authorities enhanced their supervision of the national oil company (Société Nationale des Hydrocarbures, SNH), reviewing the transfer of oil revenue to the budget. Those efforts were also significantly renewed in 2005 as part of the authorities' broader commitment to enhance fiscal transparency and reporting in the context of the implementation of their programmes with the IMF.[93] He notes that further steps still have to be taken to enhance accountability, improve the use of oil revenue and strengthen fiscal policies to meet the country's development priorities. Notwithstanding substantial oil-generated resources over the last more than 30 years, Cameroon has remained a low-income country with relatively weak social indicators. He tries to identify why and how transparency matters in Cameroon's oil sector, stressing in particular that fiscal transparency can help

[92] 20 countries have endorsed EITI, including the eight sub-Saharan African oil producing countries (see www.eitransparecy.org). The Cameroonian authorities announced in March 2005 that they would adhere to the EITI principles and work with other stakeholders in the oil sector to improve transparency.

[93] An IMF staff-monitored programme agreed in early 2005 was replaced in October 2005 by a medium-term economic programmes supported by the Fund through a Poverty Reduction and Growth Facility arrangement.

economic development and poverty reduction. To this end, the government needs to include in the state budget all the oil revenue it receives and to make related government receipts more predictable, thereby allowing notably more and steadier government spending. He further points out that enhanced oil transparency can lead to stronger accountability and in turn contribute to improved governance and strengthened business confidence. He then reviews the main benefits of increased transparency in the oil sector and identifies key specific gaps in Cameroon, underlining in particular, progress that could be achieved in the fiscal area.

This study will add to the existing literature through its attempt at analysing the available local and regional legislation that touches on the human rights responsibilities of oil MNCs in Cameroon, within the framework of the human right to development and the right to a healthy environment. The plethora of literature which exists on this subject deals mostly with environmental degradation and forced displacement whereas this study focuses more on the human right to development and the right to a healthy environment as inalienable rights of Cameroonians, which oil companies and the state have failed to promote.

The relationship between regulation, corporate human rights responsibility, and the enjoyment of the right to development and a healthy environment, can be explained from a number of theoretical perspectives.

The Libertarian Theory

Libertarianism is associated with the idea of a minimal state,[94] restricted to the narrow functions of protecting citizens from each other (and from non-citizens), and providing for the enforcement of private contracts. Typically, libertarians assume that this is necessarily accompanied by the economic institutions of a pure form of capitalism, including strong private property rights, low or no taxation, and free competition among potential producers

[94] Nozickian libertarianism, allows people voluntarily to contract into a more than minimal state, if that is what they wish to do. See Robert Nozick, Anarchy, State, and Utopia 318-20 (1974). For present purposes I ignore "left-libertarianism," which combines principles of individual liberty with restrictions on the type of property rights individuals may form. See Michael Otsuka, Libertarianism Without Inequality 114-31 (2003); Hillel Steiner, An Essay on Rights 268 (1994); Peter Vallentyne, Introduction: Left-Libertarianism--A Primer, in Left-Libertarianism and Its Critics: The Contemporary Debate 1, 15-16 (Peter Vallentyne & Hillel Steiner eds., 2000).

of goods and services.[95] Libertarianism can take various forms, but here Deontological libertarianism will be contrasted with Consequentialist libertarianism. Deontological libertarianism, pioneered by Robert Nozick, is based on a strict doctrine of natural rights, violation of which is never permitted, whatever the consequences.[96] The justification for such a theory is claimed to be a particular rights-based theory of justice.[97] Proponents of consequentialist libertarianism, by contrast, argue for the free market and strong individual rights to property, not on the basis of an antecedent theory of justice, but in terms of the beneficial consequences such as wealth creation and efficiency that such arrangements may bring. Pure consequentialist libertarianism is rare, if it exists at all, but there are hybrid forms of libertarianism that combine deontological and consequentialist reasoning.

Libertarianism is a theory which broadly states that people lead better lives when they are left to make their own decisions in both their social and economic lives. Consequently, the role of government in a libertarian state should be minimal and limited to protection and enforcement of contracts.

The libertarian position resists government control over regulation of, and influence upon economic and social phenomena. In short, it argues against economic and social regulation, advocating instead reliance on free markets — where "free" means uninhibited by public-law institutions. Libertarianism holds that the government's activity should be limited, wherever possible, to the protection of property rights and the enforcement of contracts. What argument justifies such a position? One standard version of the argument runs as follows: Decisions have consequences. Consequences can be either desirable or undesirable. When decision-makers are personally accountable for the consequences of their decisions, those consequences tend to be desirable. When, on the other hand, decision-makers are not personally accountable for the consequences of their decisions, those consequences tend to be undesirable, however benign the decision-makers' intentions may be. Therefore, the elimination of much government regulation together with an increased reliance on unregulated market forces would produce an improved state of affairs.

The libertarian premise that good intentions cannot accomplish what accountability can is both necessary and puzzling. It is necessary to preempt

---

[95] Loren E. Lomasky, Persons, Rights, and the Moral Community 125-26 (1987).

[96] Nozick, supra note 94, at pp ix-xi

[97] Ibid. at 163

the alternative proposal that decision-makers act beneficently. If beneficence is typically sufficient to produce desirable consequences, then the call for accountability loses its importance; the libertarian argument could call for beneficence instead. It is precisely because beneficence without accountability leads to undesirable consequences that the libertarian call for accountability is necessary. Beneficence is insufficient; accountability is necessary.

The supposition that accountability can solve problems that beneficence cannot is also puzzling. Having good intentions presumably entails full consideration for the consequences of one's behaviour. Suppose, for example, that I have good intentions towards you but know that I will not be accountable for the consequences of any decision I make with respect to you. How will I act? Given that I have good intentions, I will behave as if I were accountable for the consequences of my decision. To subject you to consequences that I would not subject myself to would constitute a betrayal of my good intentions. Or, if the libertarian argument implicitly defines "good intentions" to mean something other than adherence to the Golden Rule, then it is unclear why libertarians should not prescribe adherence to the Golden Rule instead of personal accountability.

Thus libertarianism, like many other critical theories, promises emancipation. Embracing libertarianism's tenets offers freedom from the tyranny of regulation. "Tyranny," like "totalitarianism," is a heavy term. These terms are, nevertheless, often included in libertarianism's description of government regulation.[98] Regulation is not just a waste of money, it is tyrannical. Understanding its inherent and inescapable vices will set us free, where the "us" is both those of us subject to regulation and those of us whom regulation is supposed to, but cannot, benefit. Steven P. Croley (2000) points out that, exposing public-law enthusiasts to the hopelessness of regulation will rescue America, and hasten their freedom. It may not get them to Heaven, but at least they can avoid Hell.[99]

Both of these forms of libertarianism endorse full self-ownership. They differ with respect to the liberties persons have to use, or the moral powers they have to acquire, ownership of natural resources. Natural resources are all the resources in the world, in their unimproved form, that were not created

[98] See, e.g., Milton Friedman & Rose D. Friedman, Free To Choose 38-69 (1980 ed.).

[99] Steven P. Croley. This essay is an edited version of remarks given at a 1994 meeting of the University of Michigan Federalist Society with the theme "My Road to Hell Is Paved With Your Good Intentions."

by any non-divine agent. These include space, land, air, and minerals in their original unimproved state. The most well-known versions of libertarianism are right-libertarian theories, which hold that agents have a very strong moral power to acquire full private ownership of unowned things. Left-libertarians, by contrast, hold that natural resources (such as space, land, minerals, air, and water) belong to everyone in some egalitarian manner and thus cannot be privately appropriated without their consent or significant compensatory payment to them.[100]

There are many different versions of left libertarianism, but two of them are relevant to this work: the equal share view and the equal opportunity for well-being view. Like right-libertarianism, each view holds that individuals have the moral power to appropriate unowned natural resources. Unlike right-libertarianism, however, both hold that ownership of natural resources is always conditional upon paying rent based on the competitive value, or supply and demand, of the rights claimed over those resources. Strictly speaking, both views deny that individuals can fully own natural resources, because their rights over them are always conditional on the payment of the competitive rent. As long as the rent payment is made, however, individuals may have all the other rights of full ownership.[101]

The two versions of left libertarianism that this thesis considers differ with respect to their view on how the rent fund is to be allocated. The equal share view holds that everyone has a right to an equal share of the value of natural resources and thus a right to an equal share of the rent fund.[102] The equal opportunity for well-being view holds that everyone has a right to whatever share of the value of natural resources-and hence of the rent fund-provides them with an equal opportunity for well-being.[103] Under this view,

[100] Peter Vallentyne, "Left-Libertarianism: A Primer, in Left Libertarianism and Its Critics: The Contemporary Debate" (200),1 (Peter Vallentyne & Hillel Steiner eds., 2000). For more on left libertarianism, see generally The Origins of Left-Libertarianism (Peter Vallentyne & Hillel Steiner eds., 2000). For a critical assessment of left libertarianism, see Barbara H. Fried, Left-Libertarianism: A Review Essay, 32 Phil. & Pub. Aff. 66 (2004), and Peter Vallentyne et al., Why Left-Libertarianism Is Not Incoherent, Indeterminate, or Irrelevant: A Reply to Fried, (2005), 33 Phil. & Pub. Aff. 201.

[101] Ibid, at pp 5-11.

[102] See, e.g., Hillel Steiner, An Essay on Rights (1994).

[103] See, e.g., "Michael Otsuka, Libertarianism Without Inequality", (2003). Though the version that I invoke here differs in some ways from Otsuka's view, the differences are not essential for present purposes.

the rent fund may be divided up unequally, with more going to those who suffer from unchosen disadvantages in their genetic endowments, childhood environments, and so on.[104]

According to equal opportunity left libertarianism, each individual has a duty to pay competitive rent on the rights over natural resources claimed.[105] Moreover, the rent must be spent so as to efficiently promote equality of opportunity for well-being. For simplicity, this version assumes that the rental payment is paid to the state in the form of a tax, and that the state then uses the funds to promote equality of opportunity. If there is no state, or if the state would not distribute the funds appropriately, then the individual has a duty to distribute them directly.

The essence of this theory to this work is two-fold: first, it supports the argument that Cameroonians would lead better lives if they are active participants in the management of revenue from the oil industry. Second, it supports the argument that accountability is an essential ingredient of transparency which is much welcomed in Cameroons's oil industry.

Theory of Legitimacy

Traditionally, local communities have been the least regarded actors and therefore historically neglected in policy and other related discussions relating to mineral development.[106] However, in recent years, local communities have been introduced as a stakeholder with 'salience' and therefore meeting community expectations is now increasingly seen as important for the survival of the firm exploiting natural resources.[107] Indeed, Waddock and

[104] For simplicity, I ignore the difference between equality of opportunity for well-being, which is not sensitive to later brute luck, and equality of brute luck well-being. See generally, Peter Vallentyne, Brute Luck, Option Luck, and Equality of Initial Opportunities, (2002), 112 Ethics 529.

[105] See Vallentyne, supra note 100, at pp 5-11.

[106] K. Mate, Communities, Civil Society Organisations and the Management of Mineral Wealth, Mining, Mineral and Sustainable Development, International Institute for the Environment and Development, World Business Council for Sustainable Development, No. 16 (2002)

[107] Uwafiokun Idemudia, "Community Perceptions and Expectations: Reinventing the Wheels of Corporate Social Responsibility Practices in the Nigerian Oil Industry", (2007), Business and Society Review, Blackwell Publishing, 372.

Boyle[108] asserted that Corporate Community Relations (CCR) is no longer a buffer between the organization and its environment ; rather, it is a function that intergrates stakeholder interests, particularly those of its employees and the surrounding communities with those of the corporation[109] This changing understanding of CCR is due to the realization that CSR is a collaboration between the corporation and communities, and the need to develop mutually beneficial stakeholder relationships. Underlying these changing understanding of CCR are two useful theoretical positions that can assist in gaining an insight into corporate-community relations. The first is the legitimacy theory. Legitimacy can be described as the generalized perception that the actions of an entity are desirable or appropriate within some socially constructed system of norms, values, beliefs, and expectations.[110] Simply put, a corporation is legitimate when it is judged to be just and worthy of support by the community.[111] Legitimacy theory relies on the notion of social contract between the company and community and on the maintained assumption that companies will adopt strategies to show the community that the organization is attempting to comply with the community's expectations.[112] This is because corporations as one kind of social arrangement require legitimacy to maintain functional, long-term relationships with the various communities on which they depend.[113] Legitimacy is therefore not a characteristic of the corporation, but a measure of societal perceptions of the adequacy of corporate behaviour.[114] Seth[115] thus asserts that legitimacy gaps arise when societal expectation of corporate behaviour differs from societal perceptions

[108] A. S. Waddock and M. Boyle, "The dynamics of change in corporate community relations", (1995), California Management Review, 37, pp 125 – 140.

[109] A. Boehm, 'Corporate Social Responsibility: a contemporary perspective of community and corporate leaders', (2002), Business and Society Review, 107, p 171 – 194.

[110] M. C. Suchman, "Managing legitimacy: strategic and institutional approaches," (1995), Academy of Management Review 4 pp 571 – 610.

[111] J. Dowling and J. Pfeffer, "Oganisational legitimacy: social value and organizational behaviour," (1975), Pacific Sociological Review 18, pp 122 – 138.

[112] H. Jenkins, "Coporate Social Responsibility and the mining industry: conflicts and constructs," (2004), Corporate Social Responsibility and Environmental Management Journal 11, pp 23 – 34.

[113] J. Nasi, S. Nasi, N. Phillips and S. Zyglidopoulos, "The evolution of corporate responsiveness: an exploratory study of Finnish and Canadian forestry companies," (1997), Business and Society Review 36, pp 296 – 321.

[114] Supra note 110.

[115] P. S. Seth, "Dimensions of corporate social responsibility: an analytical framework," (1975), California Management Review 17, pp. 58 – 64.

of corporate behaviour.[116] The loss of legitimacy can often be followed by a breakdown in CCR, and the loss of the associated benefit of legitimacy. For example, companies that are positioned favourably in communities (i.e., have legitimacy) are treated diferentially and respectfully and their mistakes are given the benefit of doubt, which is not the case with companies without legitimacy.[117]

The second closely related theoretical perspective is Burke's[118] concept of an implicit psychological contract between companies and communities. Burke[119] asserts that the psychological contract, unlike a social contract that is explicit, contains implicit expectations that companies and communities have for each other. It remains beneath the surface of the relationship and it is dynamic in character, continually changing, and frequently unacknowledged. The psychological contract is a manifestation of the ideals, ego ideals, which one part to the contract has for the other. Burke[120] asserts that while the psychological contract is unwritten, each party tacitly assumes that such a contract exists and each expects the other to act in accordance with it.

---

[116] Supra note 113.

[117] M. E Burke, Corporate Community Relations: The Principle of the Neighbour of Choice (London: Quorum Books, 1999).

[118] Ibid., pp 1 – 13.

[119] Ibid., p 4.

[120] Ibid., pp 4 – 5.

2

THE LEGAL FRAMEWORK FOR REGULATING CAMEROON'S OIL INDUSTRY

2.0. Introduction

Cameroon, the land of abundant natural resources, the island of peace and bread basket of the Central African Sub-Region, has many apparently very attractive laws. For example, and in line with Regulation No. 17/99/CEMAC – 020 –CM -03 relating to the CEMAC investment charter which provides that Member States shall ensure the promotion of legal and judicial security and the strengthening of the rule of law,[121] the Cameroon government has put in place the so-called "Cameroon Investment Charter." This charter creates an investment-promotion framework in accordance with the overall development strategy aimed at increased and sustainable growth, job creation in all branches of economic activity, and social well-being of the people.[122] The Cameroon Investment Charter is a totality of specified rights, liberties, obligations and powers granted by the government to investors. Its incentives are identical for foreign and domestic investors and provide fourteen guarantees to investors including property ownership, ability to repatriate capital and income, prior compensation in case of expropriation, freedom of movement within Cameroon, and free egress of personnel.[123] The

[121] Item 4.

[122] Section 6 of Law No. 2002/004 of 19th April 2002, instituting the Investment Charter of Cameroon.

[123] Ibid. See section 10.

investment-promotion framework provided by the Charter will be meaningful if its implementation is effective. However, an evaluation of the effective implementation of this Charter, less than ten years of its existence, may not provide an accurate picture. Nevertheless, drawing from the weaknesses of the previews investment codes, it is hoped that the implementation of the charter will be appealing.

Cameroon is a signatory to the 1993 Port Louis Treaty, which created the Organisation for the Harmonisation of Business Laws in Africa (OHADA).[124] The purpose of this treaty was to create a secured legal and judicial framework in Africa so as to attract foreign investments.[125] In addition to the above, Cameroon has a very attractive Labour Code. The framework created by the Labour Code is in fact supportive of a flexible and efficient labour market.[126] Cameroon has also signed seven Bilateral Investment Treaties for the mutual protection of the parties' foreign investments.[127]

This seemingly attractive investment climate is further brightened by the abundance and availability of natural resources. It is within this framework that investors are vying for licenses to explore and exploit petroleum oil in Cameroon. The investment climate encourages investors to invest in the exploitation of natural resources. Among all these natural resources (primary goods), this thesis focuses its analysis on petroleum because of the important place it occupies in the economy and because its exploitation has far reaching socio-economic consequences for both the government and the citizenry. Before these investors qualify to deposit applications to obtain an authorization to explore and exploit oil in Cameroon, they must also be duly qualified to do business in Cameroon. In order to qualify to do business in Cameroon, and by extension, qualify to apply for a license to explore and exploit petroleum oil in Cameroon, an investor must comply with Cameroonian company law. It is important to point out that all petroleum investment in Cameroon is in fact effected by business organizations, subject to Cameroonian company law.

124 OHADA – Organization pour L'Harmonisation en Afrique du Droit des Affaires

125 Article 1 of the 1993 Port Louis Treaty.

126 See Preamble of the 1990 Labour Code.

127 Since independence, Cameroon has signed seven bilateral treaties. The first was signed with the Republic of Germany in 1962; the second with Switzerland in 1963; the third with the Netherlands in 1965; the forth with the Belgio-Luxemburg Economic Union in 1980; the fifth with Romania in 1980; the sixth with the USA in 1980, and the seventh with the UK in 1982.

2.1. Applicable Law on the Establishment of Oil Companies

The procedure for creating a company under Cameroon Business Law is governed by the OHADA (Organisation for the Harmonisation of Business Laws in Africa) Uniform Act (UA) on Commercial Companies and Economic Interest Groups (CCEIG).[128] OHADA is a regional integration arrangement made up of sixteen Central and West African Countries.[129]

Unlike other regional integration arrangements in Africa, OHADA's objectives to its member states is tightly focused to harmonise their business law such that they have a single modern legal framework for their economic activities and to promote arbitration as a means of settling contractual disputes.[130] OHADA is an organization created by the Port Louis Treaty in 1993,[131]and amended in 2008. The main objective of the Treaty is to provide legal and judicial security within members States so as to attract investors.[132] This task of securing a viable legal and judicial environment was assigned to OHADA, which to date has in place nine[133] UAs, among which is the UA on CCEIG.

---

[128]See generally Book 1 of this Uniform Act.

[129]These countries are: Benin, Burkina faso, Cameroon, The Central African Republic, Chad, Comoros, The Republic of Congo, Cote d'Ivoire, Equatorial Guinea, Gabon,Guinea-bissau, Guinea (Conakry), Mali, Niger, Senegal and Togo. Congo-Kinshasa has fulfilled all the conditions to become a member except turning over the documents to Senegal as repository.

[130]See Preamble Of the Port Louis Treaty of 1993

[131]Ibid. Art. 1

[132]Art 3 Of the Port Louis Treaty.

[133] The Uniform Act Regulating Securities adopted on the 17th of April 1997, which entered into force on the 1st of January 1998; The Uniform Act Relating to General Commercial Law adopted on the 17th of April 1997, which entered into force on the 1st of January 1998; The Uniform Act Relating to Commercial Companies and Economic Interest Groups adopted on the 17th of April 1997, which entered into force on the 1st of January 1998; The Uniform Act Organising Simplified Recovery Procedures and Measures of Execution adopted on the 10th of April 1998, which entered into force on the 10th of July 1998; The Uniform Act Organising Collective Proceedings for Wiping Off Debts adopted on the 10th of April 1998, which entered into force on the 1st of January 1999; The Uniform Act Regulating Arbitration adopted on the 11th of March 1999, which entered into force on the 11th of June 1999; - The Uniform Act on Accounting adopted on the 24th of March 2000, which entered into force on the 1st of January 2001 for Enterprise accounts and the 1st of January 2002 for Combined Accounts; The Uniform Act Regulating the Transportation of goods by land adopted on the 22nd of April 2003, which entered into force on the 1st of January 2004: The Uniform Act on Cooperatives adopted in December of 2010. Others are still in preparation amongst which are the Uniform Act Regulating Contracts, the Uniform Act on Labour Relations, and the Uniform Act on Evidence.

This last UA requires that with the exception of sleeping partnerships, all companies shall be registered in the Trade and Personal Property Credit Register.[134] The Uniform Act recognizes the fact that a company may operate through a division and thus provides that a division shall be a commercial, industrial or service-providing establishment which belongs to a company or a natural person and which has been granted a certain degree of autonomy in its management.[135] The division shall however, not have a separate legal personality distinct from that of the parent company or the natural person who owns it. Thus, the rights and obligations arising from its activities or its existence shall be considered to be those of the parent company.[136]

Of great importance is the fact that the Uniform Act recognizes that a division may be an establishment of a foreign parent company. It provides that such a division shall be governed by the law of the Contracting State,[137] in this case, Cameroonian law, so long as neither international law nor any international agreement entered into by Cameroon provides otherwise. Such a division must however be registered in the Trade and Personal Property Register in accordance with the provisions organizing the said registry.[138] The Uniform Act further provides that where the division is owned by a foreigner (the division – or, more precisely, its assets in Cameroon presumably subject to relevant liabilities – must be transferred to a Cameroonian business organization), it shall be attached to a company in existence or to be created, governed by the laws of the Contracting States not later that two years after the branch is set up, unless this obligation is waived by order of the minister in charge of trade in the Contracting State in which the subsidiary is located.[139] This therefore calls for an examination of the ramifications of non-domestication.

2.2. The Implications of Non-Domestication

Non-domestication may arise from two kinds of situations. Firstly, it may arise from a situation where a waiver of domestication is expressly obtained.

[134] Art. 97.

[135] Art. 116.

[136] Art. 117.

[137] Art.118.

[138] Art. 119.

[139] Art. 120.

Secondly, it may also arise from a situation where an express waiver is not obtained but the government does not object to the company's operations. It is important to point out that the oil industry in Cameroon is largely dominated by foreign companies.[140] These companies are systematically granted waivers,[141] meaning that the internal affairs of these companies are governed by the laws of their countries of incorporation and therefore subject only to Cameroon's public policy considerations.

2.3. Contractual Arrangements for the Exploitation of Petroleum Oil in Cameroon

One obvious but highly relevant feature of the oil sector is that its exploration and development must take place where the resources are located. Ventures in this sector are of a high-risk nature in the physical, commercial, and political sense as it is difficult to determine in advance the existence, extent and quality of mineral reserves as well as production costs and the future price in the world market. Profitability is not assured, and the fact that the resource is finite requires the continual acquisition of interests in new deposits.

There are four basic contract types in the petroleum industry: concessions, production-sharing agreements, service contracts, and joint ventures. Each form can be used to accomplish the same purpose. The differences between the types of contracts are of a conceptual nature, mainly with regard to levels of control granted to the foreign contractor, to the compensation arrangements, and to the levels of involvement by National Oil Companies (NOCs). The Cameroon Petroleum Code makes provision for the usage of either Concession Contracts (CC) or Production-Sharing Contracts (PSC).[142]

---

[140] The oil companies in Cameroon include :ADDAX, EUROIL, EXXON MOBIL, KOSMOS ENERGY, PECTEN,PERENCO,PETRONAS, STERLING OIL, TOTAL E&P, TROPHY, TULLOW and TURNBERRY. Of all these companies, TOTAL E&P is the largest in terms of production activities.

[141] Article 120 of the UA on CCEIG which provides that where the subsidiary is owned by a foreigner, it shall be attached to a company in existence or to be created, governed by the laws of one of the Contracting States not later that two years after the branch is set up, unless this obligation is waived by order of the minister in charge of trade in the Contracting State in which the branch is located.

[142] Art. 13 of Law No. 99/013 of 22 December 1999, instituting the Petroleum Code of Cameroon.

2.3.1. Concession Contracts

With respect to concession contracts, the Code[143] provides that they shall be signed for the purpose of authorizing an oil company to explore for hydrocarbons. The contract determines the rights and obligations of the State and the oil company throughout the duration of the contract. If during the term of the contract oil is discovered in commercial quantity, the holder of the contract has the right to exploit it.[144] The oil company finances all the petroleum operations and disposes of the oil extracted during the validity of the contract, in conformity with the terms of the concession contract, taking into account the right of the State to receive royalties.[145]

2.3.2. Production Sharing Contracts (PSC)

A PSC is a contract between the host government and a foreign oil company, which gives to the latter the exclusive right to explore and exploit oil from a particular oil field, which is a subject matter of the contract.[146] The oil company bears all the cost of production and receives a re-imbursement of only the part of the production cost referred to as "cost oil".[147] In the mid 1960s, the Indonesian government introduced production-sharing contracts in response to increasing criticism and hostility towards the existing concession system. The oil is owned by the state, which brings in a foreign company to explore and, in case of commercial discovery, develop the resource. The company operates at its sole risk and expense, and receives a specified share of production as a reward.

Thus, the main difference from concessions is the ownership of the mineral resource. Whereas under concessions, all crude oil produced belongs to the company, under PSCs, it is owned by the host government, and the share of production allocated to the company can be regarded as payment or compensation for the risk taken and services rendered.

The Cameroon government, through its State-owned National Hydrocarbons Corporations (SNH), has over the years signed a series of

---

[143] Ibid. Art. 14.

[144] Ibid.

[145] Ibid.

[146] Ibid. Art. 15.

[147] Ibid. Art. 16.

PSCs. These include the PSC between SNH and the Swiss-based Glencore and Afex Global Limited to explore for oil in the Matanda block of the country's Douala-Kribi/Campo basin;[148] PSC between SNH and Perenco Cameroon for oil exploration in the Elombo block (former Ebodje permit) situated offshore in the Douala/Kribi-Campo basin;[149] the BowLeven subsidiary, Euroil Ltd has also signed a PSC with SNH for the Bomono permit extending to the Douala/ Kribi-Campo basin;[150] Kosmos Energy signed a PSC covering the Ndian River Block located predominantly onshore.[151]

When an oil company has successfully signed either a Concession contract or a PSC, it can then start its activity in either exploring or exploiting the oil. At this stage, the oil company is governed both by domestic laws as well as some rules of international law applicable to the oil industry. They also operate subject to the contract provisions.

2.4. Applicable Law on Operation

During the duration of the CC or PSC, the oil company is regulated by local legislation, international law and the private code of conduct.

2.4.1. Local Legislation

2.4.1.1. The Petroleum Code

The main piece of legislation governing the oil industry in Cameroon is Law No. 99/013 of 22 December 1999, instituting the Petroleum Code (the Code) of Cameroon, together with Decree No. 2000/465 of 30 June 2000 laying down modalities for the application of the Code. The Code in its Part V, lays down the rights and obligations attached to petroleum activities. It provides that the holder of a petroleum contract, whether a CC or PSC, must conduct its activities with due diligence, taking into consideration, the rules of international law and practice applicable to the industry.[152] The Code requires that if the holder of a petroleum contract requires services from another

[148] See http://africanpress.wordpress.com/2008/04/12/cameroon-signs-oil-production-sharing-contract. (last accessed on July 7 2010).

[149] See http://www.oilvoice.com/n/Perenco_Signs_ProductionSharing_Contract_in_Cameroon/db5 (last accessed on July 7 2010).

[150] See http://www.rigzone.com/news/article.asp?a_id. (last accessed on July 7 2010).

[151] See http://www.kosmosenergy.com, (last accessed on July 7 2010).

[152] Ibid. Art. 71.

company, it should give priority to a Cameroonian company for the provision of such services.[153] It equally requires the holder of a petroleum contract to employ as a matter of priority, qualified Cameroonians in their operations.[154] In furtherance of this requirement, the petroleum or oil company is expected to design and sponsor a training programme at the beginning of its operations, so as to train qualified Cameroonians, in line with the petroleum contract.[155] The existence of this provision does not seem to have any significant impact because it is not mandatory enough to deliver the required goods. This requirement would be more effective at providing work opportunities if it expressed in numerical terms, the number of people to be trained, rather than allow it to be determined by the petroleum contract which often is a secret between the government and the oil company.[156] The petroleum company also has an obligation to satisfy the internal market first if need be and at the request of the Minister in charge of Hydrocarbons, under conditions to be defined by decree.[157] The obligation to satisfy the internal market is an important issue which deserves better attention than has been provided so far. The importance of this issue is down-played by the use of the phrase "if need be". This phrase is too flexible and subjective to be employed in such circumstances. Further, the determination of need is left at the discretion of the minister who may not see the need whereas in actual fact, there is a need.

With respect to environmental issues, the Code obliges the holder of a petroleum contract in all circumstances to conduct its activities in such a way as to conserve natural resources and the essential characteristics of the environment and the ecosystem.[158] Since operations associated with the exploration and exploitation of oil has a potential to damage the environment, the contract holder is obliged to undertake an environmental impact assessment prior to the commencement of activities.[159] Some oil companies have gone past the Code by carrying out not only the environmental impact

[153] Ibid. Art. 76.

[154] Ibid. Art. 77.

[155] Ibid.

[156] This researcher while on field work to Bamuso Sub-Division in Ndian Division, precisely in Mofako village, where Kosmos Energy installations were located for the purpose of carrying out seismic studies, sort to talk to the authorities of the company, who vehemently refused to talk, preferring to give a phone number which never went through.

[157] Ibid. Art. 79.

[158] Ibid. Art. 82.

[159] Ibid. Art. 83.

assessment, but also have undertaken an environmental and social impact assessment prior to commencement of activities.[160] This assessment permits the oil company to evaluate the direct and indirect consequences of the petroleum activities on the ecological equilibrium and on the social life of local inhabitants. Companies definitely go beyond the legal obligation so as to reassure the local communities that oil exploitation will benefit them. Apart from the Petroleum Code, there are other pieces of legislation aimed at regulating notably down stream activities in the oil industry in Cameroon.[161] They include:

- Law No. 96/147 of August 5th 1996 regulating the transport of hydrocarbon by pipeline from other countries. This law was urgently enacted to regulate the construction and exploitation of the Chad-Cameroon pipeline project. It was the basis of the controversial Convention of Establishment between Cameroon Oil Transportation Company (COTCO) and the Republic of Cameroon.[162]
- Law No. 98/15 of July 14th 1998 relating to establishments classified as dangerous, unhealthy or obnoxious.
- Decree No. 2000/935/PM of 13 November 2000 laying down the conditions for exercising activities in the down-stream petroleum sector. This sector involves the distribution of petroleum products.

2.4.2. Rules of International Law

In addition to domestic legislation regulating expressly or implicitly the petroleum industry, there also exist rules of international law, which regulate the activities of oil companies operating in Cameroon. These rules for the purpose of convenience can be examined under 'hard law' and 'soft law'.

2.4.2.1. Soft Law

Soft laws are rules of international law which are not legally binding, but which are respected as a matter of custom. These rules emanate from

---

[160] See http://www.kosmosenergy.com/cameroon.html. (Last accessed on July 7th 2010)

[161] 'Down stream activities' in the Oil Industry refer to the distribution or marketing of Petroleum Products.

[162] For a discussion on COTCO, See infra, chapter eight.

international organizations such as the United Nations (UN), The Organization for Economic Cooperation and Development (OECD), and the World Trade Organization (WTO).

With respect to the OECD, the Guidelines for Multinational Enterprises (the Guidelines) are recommendations addressed by governments to multinational enterprises. They provide voluntary principles and standards for responsible business conduct consistent with applicable laws. The Guidelines aim to ensure that the operations of these enterprises are in harmony with government policies, to strengthen the basis of mutual confidence between enterprises and the societies in which they operate, to help improve the foreign investment climate and to enhance the contribution to sustainable development made by multinational enterprises. The Guidelines are part of the OECD Declaration on International Investment and Multinational Enterprises, the other elements of which relate to national treatment, conflicting requirements on enterprises, and international investment incentives and disincentives.

However, the Organization for Economic Cooperation and Development Guidelines for Multinational Enterprises which are regarded as the only existing code of conduct for international business are, as the name suggests, guidelines only and are not legally binding on MNCs. They are voluntary in nature. The voluntary and nonbinding nature of the Guidelines has led to criticisms that they do not represent a genuine attempt to control MNCs but are rather designed to deflect criticisms of their activities.[163] A further criticism is that the very objective of the OECD is to protect business and this, according to some observers, is made clear in the Guidelines.[164] The initiation of a Multilateral Agreement on Investment (MAI) within the OECD in 1995 appeared to give much credence to the criticism that the objective of the OECD is to protect business and the Guidelines merely designed to deflect criticisms.

Another international organization that is worth examining is the United Nations Organization (UN). This is the world's most representative body with a potential to control MNCs. The UN attempted to control MNCs through

---

[163] R. Jenkins, 'Corporate Code of conduct: self-regulation in a Global Economy', UNRISD

Programme on Technology, Business and Society. Paper No. 2. April 2001, p. 4.

[164] E. V. K. Fitzgerald, 'Regulating Large International Firms' UNRISD Programme on Technology,

Business and society, Paper No. 5, November 2001, p. 13.

the use of codes of conduct, but this approach was abandoned with the abolition of the United Nations Commission on Transnational Corporations in 1994. Unfortunately, the UN changed its policy from regulation of MNCs to facilitation of foreign direct investment and eventually to co-operation with business following the establishment of the Global Compact by the UN Secretary General in 1999. Thus, the UN prefers co-regulation and self-regulation by business over the use of legally binding frameworks. For example, like the Global Compact, the UN Norms on the Responsibilities of Transnational Corporations and Other Business Enterprises with Regard to Human Rights, adopted by the UN Sub-Commission for the Protection and Promotion of Human Rights in 2003, are not legally binding.[165]

The UN General Assembly Resolution 3281 provides in article 2 (2) (b) that each State has the right to regulate and supervise the activities of transnational corporations within its national jurisdiction and take measures to ensure that such activities comply with its laws, rules and regulations and conform with its economic and social policies. It goes further to provide that transnational corporations shall not intervene in the internal affairs of the host State.[166] On its part, the UN General Assembly Resolution 1803 provides in part, that where authorization to invest is granted to foreign capital, such capital and the earnings on such capital, shall be governed by the terms thereof (terms of the authorisation), by national legislation in force and by international law. It further provides that the profit derived must be shared in the proportion freely agreed upon, in each case, between the investor and the recipient State, with due care being taken to ensure that there is no impairment, for any reason, of that State's sovereignty over its natural wealth and resources.[167] Equally, Resolution 3202 makes provision for the regulation and control of the activities of transnational corporations.[168]

However, a controversy surrounds the binding nature of these GA resolutions. The UN Charter does not contain any general provisions on the legal effects of GA resolutions. Opinon is therefore divided over the issue as

[165] Edwin Mujih, "The Regulation of Multinational Corporations operating in Developing Countries: A Case Study of the Chad-Cameroon Pipeline Project", (2004), Social Responsibility International Journal.

[166] GA Res.3281 (xxix), 29th Sess., Supp. No.31 (1974).

[167] Art. 1 (3) of General Assembly Resolution 1803 (XVII) of 14 December 1962, on Permanent Sovereignty over Natural Resources.

[168] See Part V of UN General Assembly Resolution 3202 on the Programme of Action on the Establishment of a New International Economic Order, May 1 1974.

to whether the UNGA resolutions are binding or not. Proponents of the non-binding nature of the UNGA resolutions[169] argued that:

> All that the GA resolution can do is to discuss and recommend and initiate studies and consider reports from other bodies. It cannot act on behalf of all the members as the Security Council does and its decisions are not directions, telling the member states what they are, or are not to do. In principle, its functions are similar to those of the assembly of the League and like that body, must rely on cooperation among members and not on power for it has no power.[170]

However, some jurists[171] are of the view that the UNGA resolutions have weight in transnational transactions. Brownlie observes that :

> In general, these resolutions are not binding on member states but when they are concerned with general norms of international law, then acceptance by a majority vote constitutes evidence of the opinions of governments in the widest form for the expression of such opinion. Even when they are framed as general principles, resolutions of this kind provide a basis for the progressive development of the law and the speedy consolidation of customary rules.[172]

On his part, George Lauterpacht while reiterating the opinion that GA resolutions are legally binding on member states equally observed as follows:

> Whatever may be the content of the recommendation and whatever may be the nature and the circumstance of the majority by which it has been reached, it is nevertheless a legal Act of the UN, which members are under a duty to treat with a degree of respect appropriate to a resolution of the GA.[173]

---

[169] J. L. Briely and D.H.N Johnson.

[170] J.L. Briely, The Basis of Obligation in International Law, Oxford Clarendon Press, 1958.

[171] Ian Brownlie and George Lauterpacht.

[172] Ian Brownlie, Principles of Public International Law, 6th Ed., 2003.

[173] George Lauterpacht, Private Law Sources and Analogies of International Law, Archon Books,

George Lauterpacht equally emphasised the importance of not allowing the principle that the UNGA have only a recommending force to obscure their importance and weight in international interactions.[174]

Looking at the arguments of the proponents of the non- binding nature of the UNGA resolutions, one is tempted to think that they based their arguements on Art. 38 of the statute of the International Court of Justice (ICJ) which deals with the sources of international law. They argue that the UNGA resolutions are not listed as a source of international law under that article. This contention could be said to be a mistaken one on the basis of the fact that Art. 38 of the statute of the ICJ does not provide an exhaustive list of the sources of international law. Consequently, UNGA resolutions may be forcefully argued to have a force of law if approved or adopted by a vast majority of the members of the UN. It may therefore be on this score that the decision in the case of *Texaco Overseas Co. V. Libya*[175] could be said to be very instructive. In that case, the sole arbitrator, Professor Dupuy held that Libya was bound by Resolution 1803 and therefore liable to compensate the plaintiff for its interest and property in the country. The sole arbitraror based his decision on the fact that approval of resolution 1803 cuts accross the geographical area of the globe and therefore saw it as constituting of existing customary rules of international law. The decision in *Liamco V. Libya*[176] equally re-inforces Professor Dupuy's decision. In *Liamco V. Libya*, the arbitrator observed that resolution 1803 created rules of international law.

The World Trade Organization (WTO) is another organization that seeks to protect rather than regulate MNCs. As the most important body involved in international regulation of commerce, the WTO seems to be the only international body with real power to enforce judgments against MNCs, thus effectively regulating them. Unfortunately, the devotion of the WTO to free trade means that it is seen by some critics[177] as part of the problem rather than the solution, as most of its decisions have been in favour of MNCs.[178] The WTO agreements cover goods, services and intellectual property. They spell out the principles of liberalization, and the permitted exceptions. They include

---

1970.

[174] Ibid.

[175] Texaco Overseas Co. V. Libya, reprinted in 20 I.L.M 1, 75 (1981).

[176] Libyan American Oil Co. (LIAMCO) v. Libya, reprinted in 20 I.L.M. 1, 53 (1981).

[177] See note 179, infra.

[178] Ibid. at p. 95.

individual countries' commitments to lower customs tariffs and other trade barriers, and to open and keep open services markets. They set procedures for settling disputes. They prescribe special treatment for developing countries. They require governments to make their trade policies transparent by notifying the WTO about the laws in force and the measures adopted, and through regular reports by the secretariat on countries' trade policies. These agreements are often called the WTO's trade rules, and the WTO is often described as "rules-based", a system based on rules. But it is important to remember that the rules are actually agreements that governments negotiated. The rules and resolutions emanating from these organizations are not binding, although there is controversy as to the binding nature of United Nations General Assembly Resolutions.

2.4.2.2. Hard Law

Hard law here refers to binding rules of international law as may be found in instruments like the United Nations Charter, the Universal Declaration of Human Rights, the International Covenant on Civil and Political Rights, the International Covenant on Economic, Social and Cultural Rights, and the African Charter on Human and Peoples' Rights. It is necessary to indicate that Cameroon has signed and ratified all these instruments.

Although the existence of the norms embodied in these documents cannot be denied, there has been controversy about their binding character and practical effect. L. B. Sohn argues[179]in particular, that most of these documents are 'soft law,' rather than 'hard law.' According to this view, these documents contain no more than mere guidelines, which states need not follow. Furthermore, there are no effective means of implementing the documents, and violators go unpunished.[180] The better view definitely is that these documents have become a part of international customary law and, as such, are binding on all states. Some of the documents provide appropriate means of implementation, leading to a proper condemnation of violators.

It is difficult to proceed against great sovereign states, and even more difficult to punish them in any meaningful fashion. States function through individuals. Eventually means are likely to be found to punish those who are truly responsible for a state's misbehaviour. Although the law ideally treats

---

[179] Louis B. Sohn, "The New International Law: Protection of the Rights of Individuals rather than States", (1982), 32 Am. U. L. Rev. 1.

[180] Ibid.

all parties equally, it is well known that the legal enforcement system is less effective against those who are powerful than against those who are poor and weak. Victor Hugo described this in his great romances, *The Count of Monte Cristo* and *Les Miserables.*[181] Emile Zola and Charles Dickens observed that even domestic law is imperfect in this respect.[182] It is also well known that powerful multinational corporations and great transnational consortia often have been able to act outside the law, with only minor punishments. Once governments became willing to enforce stronger sanctions, punishing responsible officers as well as the corporations themselves led to more cautious attitudes on the part of officers.

On the international scene, it is difficult to persuade governments, which as a group are the international lawmakers, to agree on enforcement against themselves, in the event that they violate international law. It is not the law that is soft, but the governments. Usually hiding behind the vital interests of the state, 'raison d'état,' they find it difficult to declare punishable an act that they may some day wish to commit.

2.4.2.2.1. The U.N. Charter. Although it is easy to wave off the Charter of the United Nations with the back of the hand and stigmatize it as being ineffective, most such critics seem not to have reviewed the Charter carefully enough and, therefore, do not have a mastery of its exact content. This constitution of the world, the highest instrument in the intertwined hierarchy of international and domestic documents, prevails expressly over all other treaties, and implicitly over all laws, anywhere in the world.[183] The Charter was not meant to be a temporary document, to be easily and perpetually amended, but, rather, to be

---

[181] Ibid.

[182] C. Dickens, Bleak House (1853). The following passage demonstrates Dickens' dim view of the legal system:

This is the Court of Chancery; which has its decaying houses and its blighted lands in every shire; which has its worn-out lunatic in every madhouse, and its dead in every churchyard; which has its ruined suitor, with his slipshod heels and threadbare dress, borrowing and begging through the round of every man's acquaintance; which gives to monied might the means abundantly of wearying out the right; which so exhausts finances, patience, courage, hope; so overthrows the brain and breaks the heart; that there is not an honourable man among its practitioners who would not give—who does not often give—the warning, 'Suffer any wrong that can be done you, rather than come here!

[183] U.N. Charter, art. 103.

a lasting expression of the needs of humanity as a whole. Its basic provisions, constituting the *jus cogens*, are broad in scope and sufficiently flexible to permit their interpretation to be adjusted to the needs of each generation. It is no secret that although the wording of the Charter has changed little since its inception, only with respect to the membership of its two executive organs, the meanings of several provisions have been greatly expanded in practice by commonly accepted interpretations. In attempting to explain this scenario, L. B. Sohn contends that:

> As nature abhors a vacuum, constitutional documents abhor strait-jackets. Great ideas cannot be imprisoned; they must be able to move freely from one part of the earth to another. The U.N. Charter contains several such ideas, which revolutionized the world, although no one knew in 1945 how successful the drafters of the Charter would be in planting in that document the seeds from which many mighty trees would grow.[184]

The most influential of these ideas are that human rights are of international concern, and that the United Nations has the duty to promote 'universal respect for, and observance of, human rights and fundamental freedoms for all without distinction as to race, sex, language and religion.'[185] It is the duty of the international community not only to respect human rights but also to promote their 'universal respect' and to ensure that they are observed throughout the globe.[186] All members of the United Nations - not only the original 50, but the more than 192[187] members today - have pledged to 'take joint and separate action,' in cooperation with the United Nations for the achievement of these great purposes.[188] In the Charter's preamble, the peoples of the United Nations as well as their governments, have reaffirmed their 'faith in fundamental human rights, in the dignity and worth of the human person, in the equal rights of men and women and of nations large and small.'[189] In that statement, the authors of the Charter anticipated not only the racial

---

[184] Cf. note 179, supra, at p. 6.
[185] U.N. Charter, art. 55(c).
[186] Ibid.
[187] http://www.un.org/en/members/growth.shtml
[188] Ibid. art. 56.
[189] Ibid. preamble.

revolution, but also the dignity and worth of the human person. The charter therefore anticipated that the human person had the right to lead a dignified life as well as live in an environment free from contamination. It implies that all peoples, both physical and moral, have to take measures to ensure that this should be the case. The United Nations deals principally with nation states. However, the various nation states are made up of different constituent parts. Hence, the aspirations of the United Nations Charter are to be applicable on these constituent parts.

2.4.2.2.2. The Universal Declaration of Human Rights. Although the U.N. Charter mentions human rights in many places, it did not prepare a more detailed document paralleling the national bills or declarations of the rights of man and of the citizen. It was promised at San Francisco that the United Nations would commence the drafting of an International Bill of Rights, as one of the first items of business. The Commission on Human Rights was established in 1946, only a few months after the Charter came into force, and was asked to prepare such a document.[190] It soon became obvious that the task could take a long time and, in view of the urgency of the matter, that the first step should be a declaration of general principles, to be followed later by a document containing more precise obligations.

Two years later, the first document, the Universal Declaration of Human Rights,[191] was ready. On December 10, 1948, the General Assembly, after some amendments, approved it unanimously. Although some delegations emphasized that the Universal Declaration of Human Rights was not a treaty imposing legal obligations,[192] others more boldly argued that it was more than an ordinary General Assembly resolution; that it was a continuation of the Charter and shared the dignity of that basic document. It merely expressed more forcefully, rules that already were recognized by customary international law. Under the latter view, the Declaration would possess a

---

[190] E.S.C. Res. 5(I), 1 U.N. ESCOR Supp. (No. 1) at 163, U.N. Doc. E/1 (1946).

[191] Approved Dec. 10, 1948, G.A. Res. 217A, U.N. Doc. A/810 at 56 (1948) [hereinafter cited as Universal Declaration]. Among the rights included in the Universal Declaration are the following: the right to life, liberty, and security of person (art. 3); the right to be free from arbitrary arrest, detention, or exile (art. 9); the right to marry and found a family (art. 16); the right to freedom of thought, conscience, and religion (art. 18); and the right to education (art. 26).

[192] Mrs. Roosevelt was obliged to state on behalf of the United States that the Declaration 'was not a treaty or international agreement and did not impose legal obligations.' 3 U.N. GAOR (pt. 1, 3d Comm.) at p. 22 (1948).

binding character.[193] In particular, Professor Cassin, one of the principal authors of the Declaration, explained that the Declaration was 'destined to guide Governments in the determination of their policy and their national legislation,' that it 'could be considered as an authoritative interpretation of the Charter of the United Nations and as the common standard to which the legislation of all the Member States of the United Nations should aspire,' and that it 'was a development of the Charter which had brought human rights within the scope of positive international law.'[194] The Declaration itself proclaims that it is 'a common standard of achievement for all peoples and all nations.' It calls upon every individual and every organ of society to strive, 'by progressive measures, national and international, to secure . . . universal and effective recognition and observance of the rights and freedoms therein.'[195]

Even if governments and scholars were originally in disagreement regarding the importance, status, and effect of the Universal Declaration, practice in the United Nations soon caught up with the doubters. Many of the governments that originally were skeptical about the value of the Declaration did not hesitate to invoke it against other countries. Thus, the United States invoked it in the so-called *Russian Wives Case*, and the General Assembly declared that Soviet measures preventing Russian wives from leaving the Soviet Union in order to join their foreign husbands were 'not in conformity with the Charter,' citing Articles 13 and 16 of the Declaration in support of its conclusion.[196] The Soviet Union, which originally claimed that the Declaration violated the Charter's prohibition against interference in a state's internal affairs, later voted for many resolutions charging South Africa with violations of the Universal Declaration.[197]

The Declaration thus is now considered to be an authoritative interpretation of the U.N. Charter, spelling out in considerable detail the meaning of the phrase 'human rights and fundamental freedoms,' which Member States agreed in the Charter to promote and observe. The Universal Declaration has joined the Charter of the United Nations as part of the constitutional structure of the world community. The Declaration, as an authoritative listing of human

---

[193] Louis B. Sohn, A Short History of the United Nations Documents on Human Rights, in Commission to study the Organisation of Peace, 18th Report, The United Nations and Human Rights 39, 68-70 (1968).

[194] Ibid at p. 70.

[195] Universal Declaration, supra note 191.

[196] G.A. Res. 285(III), U.N. Doc. A/900 (1949).

[197] See, S.C. Res. 182, 18 U.N. SCOR Supp. (Oct.-Dec. 1963) at 103, U.N. Doc. S/5471 (1963).

rights, has become a basic component of international customary law, binding on all states, not only on members of the United Nations. Thus, multinationals, and by extension oil multinationals, operating across borders are answerable to this international constitution.

2.4.2.2.3. The Covenants. A cursory look at the environment of human rights may put in perspective the role of the two international covenants as binding international legal instruments pursuant to which oil multinationals may be regulated. The theoretical nature of human rights has been debated forcefully for a long time, without resolution. In the play *Antigone*, Sophocles[198] described Antigone's dilemma when King Creon prohibited the burial of her brother, who had been killed while rebelling against the King. When she was arrested for violating that order, she defended her action by claiming that the King could not override the 'immutable, unwritten laws of heaven.' The King replied that traitors must be punished; a state must have laws and they must be obeyed in all things, just and unjust alike, otherwise, there will be anarchy, and there is no evil worse than anarchy.[199]

Similarly, when rebelling against the English King, the American revolutionaries in 1776 relied in their Declaration of Independence on the concept of 'inalienable rights' endowed by their Creator.[200] In the same spirit, the French National Assembly in 1789 set forth in the Declaration of the Rights of Man and of the Citizen 'the natural and imprescriptible rights of man.'[201] In 1973, Jacques Maritain pointed out that:

> The human person possesses rights because of the very fact that it is a person, a whole, a master of itself and of its acts . . . by virtue of natural law, the human person has the right to be respected, is the subject of rights, possesses rights. These are things which are owed to a man because of the very fact that he is a man.[202]

[198] See supra, note 179, at p. 7.

[199] Ibid.

[200] Ibid.

[201] Declaration of the Rights of man and of the citizen art. 2 (1789), see also I. Brownlie, Basic Documents on Human Rights 8-10 (1971).

[202] J. Maritain, "The Rights of Man and Natural Law" 65 (D. Anson trans. 1951). See also M. Cranston, "What are Human Rights?" 11 (1973) (noting the resurgence of natural law; as a living, as well as an ancient, concept, it is potentially fallacious despite claims that it is binding all over the globe).

The United Nations' concept of human rights embraces this natural law concept of rights, rights to which all human beings have been entitled from time immemorial and to which they will continue to be entitled as long as humanity survives. Thus, both the Universal Declaration of Human Rights and the two Covenants assert in the first paragraphs of their preambles that the 'recognition of the inherent dignity and of the equal and inalienable rights of all members of the human family is the foundation of freedom, justice and peace in the world.'[203] In 1977, in specifying the guiding concepts for future human rights work within the United Nations' system, the General Assembly listed among those concepts the natural law idea that 'all human rights and fundamental freedoms of the human person and of peoples are inalienable.'[204]

These 'inalienable' rights, both permanent and universal, differ from rights, bestowed by positive law, that a state can give and take away. The distinction between these two categories of rights becomes evident when a state attempts to limit human rights in the interest of the community during an emergency. Thus, the International Covenant on Civil and Political Rights permits states to derogate from certain of its provisions, when a public emergency threatens the life of the nation.[205] In contrast, the Covenant does not permit derogation from certain inalienable rights, including the right to life, freedom from torture or cruel, inhuman, or degrading treatment or punishment, freedom from slavery and servitude, non-applicability of retroactive laws, right to recognition as a person before the law, and the right to freedom of thought, conscience, and religion.[206] The ICCPR has been adopted by Cameroon. So it is part of Cameroon positive law. The Cameroon Constitution puts international treaties above domestic laws;[207] so Cameroonians can not be deprived of the inalienable rights.

When the Commission on Human Rights finished the Universal Declaration, it began preparing the other part of the International Bill of Rights; a Convention containing precise obligations that would be binding on the State Parties. It proved impossible to formulate in a parallel manner, all the rights listed in the Universal Declaration. It became necessary to divide the materials into two categories: civil and political rights, and economic,

---

[203] See the preambles of the Universal Declaration, the ICCPR, and the ICESCR.

[204] G.A. Res. 32/130, 32 U.N. GAOR Supp. (No. 45) at 151, U.N. Doc. A/32/45 (1977).

[205] See the ICCPR, art. 4(1).

[206] Ibid. arts. 6, 7, 8, 11, 15, 16, 18.

[207] Art 45 of the Cameroon Constitution.

social, and cultural rights.[208] These two categories were embodied in two separate Covenants, each differing from the other in several respects. The main difference was in their treatment after coming into force. States parties were to give the Covenant on Civil and Political Rights immediate effect through appropriate legislative or other measures and by making available an effective remedy to any person whose rights have been violated.[209] In contrast, each State Party to the Covenant on Economic, Social and Cultural Rights agreed only to take steps, to the maximum of its available resources, toward a progressive realization of the rights recognized in that Covenant.[210] The latter Covenant thus contained a loophole because a state's obligation was limited to the resources available to it; thus a poor state could proceed slowly, progressing only as fast as its resources permitted. If its resources should diminish, for example, during an economic crisis, its progress could also decline. Resource rich developing countries are likely to cling to this provision whenever the citizenry demand economic advancement. In contrast, the Covenant on Civil and Political Rights permits no such excuses; a state must guarantee civil and political rights fully on ratification.[211]

Although doubts were expressed about the legal force of the Declaration,[212] the Covenants are now binding on a vast majority of member states, Cameroon being one of them.[213]

2.4.2.2.4. The African Charter on Human and Peoples' Rights. The African Charter on Human and Peoples' Rights, also known as the Banjul Charter on Human and Peoples' Rights, was adopted by the 18th Assembly of Heads of State and Government of the Organization of African Unity (OAU), held in Nairobi in June 1981. It entered into force on October 21, 1986, after the deposit of the 26th instrument of ratification, the number required by its Article 63(3). By April 16, 1987, there were 33 states parties to the Charter,[214]

---

[208] 13 U.N. ESCOR at 405-19, U.N. Doc. E/SR.524 (1951); G.A. Res. 543(VI), 6 U.N. GAOR Supp. (No. 20) at 36, U.N. Doc. A/2119 (1952); 9 U.N. GAOR Annex (Agenda Item 58) at 7-15, U.N. Doc. A/2808 (1954).

[209] Covenant on Civil and Political Rights, supra note 38, art. 2(2), 3(a). See also United Nations Action in the Field of Human Rights, U.N. Doc. ST/HR/2/Rev. 1 (1980).

[210] Covenant on Economic, Social and Cultural Rights, art. 2(1), (3).

[211] Covenant on Civil and Political Rights, art. 2(1), (3).

[212] Supra, note 198.

[213] See Multilateral Treaties Deposited with the Secretary-General of the United Nations.

[214] See Richard N. Kiwanuka, "The Meaning of 'People' in the African Charter of Human and

which makes it the largest regional human rights system in existence.[215] This is a regional instrument which is binding on all member States of the African Union. It provides in its Article 21 that:

> 1. All peoples shall freely dispose of their wealth and natural resources. This right shall be exercised in the exclusive interest of the people. In no case shall a people be deprived of it.
> 2. In case of spoliation, the dispossessed people shall have the right to the lawful recovery of its property as well as to an adequate compensation.
> 3. The free disposal of wealth and natural resources shall be exercised without prejudice to the obligation of promoting international economic cooperation based on mutual respect, equitable exchange and the principles of international law.
> 4. States parties to the present Charter shall individually and collectively exercise the right to free disposal of their wealth and natural resources with a view to strengthening African unity and solidarity.
> 5. States parties to the present Charter shall undertake to eliminate all forms of foreign economic exploitation particularly that practiced by international monopolies so as to enable their peoples to fully benefit from the advantages derived from their national resources.

Cameroon signed this Charter on 23rd July 1987, ratified same on 20th June 1989 and deposited it on 18th September 1989.

A careful examination of this provision indicates that oil companies operating for example in Cameroon can be held accountable either directly or indirectly for any violation of the rights of the citizens. The binding nature of this Charter is buttressed by the Bakweri Land Claims Case brought against Cameroon,[216] which is discussed more detailly in chapter six. Oil companies doing business in Cameroon actually operate within a well-defined legal framework. National laws prescribe both entry requirements as well as the

Peoples' Rights", (1988), 82 Am. J. Int'l L., at 1.

[215] The European Convention has 21 parties, while the American system covers 19 states.

[216] See Ndiva Kofele-Kale, "Asserting Permanent Sovereignty Over Ancestral Lands: The Bakweri Land Litigation Against Cameroon", (2007), Ann. Sur. Int'l Law.

standards to be respected during operations. On the other hand, international instruments through hard and soft law, have provided extensive benchmarks for the protection and promotion of human rights by oil companies whereever they operate. The legal framework for the exploitation of petroleum in Cameroon discussed herein above is intended to enhance the enjoyment of human rights by Cameroonians. Why should oil companies be obliged to protect and promote human rights while carrying out their operations? An answer to this question demands an examination of the basis of the rights.

3

ESTABLISHING THE RIGHTS HOLDER

3.0. Introduction

Oil exploitation and human rights have over the years had a very uneasy relationship. Human rights organizations, activist and journalists have all castigated oil companies for complicity in human rights violations. They have also castigated the government for complicity with oil companies in human rights violation. This negative publicity has forced some oil companies to search for face saving strategies so as to improve their image and ensure that their activities meet up with minimum human rights standards. These criticisms have also pushed states to try to align with some of the pronouncements contained in the *grundnorm* with respect to human rights. The negative socio-economic effects of oil development in Cameroon are not a secret. While Cameroonians as a nation have witnessed the effects of what may be referred to as a "resource curse",[217] people in areas where oil exploitation activities are located like in Ndian Division, those living along the Chad – Cameroon pipeline, and other oil fields, have experienced the negative effects of oil exploitation more than the rest of the country. Standards of living are extremely low, with a vast majority of Cameroonians living on less than one dollar a day;[218] social amenities are non-existent, and even where they exist, they are inefficient. The road network is deplorable (some areas in Ndian

[217]See Richard M Auty, "Sustaining Development in Mineral Economies: The Resource Curse Thesis" (1993). The concept of resource curse denots an inverse relationship between the availability of resources and the level of development.

[218]See Zeufack Albert, supra, note 10

Division see vehicles once a week, on market days only). To say the least, Cameroonians do not really feel a positive impact from the oil that comes out of their national territory (terrestrial or maritime). The socio – economic consequences of oil exploitation in Cameroon, are far from being positive. This chapter argues that the rich natural resource – oil actually belongs to Cameroonians and not only to those who have the opportunity of exploiting it. In examining the question as to who owns natural resources found within a national territory, whether they belong to the citizens or the state, this chapter looks at the international law principle of permanent sovereignty over natural resources. Based on this principle, this chapter equally argues that Cameroonians are supposed to be the primary beneficiaries of this activity, but the reality seems to be the contrary.

3.1. The Principle of Permanent sovereignty Over Natural Resources.

This principle seems to have originated from the understanding that those who own natural resources should reap the benefits. But this original intention was punctured somewhere along the line. For quite some time, the principle of permanent sovereignty over natural resources (PSNR) was a source of great controversy, which generated heated debates among legal scholars, representatives of developed, and developing countries, and multinational oil corporations.[219] Those arguing in favour of sovereignty of developing countries over their natural resources saw resources as a back bone of economic development.[220] This vision notwithstanding, the developing countries who championed this course and in whose favour the arguments were presented, have not been able to see their dreams materialize,[221] more than half a century since this concept came to the fore.[222] This may be explained following Ndiva Kofele-Kale's (1995)[223] reasoning that rulers of developing countries apparently

---

[219] See Ruth Gordon, "Racing U.S. Foreign Policy", (2003), 17 Nat'l Black L.J. 1, 3, See also David J. Halperin, "Human Rights and Natural Resources", (1968), 9 Wm. & Mary L. Rev. 770 (discussing a state's power to exploit natural resources).

[220] See supra note 74.

[221] See supra note 75.

[222] James N. Hyde, Permanent Sovereignty over Natural Wealth and Resources, (1956), 50 Am. J. Int'l L. 854.

[223] See Ndiva Kofele-Kale, Patrimonicide: The International Economic Crime of Indigenous Spoliation, (1995), 28 Vand. J. Transnat'l L. 48, 116. (He indicates that for those countries "that have been victims of looting on a massive scale, indigenous spoliation has become the single most important obstacle to economic development").

interpreted PSNR as conferring ownership of their nations' resources on themselves, thereby perceiving a license to corner the countries' wealth where none exists. After independence, kleptocratic leaders adapted the extractive structure of the colonial period.[224]

At the centre of the arguments in favour of the concept of PSNR was the protection of a country's natural resources against foreign spoliation. Evidently, there is no gainsaying now that "the wealth and natural resources of a country can be spoliated as thoroughly and efficiently by a native as well as by a foreigner,"[225] which deserves even a higher level of condemnation than foreign spoliators deserved. This is evidenced by the resource curse concept. To turn the hand of the clock on the current state of affairs means that a proper interpretation of instruments has to be made in relation to the question of who owns natural resources as between the government and the citizens.[226] In line with this, this chapter asserts that the right to permanent sovereignty over natural resources is vested in peoples, not states, and that the term "peoples" should be used to mean the owners of natural resources. Consequently, the government which should play a sovereign role should be considered as a mere trustee.[227] However, this may not be the solution because holding that the resources belong to the people is one thing, and ensuring that governments act as faithful trustees and competent managers of these resources is an entirely different and much more difficult matter to handle.

3.1.1. Evolution of the Concept.

The concept of PSNR entered the international legal lexicon close to fifty years ago. Its genesis has been traced to General Assembly Resolution 626 (VII) of December 21, 1952 entitled, Right to Exploit Freely Natural Wealth and Resources.[228] However, the most significant expression of the principle is contained in General Assembly Resolution 1803 (XVII) of 1962 which declares that both people and nations have a right to exercise sovereignty over natural resources.[229] Indeed, the controversy over the legal status of PSNR

---

[224] Ibid.

[225] W. Michael Reisman, "Sovereignty and Human Rights in Contemporary International Law", (1990), 84 Am. J. Int'l L. 866, 872.

[226] See infra, discussion on PSNR, State or People Centered ?

[227] Kofele-Kale, Patrimonicide, supra note 223, at p. 97.

[228] See G.A. Res. 626 (VII), U.N. Doc. A/2361 (Dec. 21, 1952); Ian Brownlie, Principles of Public International Law (6th ed. 2003).

[229] See G.A. Res. 1803 (XVII), U.N. Doc. A/5217 (Dec. 14, 1962). For an excellent discussion of

dates as far back as the negotiation stages of earlier resolutions on the subject.[230] One very important question which the landmark Resolution 1803 did not address was the issue of who actually had the right over natural resources, the people or the State. This led to doubts being cast on the legal validity of the concept of PSNR. Kofele-Kale[231] advanced that the reason for doubting the validity of the concept as a legal principle was the difficulty of ascertaining who or what the concept relates to. This was definitely so because, quite an important notion – peoples – which is used in the concept, is opened to a variety of definitions. A definition of "peoples" is necessary to provide some understanding. In doing so, the dominant theories of treaty interpretation will be used so as to demonstrate that the right to PSNR is a peoples' right, and that the definition of peoples contemplated in relevant international texts is one that encompasses all of the population.

3.2. Methods of Treaty Interpretation

The concept of PSNR is mentioned in resolutions of the UN General Assembly,[232] and also in international conventions or treaties.[233] What is common to these

---

the origins of the Resolution, see Karol N. Gess, Permanent Sovereignty Over Natural Resources: An Analytical Review of the United Nations Declaration and Its Genesis, 13 ICLQ 398 (1964). Shortly after its passing, the Resolution was described as "the capstone of more than ten years of consideration of the subject by the General Assembly, the Human Rights Commission, the Economic and Social Council and a special Commission on Permanent Sovereignty over Natural Resources." Stephen M. Schwebel, The Story of the U.N.'s Declaration on Permanent Sovereignty over Natural Resources, 49 A.B.A.J. 463, 463 (1963). Resolution 1803 was adopted with the objective of "determining the nature of the right of permanent sovereignty over natural resources, the manner in which the right should be exercised and what measures should be taken into account in accordance with international law." Lorne S. Clark, International Law and Natural Resources, 4 Syracuse J. Int'l L. & Com. 377, 380 (1977).

[230] P.J. O'Keefe, The United Nations and Permanent Sovereignty Over Natural Resources, (1974), 8 J. World Trade L. 239, 244-245.

[231] Kofele-Kale, Patrimonicide, Supra note 223.

[232] UN General Assembly Resolutions on permanent sovereignty over natural resources (PSNR) in addition to those already mentioned include: Charter of Economic Rights and Duties of States, G.A. Res. 3281 (XXIX), art. 2, U.N. Doc. A/9631 (Dec. 12, 1974) ("Every State has and shall freely exercise fully permanent sovereignty, including possession, use and disposal, over all its wealth, natural resources and economic activity."); Declaration on the Establishment of a New Economic Order, G.A. Res. 3201 (S-VI), P 4(e), U.N. Doc. A/9559 (May 1, 1974) (providing for "full permanent sovereignty of every State over its natural resources and all economic activities"); Permanent Sovereignty over Natural Resources, G.A. Res. 3171 (XXVIII), U.N. Doc. A/9030 (Dec. 17, 1973).

[233] See, e.g., European Energy Charter Conference, Energy Charter Treaty, Dec. 17, 1994, 34

United Nations resolutions and international conventions, is the fact that all of the provisions are susceptible to a variety of interpretations.[234] For the purpose of this chapter, the intentions of the drafters of these various provisions have to be captured so as to get rid of any vagueness or ambiguity that characterizes the instruments.

Over the years, a number of rules for the interpretation of treaties have emerged, prominent[235] among them appearing in the Vienna Convention on the Law of Treaties (Vienna Convention).[236] This convention is believed by many to represent a codification of customary international law on treaty interpretation.[237] By virtue of the Vienna Convention, the most important

I.L.M. 360, 394 (1995); United Nations Convention on the Law of the Sea arts. 56, 93, Nov. 16, 1994, 1833 U.N.T.S. 397 (announcing that "in the exclusive economic zone, the coastal State has sovereign rights for the purposes of exploring and exploiting, conserving and managing the natural resources" and providing for the "sovereign right of States to exploit their natural resources"); United Nations Framework Convention on Climate Change, Mar. 21, 1994, 1771 U.N.T.S. 107; United Nations Convention on Biological Diversity, June 5, 1992, 31 I.L.M. 818; Vienna Convention on Succession of States in Respect of State Property, Archives, and Debts art. 38.2, U.N. Doc. A/CONF.117/14 (Apr. 7, 1983), reprinted in 22 I.L.M. 306 (1983); Organization of African Unity: Banjul Charter on Human and Peoples' Rights, OAU Doc. CAB/LEG/67/3 rev. 5, (Jan. 7-19, 1981), reprinted in 21 I.L.M. 58 (1982); Vienna Convention on Succession of States in Respect of Treaties art. 13, U.N. Doc A/CONF.80/31 (Aug. 22, 1978), reprinted in 17 I.L.M. 1488 (1978) (affirming permanent sovereignty over natural wealth and resources); International Covenant on Civil and Political Rights, G.A. Res. 2200 (XXI), arts. 1(2), 47, U.N. Doc. A/6316 (Dec. 19, 1966), reprinted in 6 I.L.M. 368 (1967) (protecting people's right to utilze their natural wealth and resources to their fullest extent); International Covenant on Economic, Social and Cultural Rights, G.A. Res. 2200 (XXI), arts. 1(2), 11(2)(a), 25, U.N. Doc. A/6316 (Dec. 19, 1966), reprinted in 6 I.L.M. 360 (1967) (protecting people's right to dispose of their natural wealth and resources freely).

234 Antony Anghie, "The Heart of My Home: Colonialism, Environmental Damage, and the Nauru Case", (1993), 34 Harv. Int'l L.J. 445, 473, (noting the lack of clarity in the language of the instruments espousing the principle of PSNR, particularly the content of the right and the meaning of the term "peoples," leaving them open to several conflicting interpretations).

235 Mark J. Kadish, "Article 36 of the Vienna Convention on Consular Relations: A Search for the Right to Consul", (1997), 18 Mich. J. Int'l L. 565, 590 (stating that the Vienna Convention on the Law of Treaties governs the interpretation of treaties).

236 Vienna Convention on the Law of Treaties arts. 31-33, May 23, 1969, 1155 U.N.T.S. 331, 340.

237 Some scholars dispute the assertion that the Vienna Convention codifies customary international law on treaty interpretation. See, e.g, Philip M. Nichols, "GATT Doctrine", (1996), 36 Va. J. Int'l L. 379, 429, (stating that "whether the interpretive method suggested by the Vienna Convention has become customary is debatable" and citing to the conclusion of another scholar that Articles 31 and 32 of the Vienna Convention constitute an innovative scheme that does not represent a codification of custom).

way of determining meaning from a treaty provision is through a textual interpretation.[238] This method of interpretation could be justified on the ground that the drafters of the text may no longer be available to be interviewed. In this connection, an examination of the legislative history of the text is made. This is what may be referred to as the *travaux preparatoires*. The essence of this effort is to determine the intention of the treaty framer so as to avoid ambiguity. Some scholars have even gone further to suggest that the Vienna Convention does not necessarily require that an ambiguity be discovered before the preparatory texts are examined.[239] According to them, the *travaux preparatoires* or legislative history should be examined simultaneously with the corresponding text as well as other materials.[240] Laurence R. Helfer and Anne-Marie Slaughter (1997),[241] pointed out that it is common practice in international law to resolve potentially troublesome questions of textual interpretation by reference to a treaty's object and purpose. They say that:

> Treaties should be interpreted in good faith and in accordance with the ordinary meaning of the terms in pertinent provisions, keeping in view the object, purpose, and the overall text of the treaty.

Apart from the method of interpretation contained in the Vienna Convention, other interpretative methods are substantially similar. For example, Mark Villigier[242] identifies at least five methods of treaty interpretation whose origins long precede the Vienna Convention and which were considered by the International Law Commission in drafting the Vienna Convention's interpretative scheme contained in Articles 31 and 32. The methods highlighted include: textual interpretation, which concentrates entirely on the text of the treaty; subjective interpretation, which often utilizes extrinsic material other than the travaux prèparatoires; contextual

[238] Vienna Convention on the Law of Treaties, supra note 37, 1155 U.N.T.S. at 340, art. 31.

[239] Michael S. Straubel, "Textualism, Contextualism and the Scientific Method in Treaty Interpretation: How Do We Find the Shared Intent of the Parties"?, (1994), 23 Wayne L. Rev. 1191, 1205.

[240] Ibid.

[241] "Toward a Theory of Effective Supranational Adjudication", (1997), 107 Yale L.J. 273, 378. See also Pemmaraju Sreenivasa Rao, "Multiple International Judicial Forums: A Reflection of the Growing Strength of International Law or Its Fragmentation?", (2004), 25 Mich. J. Int'l L. 929, 952.

[242] Mark Villigier, Customary International Law and Treaties 327 (1985).

interpretation, which seeks to locate the treaty text within a wider context; teleological interpretation, which goes beyond the text in order to achieve the treaty's goals; and logical interpretation, which utilizes reasoning and abstract legal principles.[243] It is important to bear in mind that in the interpretation of a treaty, one should consider not only the particular treaty's context, but also the wider context of conventional or customary international law.

With the foregoing in mind, this chapter now proceeds to interpret the provisions of international instruments on the PSNR with a view to determining the scope of the principles' application. This will assist in determining whether the petroleum oil with which Cameroon is endowed, belongs to the State or to the people of Cameroon. The treaty interpretation shall be based on the text of the treaty and attention shall also be paid to the object and purpose of the treaty.

3.3. PSNR, State or People Centered?

An omission which has already been pointed out in Resolution 1803 is the fact that it is not clear as to who possesses the right of permanent sovereignty over natural resources, as between the State and the people. Going by this resolution therefore, it is not clear whether petroleum oil in Cameroon belongs to the State or to Cameroonians. This lacuna gives room for questioning the legal validity of the principle of PSNR. More important is how this omission affects full and proper enjoyment of PSNR. A threefold interpretation has emerged regarding the scope of the concept and the bearers of the right of permanent sovereignty over natural resources. The right to PSNR has been viewed alternatively as a right vested exclusively in peoples, solely in states (or nations), or jointly in peoples and states. Does the right to petroleum oil belong to Cameroonians, to the State or jointly to Cameroonians and the State?

Cameroon's national legislation[244] arrogates the right to natural resources generally to the State. However, this right is a right of sovereignty rather than a right of ownership *stricto senso*. This is in consonance with international law as evidenced by the hierachy of norms provided for by Article 45 of the

---

[243] Philip M. Nichols, "Corruption in the World Trade Organization: Discerning the Limits of the World Trade Organization's Authority", (1996), 28 N.Y.U. J. Int'l & Pol. 711, 742 n.105.

[244] See generally the preamble of the 1996 Constitution. See also Art, 3 of Law No. 99/013, instituting the Petroleum Code of Cameroon.

1996 Constitution of Cameroon. The concept of ownership entails the right to enjoy, manage and dispose of property in a manner deemed necessary. Going by the methods of interpreting texts examined above, it is clear that this is not the intention of the legislator. Jurists and legal commentators sometimes speak of PSNR as a right of states. Schwebel notes with regard to the 1962 resolution that "much of the resolution consists of an affirmation of the permanent sovereignty of states over their natural wealth and resources".[245] Some observe that because the concept of PSNR emanated from relations between multinational resource extraction corporations and their host states, the right of the state to legislate for the common good in the area of natural resources and national economic activities has become the primary construction given to the principle of permanent sovereignty over natural resources.[246] Judge Skubiszewski, in a dissenting opinion in the *East Timor case*,[247] adverted attention to the issue of each member of the UN respecting every other state's right to permanent sovereignty over natural resources.[248] In the Liamco case, the sole arbitrator, noted that resolutions such as Resolution 1803, "if not a unanimous source of law, are evidence of the recent dominant trend of international opinion concerning the sovereign right of States over their natural resources."[249] As a matter of fact, a good number of international instruments dealing with the subject mention only the state with reference to the right.[250] Some scholars like James Crawford, are hesitant, but nevertheless lean toward the fact that the right is state oriented when he says that it is possible that:

[245] Stephen M. Schwebel, "The Story of the U.N.'s Declaration on Permanent Sovereignty over Natural Resources", (1963), 49 A.B.A.J. 463. Resolution 1803 was adopted with the objective of "determining the nature of the right of permanent sovereignty over natural resources, the manner in which the right should be exercised and what measures should be taken into account in accordance with international law." See also Lorne S. Clark, "International Law and Natural Resources", (1977), 4 Syracuse J. Int'l L. & Com. 377, 380.

[246] Kofele- Kale, Patrimonicide, supra, note 223, p. 92.

[247] East Timor (Port. v. Austl.), 1995 I.C.J. 90 (June 30).

[248] Ibid. at p. 276

[249] Libyan American Oil Co. (LIAMCO) v. Libya, reprinted in 20 I.L.M. 1, 53 (1981), See also Klockner v. Cameroon 15 I.L.M. 2, 75 (1970).

[250] For example, the following treaties consistently vest the right to permanent sovereignty in states only: United Nations Convention on Biological Diversity, supra note 233; United Nations Convention on the Law of the Sea, supra note 233; United Nations Framework Convention on Climate Change, supra note 233; Energy Charter Treaty, supra note 233, art. 18.1.

> the notion of permanent sovereignty ... is equivocal as between a right of peoples and a right of States at the moment, but also suspecting that the question of permanent sovereignty in relation to independent States is a right of States rather than peoples[251].

Construing this right as vested in the state, is tantamount to saying that the state holds it exclusively and that only the government, as a representative of the state, can exercise it. It would also mean that the people would be unable to challenge natural resource policies and actions of the government at the national and international levels, even when such policies and actions work against their wishes and aspirations. What is more is that conceiving rights of this type as exclusive to the state implies as a practical matter that all the benefits arising from their exercise would accrue only to the elites while perpetuating socio-economic inequality in the country.[252]

Another way in which the right has been viewed is that it is jointly vested in the state and in the peoples. Schrijver once observe that, "Resolution 1803 says that permanent sovereignty over natural resources is a right of nations and peoples."[253] This development is seen as evidence of the progression of international law in this area through the heavy influence of international human rights law. Some claim that the rights of permanent sovereignty and self-determination "can now be understood as being owed both to the state, and to peoples and groups within the state in different forms, notwithstanding that there may have been a time when self-determination and sovereignty over natural resources were seen as being owed exclusively to the state."[254]

The African Charter on Human and Peoples' Rights, a premier treaty on the recognition of peoples' rights,[255] can also be read as vesting rights concerning

[251] Some Conclusions, in The Rights of Peoples 159, 171 (James Crawford ed., 1988).

[252] Stephen P. "Marks, Emerging Human Rights: A New Generation for the 1980s?", (1981)33 Rutgers L. Rev. 435, 447.

[253] Schrijver, supra note 74, at 311. See also Lorne S. Clark, International Law and Natural Resources, (1977), 4 Syracuse J. Int'L. & Com. 377, 380, (stating that the 1962 Declaration sought to "enshrine the rights of peoples and nations to permanent sovereignty over their natural wealth and resources").

[254] Margot E. Salomon & Ajun Sengupta, "The Right to Development: Obligations of States and the Right of Minorities and Indigenous Peoples" 35 (2003), available at http:// www.minorityrights.org/admin/Download/pdf/IP_RTD_SalomonSengupta.pdf (accessed on June 23, 2010).

[255] Julia Swanson, "The Emergence of New Rights in the African Charter", (1991), 12 N.Y.L. Sch. J. Int'l & Comp. L. 307, 308.

the exploitation and disposal of natural resources both in the state and the people.[256] A reading of the African Charter shows that the right to wealth and natural resources is guaranteed to both peoples and states. Commenting on this, R. M. D'Sa refers to Article 21 which proclaims that 'all peoples shall freely dispose of their wealth and natural resources.' He also asserts that this right is also given to African States themselves in Article 21(4).[257] Scholars have surmised from the various instruments on the subject that peoples and states, as opposed to states only, are the holders of this right.[258] By dint of this reasoning therefore, Cameroonians and the state are holders of this right.

This joint vestiture seems to be justified on the basis of the interplay of internal and external factors in matters of economic self-determination.[259] The state acts as an intermediary in dealings with external interests on behalf of the people in a way that is essentially impossible for the people to do themselves. However, Kiwanuka points out the inherent danger in such fusion of rights in places where the interests of the state and the people diverge. He posits that equating states with "peoples" assumes that the interests of the people are adequately represented by their state, a rarity in most developing countries.[260] In consequence, equating peoples and states further strengthens the state and subjects the rights of the people to the whims of whoever controls the political process.

Some writers assume that there is really no difference between the rights of peoples and states' rights. Accordingly, they use the terms interchangeably or move from one to another with no qualms.[261] Professor Oji Umozurike, a former chairman of the African Commission on Human and Peoples' Rights, references the African Charter's recognition of the right of peoples to pursue their economic and social development and immediately adds the authority

---

[256] See Richard N. Kiwanuka, "The Meaning of "People" in the African Charter on Human and Peoples' Rights", (1988), 82 Am J. Int'l L. 80, 95.

[257] The African Charter on Human and Peoples' Rights: Problems and Prospects for Regional Action, (1983), 10 Aust. Y.B. Int'l L. 101, 118.

[258] See Kofele-Kale, Patrimonicide, supra note 223 at p. 94.

[259] Kiwanuka, supra, note 256 at p. 95.

[260] Ibid. at p. 97.

[261] See, e.g., Greta Gainer, "Nationalization: The Dichotomy Between Western and Third World Perspectives in International Law", (1983), 26 How. L.J. 1547, 1560 ("States' rights to permanent sovereignty over natural resources emerged in the United Nations General Assembly resolutions. A 1952 resolution declared that 'the right of people freely to use and exploit their natural wealth is inherent in their sovereignty.'").

of state parties to freely dispose of their national wealth and resources for the purpose of strengthening African unity and solidarity.[262] Again, the difficulty with this situation is that it exposes the right of the people to a possible hijack by those in government, which is all too common, the case in many developing countries.

Some scholars argue, which is the position adopted by this chapter, that the Declaration on Permanent Sovereignty over Natural Resources envisages that the right to sovereignty over natural resources belongs to the people or inhabitants of a given country.[263] Dufresne goes ahead to say that, because international law revolves around states, it is quite easier to lose sight of the fact that people hold the right over their natural resources. According to him, "this prerogative belongs to the people, not to the state, nor to its governmental authorities. Resolution 1803 and subsequent texts are consistent and clear in making such attribution."[264] The Human Rights Covenants provide additional support for this contention. Article 1(2) of both covenants states:

> All peoples may, for their own ends, freely dispose of their natural wealth and resources without prejudice to any obligations arising out of international economic cooperation, based upon the principle of mutual benefit and international law. In no case may a people be deprived of its own means of subsistence.[265]

Some scholars have interpreted the above provisions as vesting natural resources in peoples, not governments. Professor Antonio Cassese forcefully argues that Article 1(2) "is not merely a reaffirmation of the right of every state over its natural resources; it clearly provides that the right over natural wealth belongs to peoples."[266] Former Projects Director for Harvard's Human Rights

---

262 U.O. Umozurike, "The African Charter on Human and Peoples' Rights", (1983), 77 Am. J. Int'l L. 902, 906.

263 Robert Dufresne, "The Opacity of Oil: Oil Corporations, Internal Violence, and International Law", (2004), 36 N.Y.U. J. Int'l L. & Pol. 356.

264 Ibid.

265 The Human Rights Covenants consists of (1) the International Covenant on Civil and Political Rights, G.A. Res. 2200 (XXI), at 52, U.N. Doc. A/6316 (Dec. 19, 1966); and (2) the International Covenant on Economic, Social and Cultural Rights, G.A. Res. 2200 (XXI), at 49, U.N. Doc. A/6316 (Dec. 19, 1966).

266 Antonio Cassese, The Self-Determination of Peoples, in The International Bill of Human Rights: The Covenant on Civil and Political Rights 92, 103 (Louis Henkin ed., 1981) This view,

Programme, Makau Wa Mutua also reads Article 1 of the Human Rights Covenants as making peoples the subjects of rights enumerated therein, viewing this development as "a departure from Western notions that human rights only attach to individuals."[267] Professor Theo van Boven notes that after an initial UN reluctance in the years immediately following World War II, driven by experiences stemming from that war, to vest in peoples the right to freely dispose of natural resources was a deliberate act.[268]

It can be argued on the basis of Article 21 of The African Charter on Human and Peoples' Rights as Oloka-Onyango[269] has done, that the right belongs to states as well as peoples and may also permit a more flexible reading that confers the right directly on the people without equating the people with states. A credible case may even be made in favour of the fact that the African Commission on Human and Peoples' Rights recently has implicitly adopted this more liberal interpretation.[270]

The people-centred interpretation of the right to PSNR has a strong

---

however, has been disputed in the following terms:

Although the right of free disposal over natural resources and of free determination of the internal political, economic, and social structure are sometimes categorized as peoples' rights (as in Art. 1 para. 2 of the [Human Rights] Covenants of 1966), it is the state which is the subject of these rights. The concept of permanent sovereignty over natural resources and the non-interference rule, which functions as a correlate to the right to free determination of internal policies, do not enable a people to claim rights from states, but are claimed by states on behalf of peoples against other states.

Philipp Kunig, The Role of "Peoples' Rights" in the African Charter of Human and Peoples' Rights, in New Perspectives and Conceptions of International Law: An Afro-European Dialogue 162, 165 (K. Ginther & W. Benedek eds., 1983).

[267] Makau wa Mutua, "The Banjul Charter and the African Cultural Fingerprint: An Evaluation of the Language of Duties", (1995), 35 Va. J. Int'l L. 339, 376.

[268] Ibid.

[269] J. Oloka-Onyango, "Reinforcing Marginalized Rights in an Age of Globalization: International Mechanisms, Non-State Actors, and the Struggle for Peoples' Rights in Africa", (2003), 18 Am. U. Int'l L. Rev. 851, 890 ("Rather than privileging the interests of the state, it is possible to read the article as a direct boost to the rights and interests of peoples within the state, and of the responsibility of the state to those peoples."). Kunig presents a contrary view: For instance, Art. 21 para. 4 indicates clearly that the right to free disposal of wealth and natural resources is to be exercised by states. It is a right for the benefit of the people, and it has to be exercised on behalf of the people, but the only entity which can be the legally active subject is the state. Kunig, supra note 266 at p. 167.

[270] Ibid. at p. 890.

historical background.[271] Article 1 of the Human Rights Covenants provides that: "The precedent for treating questions of permanent sovereignty over natural resources as rights of peoples, rather than as rights of States, is thus an established one."[272] Moreover, this interpretation is in consonance with the modern trend in international law away from focus on sovereign-state rights and towards an interest in the welfare of the nationals of these states.[273]

However, the views of critics are quite the contrary. Critics have argued first of all that, all relevant legal instruments do not clearly state that PSNR is vested in peoples.[274] The interpretation would have been more defensible if supported by the text of all the resolutions and conventions on PSNR or a considerable majority of them. Secondly to them, some instruments appear to vest unambiguously the right in states with barely any reference to peoples.[275] In the same light, it could also be reasonably argued that by employing the word "sovereignty" these texts implicitly posit that control of natural resources is vested in states.[276] Also, as stated earlier, even a generous reading of some of the instruments would at best only argue that this is a right that is jointly vested in both states and peoples.[277]

There is no gainsaying the fact that some of the instruments speak of the right of peoples or a right of peoples and nations or even a right of states. At a minimum, therefore, the right to permanent sovereignty over natural resources could be viewed as a right belonging to peoples and others also (states). By analogy therefore, if governments are vested with a right, it is not necessary to also vest it in the people they represent. As Professor James Crawford has observed, "any insistence that peoples' rights are vested in governments disqualifies the right in question from being regarded as a

[271] See Crawford, at p. 170 (observing that the right to free disposal of wealth and natural resources "was originally treated as a right of peoples ....").

[272] James Crawford, The Rights of Peoples: 'Peoples' or 'Governments'?, in The Rights of Peoples, supra at pp. 55, 63.

[273] See, e.g., Claudio Grossman & Daniel D. Bradlow, "Are We Being Propelled Towards a People-Centered Transnational Legal Order?", (1993), 9 Am. U. J. Int'l L & Pol'y 1 (discussing transnational organizations that impinge upon traditional views of territorial sovereignty).

[274] See, e.g., African Charter, (arguably vesting the right in states and peoples (though not peoples exclusively)); Charter of Economic Rights and Duties of States, (referring to states only in the context of PSNR).

[275] See for e.g The Energy Charter, supra note 232.

[276] See Anupam Chander & Madhavi Sunder, The Romance of the Public Domain, (2004) 92 Cal. L. Rev. 1331, 1366.

[277] See supra, note 255 at p. 41.

peoples' right."[278] These arguments seem to erode completely the hopes of Cameroonians who may want to lay claims as having rights over the oil found beneath their soil and also beneath their territorial waters. Perhaps, a cursory look at the historical background of the principle of PSNR may revive the hopes of a people who seemingly see the presence of oil on their land as a curse and its exploitation as a missed opportunity.

Historically, peoples and their well being were at the centre of the formulation of the principle of PSNR. The concept of permanent sovereignty "was conceived as a right of peoples"[279] because the concept was viewed as "the economic corollary of the political and legal call for decolonization and self-determination."[280] There is therefore no denying the fact that the principal objective behind the emergence of PSNR was to prevent the weak or shortsighted leadership from adversely affecting the survival of the country through wide concessionary arrangements.[281] In the 1950s, during some of the earliest debates on sovereignty over natural resources, one state delegation (Saudi Arabia) emphasized that the intention behind including the phrase "means of subsistence" in the draft was to prevent a situation that occurred with much frequency in the 19th Century wherein a weak or penniless government would seriously jeopardize a country's future with its method of granting economic concessions.[282] Governments were therefore to be legally prevented from seriously disturbing the rights or destroying the interests of the people. Interpreting relevant instruments in any way that allows today's national leaders to spoliate their countries' resources with impunity, is tantamount to sinking the very foundation on which the principle of PSNR was laid.

It is apposite to posit that the principle of PSNR has two arms, namely, the sovereignty of states and the self-determination of peoples.[283] Sovereignty is only one aspect of the origin of the principle. Therefore, while sovereignty covers one aspect of the origin, it in no way extinguishes the protection

[278] Crawford, Some Conclusions, supra note 250, at 167, cited in Philip Alston, Peoples' Rights: Their Rise and Fall, in Peoples' Rights 259, 290 (Philip Alston ed., 2001).

[279] Rudolf Dolzer, "Permanent Sovereignty over Natural Resources and Economic Decolonization", (1986), 7 Hum. Rts. L.J. 217, 221.

[280] Ibid.

[281] James N. Hyde, "Permanent Sovereignty over Natural Wealth and Resources", (1956), 50 Am. J. Int'l L. 854 at pp. 857 – 58.

[282] Ibid.

[283] Schrijver, supra note 223, at p. 368.

sought for peoples under the other arm of the principle. Furthermore, a state-centered interpretation of the right is sometimes understandable, given that the state can be seen as an exclusive medium through which the rights of the people could be effectively asserted against external interests and the international community.[284] Viewed from that perspective, the state is placed in the position of an agent, having authority to act on behalf of the principal, the entire population. Acting on behalf of the people includes making national policies on natural resource exploitation beneficial to all people. Where the governments acts as an agent, they act in a subsidiary capacity and not as holders of the right.[285] The government is in a fiduciary relationship vis-a-vis the people, and has to take into consideration all the duties incumbent on an agent at common law

In as much as the principal objective of the principle of PSNR was to deter national leaders from spoliating a country's wealth and resources, the story apparently has not changed. Professor Nico Schrijver elaborates as follows:

> This 'etatist' orientation in the evolution, interpretation and application of the principle of permanent sovereignty can well be understood as part of the economic and political emancipation process of developing countries, but equating peoples and States undoubtedly further strengthens the State and subordinates the rights of the people to the whims of those in power. However, a recent tendency can be discerned indicating that the . . . rights of peoples in a non-colonial context are receiving revived attention . . . . If this tendency is consolidated, the principle of permanent sovereignty will return to its two roots [which] would certainly be a laudable development, as it implies that States should be instruments to serve the interests of peoples and not vice versa.[286]

On the basis of the foregoing, the people of Cameroon have a right to the petroleum being exploited from there, and the state is an instrument which

[284] See Philip Alston, "The Shortcomings of a "Garfield the Cat" Approach to the Right to Development", (1985), 15 Cal. W. Int'l L.J. 510, 512 (asserting in reference to the right to development that the state could serve "as the medium through which the rights of individuals are able to be effectively asserted vis-à-vis the international community").

[285] Crawford, Some Conclusions, supra note 250, at p. 167.

[286] Schrijver supra note 223 at pp. 370 – 71.

has to serve the interest of the people. The need for a return to the original conception of permanent sovereignty cannot be overemphasized. It is simply imperative.

Having shown that the right to permanent sovereignty over natural resources is vested in the peoples of Cameroon, what remains unanswered is whether "peoples" here refers to those living in the areas hosting the oil production activities or it refers to the whole nation. This worry calls for a definition of the concept of "peoples."

3.4. The Definition of the Concept of "Peoples".

No generally accepted definition of what constitutes a "people" exists,[287] though the term clearly has a wide latitude and also is used in a wider number of legal instruments. In spite of this concern for peoples and peoples' rights, the term "people" has not been authoritatively defined in any of the instruments that employ it. Moreover, it is not used to convey identical meanings in all these instruments. The African Charter, one of the legal instruments in which the term is used, departs in very significant ways from contemporary multilateral human rights instruments. One of these is the dynamic entrenchment of the concept of "peoples" into international human rights theory, a concept, however, that had long enjoyed some currency in international law.[288] As early as 1790, the decree of the French Constituent Assembly referred to both the rights of man and the rights of peoples.[289] More recently, the term has been liberally invoked "in a number of international instruments on human rights, and General Assembly resolutions, more particularly those dealing with self-determination and permanent sovereignty over natural resources."[290] For example, the Charter of the United Nations was adopted in the name of "We the Peoples" and it recognized, in Article 1(2), the principle of "self-determination of peoples." Common Article 1 of the 1966 International Human Rights Covenants deals with the right of peoples

---

[287] See Theo van Boven, "The Relations Between Peoples' Rights and Human Rights in the African Charter", (1986), 7 Hum. Rts. L.J. 183, 191.

[288] See, e.g., Virally, 'Panorama du droit international contemporain: Cours général de droit international public" , (1983), 183 Recueil Des Cours 9, 57.

[289] Brownlie, "The Rights of Peoples in Modern International Law", (1985), 9 BULL. AUSTL. SOC'Y LEGAL PHIL. 104, 107.

[290] N. S. Rembe, "Africa and Regional Protection of Human Rights" (1985); Human Rights and Development in Africa (C. E. Welch & R. I. Meltzer eds., 1984), at p.122.

to self-determination. In July 1976, a group of eminent individuals meeting in Algiers proposed to the world the Universal Declaration on the Rights of Peoples (Algiers Declaration),[291] in which a number of peoples' rights were elaborated. On its part, the Constitution of the Republic of Cameroon talks of "we the peoples".[292]

The intention of this section is to attempt to work out the meaning of the term "people" which national and international instruments deliberately leave undefined "so as not to end up in difficult discussions."[293] It will be argued that its meaning is not consistent in the various instruments, as it is always determined by the context of the particular rights referred to.

The definition and scope of the term "peoples" in international and national instruments leave fertile ground for questions and debates.[294] In the different contexts where "peoples" appear, at least four meanings are possible.[295] "Peoples" can refer to: (1) those under colonial occupation, (2) a portion of the population, especially indigenous peoples, (3) the whole of the population, or (4) a synonym for the state.[296] While each of these interpretations has merit and clearly applies in certain contexts, this chapter asserts that in relation to PSNR, "peoples" is used to encompass a country's whole population.

From the onset, the principle PSNR has always been considered to be a

---

[291] For the text, see IODC BULL., September 1976, at 47; R. FALK, Human Rights and State Sovereignty 225 (1981). For discussion of the declaration, see Pour un Droit des Peuples : Essais sur la Declaration D'Alger (A. Cassese & F. Jouve eds., 1981); Rigaux, The Algiers Declaration of the Rights of Peoples, in UN Law/Fundamental Rights : Two Topics in International Law 211 (A. Cassese ed. 1979); Falk, The Algiers Declaration of the Rights of People and the Struggle for Human Rights, in R. FALK, supra.

[292] See preamble of the 1996 Constitution of the Republic of Cameroon.

[293] Rapporteur's Report, OAU Doc. CM/1149 (XXXVII), Ann. 1, at 4, para. 13 (1981), quoted in N.S. REMBE, supra note 1, at 112. This is not the only instance where an international instrument intentionally eschews defining a crucial term. For example, the International Law Commission during its work on the draft Declaration on the Rights and Duties of States declined to define what a state was. The Commission did not believe that any useful purpose would be served by such a definition and preferred to allow the word to be interpreted according to international practice. See 1949 Y.B. INT'L L. COMM'N 289; Lachs, Development and General Trends of International Law in Our Time, 169 RECUEIL DES COURS 2, 29 (1980 IV).

[294] See, e.g., Daniel C. Turack, "The African Charter on Human and Peoples' Rights: Some Preliminary Thoughts", (1984), 17 Akron L. Rev. 365, 379 (raising one such question shortly after the conclusion of the African Charter and indicating that it would spur academic discussions).

[295] See Kiwanuka, supra, note 256, at p. 80.

[296] Ibid. See also James A. Graff, "Human Rights, Peoples, and the Right to Self-Determination, in Group Rights" 186, 186 (Judith Baker ed., 1994).

"peoples" right. The question which begs for an answer, is what specific meaning was contemplated at the time PSNR was formulated? Emeka Duruigbo[297] points out that the term "peoples" was used during deliberations leading to the formulation of the principle to refer to peoples under colonial domination who could not fit into the definition of states or nations. He says that as those peoples acquired independence, it no longer became necessary to refer to peoples in discussing PSNR. According to him, "Peoples" cannot refer to the whole population under a colonial state for the following reasons: First, after 1962 many territories in the world remained under colonial rule such that alien subjugation and domination was still a major fact of life. Dispensing with the term "peoples" on the basis of some countries' independence would have been premature and cannot satisfactorily and conclusively explain the situation[298]. A contemporary interpretation of the term is that it encompasses a whole population (even though the colonial powers created "national" boundaries that had nothing to do with any classic understanding of nationhood) and there are indications that jurisprudence under the African Charter may toe this line.[299] Professor Cassese is emphatic that the term "peoples" contained in the Human Rights Covenants refers to all the inhabitants of a country or territory:

> Literal as well as more comprehensive interpretation supports the conclusion that the words 'all peoples have the right . . .,' in Article 1 refer to any people irrespective of the international political status of the territory it inhabits. It applies, then, not only to the peoples

---

[297] Permanent Sovereignty and Peoples Ownership of Natural Resources in International Law, 38 Geo. Wash. Int'l L. Rev. 2006, citing Schrijver, supra note 223 at 9 (inferring that "the term 'peoples' was originally meant to refer to those peoples which had not yet been able to exercise their right to political self-determination"). Some scholars also believe that a more realistic interpretation of "peoples" for purposes of economic self-determination under the African Charter would show that the term is used in reference to exactly the same category of human beings that are entitled to political self-determination, which, in their opinion, are people under colonial rule or alien subjugation. See Richard Gittleman, The African Charter on Human and Peoples' Rights: A Legal Analysis, 22 Va. J. Int'l L. 667, 678-80, 682 (1982).

[298] Ibid.

[299] Ibid. citing Li-ann Thio, "Battling Balkanization: Regional Approaches Toward Minority Protection Beyond Europe", (2002), 43 Harv. Int'l L.J. 409, 464 (relaying the individual opinions of African Human and Peoples' Rights commissioners who favored the construction that "peoples" under the African Charter refers to entire populations (or those) previously colonized by European States).

> of territories that have not yet attained political independence, but also to those of independent and sovereign states. This conclusion is borne out by the *travaux preparatoires*.[300]

Alexander Kiss, writing about the International Covenant on Economic, Social and Cultural Rights (ICESCR), states that "the economic resources of a country are to be used in the interest of the population" thereby construing the covenant's reference to "peoples" to apply to the entire population.[301] He adds that "this also includes that a people may not be spoliated of its own means of subsistence for the benefit of a layer of the population."[302]

That the term "peoples" in the context of PSNR refers to the entire population is also grounded in the fact that it is the most plausible, realistic, and sustainable position once it is accepted that the right to PSNR is vested in peoples.[303]

As a synonym for states,[304] "peoples" will lose its meaning, subsume the right of peoples in states, and work against the interest of the people. It is hard to argue that the right is vested in peoples while really meaning that it is vested in states. International texts would have stated that the right resides in states instead of making unnecessary circumlocutions.

In addition, there is evidence from the *travaux preparatoires* of the Human Rights Covenants that the use of "peoples" was not an automatic reference to states. In the course of drafting the International Covenant on Economic, Social and Cultural Rights and the International Covenant on Civil and Political Rights in 1955, the United Kingdom suggested that the word "people" necessarily meant sovereign state, but this argument was discountenanced.[305] In contrast, the Chairman of the Working Party from El Salvador used two examples of "people" that did not constitute the sovereign state but were nevertheless intended to come under the Covenants' protection: a "tribe" in Tanganyika (now Tanzania) experiencing land deprivation and forced resettlement of the "people;" and the population of the Island of Nauru whose only source of natural wealth, its phosphates, was being unwisely overexploited

[300] Antonio Cassese, The Self-Determination of Peoples, in The International Bill of Human Rights: The Covenant on Civil and Political Rights 92, 103 (Louis Henkin ed., 1981).

[301] Emeka Duruigbo, note 297, citing Alexander Kiss, "The Peoples' Right to Self-Determination", (1986), 7 Hum. Rts. L.J. 165, 171.

[302] Ibid.

[303] Ibid.

[304] cf note 299 supra.

[305] cf note 301, at 859.

On the strength of the foregoing, it could be safely submitted that the term "peoples" for the purpose of this chapter refers to the entire population of a country. Consequently, the right to PSNR is vested in the entire population of a country, which is the right-holder to the exclusion of all others. By the same strand of reasoning, the use of the term "peoples" in Cameroon refers to the entire population of Cameroon, who therefore are the rightful owners of her petroleum oil, entitled to the benefits accruing therefrom. This is in consonance with the preamble of the Constitution which declares that the nation shall use its natural resources to improve the lives of its citizens. To operationalize the principle of PSNR, it may be apposite to examine the ramifications of a people-centred interpretation of the principle for the Cameroon people.

3.5. Effects of a People-Centered Interpretation of the Principle of PSNR

A people-centred construction of the principle of PSNR, gives rise to serious implications which call for a discussion. The first implication which apparently seems to be a negative one, is to the effect that a people-centred construction attracts controversy to the notion of peoples' rights.[306] The criticism of this construction coincides with that leveled against group rights to the effect that group rights have the tendency of overshadowing individual rights. The argument here is that peoples' rights pose a threat to individual rights because they are often claimed over or against individuals.[307] In this specific instance, a right of the entire Cameroon people to sovereignty over oil could endanger individual rights by restricting the private property rights of individual landowners on whose land the oil is found. It may be assumed that the alleged or real tension between individual rights and societal interests which lies at the heart of the ongoing discussion on peoples' rights and human rights finds a special manifestation in the area of natural resources. In many developing countries, the successful exploitation of natural resources is crucial for the development of the general economy; at the same time, it is also clear that the status of private property may directly and fundamentally be affected

[306] See Marks, supra note 245, at 448 ("The concept of rights of peoples is a highly controversial matter in international human rights today.").

[307] See Peter Jones, "Human Rights, Group Rights and Peoples' Rights", (1999), 21 Hum. Rts. Q. 80, 81. For further discussion of the concern that group rights can affect individual rights and interests, see Douglas Sanders, "Collective Rights", (1991), 13 Hum. Rts. Q. 368, 378-86.

by rules governing natural resources.[308]

P. Sieghart cautioned as follows:

> abstract concepts have, in the past, only too often presented great dangers to the enjoyment by individuals of their human rights and fundamental freedoms. Some of the worst violations of those rights have been perpetrated in the service of some inspiring abstraction, such as 'the one true faith', 'the nation', 'the State' (including, as a recent example, 'das Reich'), 'the economy' (including 'a strong dollar (or pound)'), and indeed 'the masses'. A 'people' is no less an abstraction than any of these: it cannot in reality consist of anything more than the individuals who compose it. If any of the individual rights and freedoms protected by modern international human rights law ever came to be regarded as subservient to the rights of a 'people'... there would be a very real risk that legitimacy might yet again be claimed on such a ground for grave violations of the human rights of individuals.[309]

Professor Peter Jones[310] avers that one of the most common fears is that the rights of a group will be held against or over its own members so that, in ascribing rights to a group, we are simultaneously placing its individual members at the mercy of the group. He goes on to argue that this fear would be without basis, if these rights were viewed from a "collective conception" instead of a "corporate conception." Under the collective conception of group rights, individuals who constitute the group hold the right jointly and the group does not possess any standing separate from the standing of the individual members. "Thus, morally, there is no group that has an existence independently of, and that can hold rights against, its own members." This is not necessarily the case under the corporate theory, which arguably makes credible the concern expressed by human rights theorists regarding group rights.[311] This fear is not entirely baseless, when judged by the old adage which

[308] Rudolf Dolzer, "Permanent Sovereignty over Natural Resources and Economic Decolonization", (1986), 7 Hum. Rts. L.J. 217, 221.

[309] The International Law of Human Rights, 1983, at 368

[310] See Peter Jones, "Human Rights, Group Rights and Peoples' Rights", (1999), 21 Hum. Rts. Q. 80, 81. See also Douglas Sanders, "Collective Rights", (1991), 13 Hum. Rts. Q. 368, 378-86.

[311] Ibid. See also Eugene Kamenka, "Human Rights, Peoples' Rights, in The Rights of Peoples", supra, at 127, 131-34, ("The rights of peoples can become rights against one's own people. They

holds that unity is strength. The fear of the aforementioned consequences should not automatically invite an objection to the concept of peoples' rights where there is sufficient reason to believe that recognizing such rights would do more good than harm.[312] It is also contended that individual and peoples rights are not necessarily in conflict and can support each other.[313] It can safely be submitted that peoples' rights in general are complementary rather than conflicting. People have become increasingly aware of the fact that some major threats to human dignity are of a collective nature. Individual human rights no longer suffice; collective rights sometimes become a necessity.[314] There may be instances in which no specific individual right is adequate to protect the group interest in question. Here, it is arguable that a new group right must be constructed. In such cases, 'peoples' rights and individual rights are not only complementary but also interdependent[315]

Looking at the other side of the coin, a people-centred construction could forever change the way business is conducted in a country like Cameroon which is endowed with petroleum. Antonio Cassese,[316] posits that this construction could be a tool of empowerment for peoples across the world to demand that the old order change and that their interests be given priority. He further submits that Article 1(2) of the Human Rights Covenants speaks of the rights of peoples to their natural resources, and consequently that sovereign governments are bound to utilize natural resources with the aim of benefiting the whole population.[317] More over, a people-centred construction gives the people the opportunity to assert themselves and challenge agreements entered into by the government and the oil companies where the provisions

regularly do. They should not.").

[312]Maleiha Malik, Communal Goods as Human Rights, in Understanding Human Rights 138, 166 (Conor Gearty & Adam Tomkins eds., 1996) (expressing support for collective rights because they can be pursued in a manner that does not occasion the erosion of extant commitments to individual rights).

[313]Theo van Boven, "Human Rights and Rights of Peoples", (1995), 6 Eur. J. Int'l L. 461, 470.

[314]See Peter R. Baehr & Koo VanderWal, Introduction Item: Human Rights as Individual and as Collective Rights, in Human Rights in a Pluralist World: Individuals and Collectivities 33, 36 (Jan Berting et al. eds., 1990);

[315]Gillian Triggs, The Rights of 'Peoples' and Individual Rights: Conflict or Harmony?, in The Rights of Peoples, at pp 141, 142-44 (discussing the concern that recognition of rights of peoples can trample or derogate from established individual rights).

[316]Antonio Cassese, The Self-Determination of Peoples, in The International Bill of Human Rights: The Covenant on Civil and Political Rights 92, 103 (Louis Henkin ed., 1981).

[317]Ibid.

or the application of such contracts are an abuse to human understanding. For example, in the Chad-Cameroon pipeline project, the Convention of Establishment between Cameroon and the consortium of oil companies concerned, had provisions which were couched in such a way as to override national laws.[318] Such obnoxious provisions could only be challenged by the collective effort of Cameroonians through civil society organizations.[319]

A people-centred construction would also mean, among other things, that oil exploration and exploitation activities that severely endanger the environment, citizenry, or communities are open to possible censure. The natural consequence of this is that the people (civil society) will have a basis on which to question government action in relation to the oil sector as well as the locus standi to confront recalcitrant oil companies. In the same light, Cameroonians will be able to monitor and question the rate at which oil is exploited because future generations also depend on it. The people will also be able to monitor and ensure that the government saves out of today's revenue in order to take care of the needs of the unborn.[320] This is to ensure that future generations are not deprived of the oil through reckless exploitation since it is an exhaustible resource.[321] It is necessary to indicate that the TOTCO (Tchad Oil Transportation Company) Convention[322] has provisions which limit what Chad can do with the oil revenue from the Chad – Camroon Pipeline project. But the COTCO (Cameroon Oil Transportation Company) Convention[323] has no such provisions.

This chapter is by no means arguing that a people-centred construction of

---

[318] See chapter eight.

[319] See Dufresne, supra note 263 at 360-62 laying the foundation for this reasoning.

[320] The situation in Cameroon is not clear because of the Colonial Pact. It is the Colonial Pact that set up the common currency for the Francophone countries, the CFA franc, which demands that each of the fourteen CFA member countries must deposit 65% (plus another 20% for financial libilities, making the dizziling total of 85%) of their foreign exchange reserves in an "operations Account at the French Treasury in Paris.... If they are in need of extra money, as they always are, they have to borrow from their own 65% in the French Treasury at commercial rates .... Amazingly, the final say on CFA arrangements belong to the French Treasury, which invests the African countries money in its own name on the Paris Bourse (the stock exchange). New African of February 2011, No. 503 p. 13.

[321] The Supreme Court of the Phillipines has expounded the concept of intergenerational responsibility in relation to natural resource exploitation. See Oposa v. Sec'y of the Dep't of Env't & Natural Res., 33 I.L.M. 173, 184 (1994).

[322] Section 28.

[323] See generally the COTCO Convention of Establishment.

the principle of PSNR should erode or undermine state sovereignty. What it seeks to highlight is that, this construction gives the people the opportunity to hold valid claims in international law against the government in relation to the control of the oil industry. It also affords the people a basis to make valid and sustainable claims under national law against oil companies. A pessimist may be tempted to argue that a people-centred construction will have disastrous consequences on the inflow of foreign investments and therefore thwart government's effort at trying to attract foreign capital which itself is a booster of economic development. However, this argument may not hold because in the current state-centred scenario, foreign investments are being attracted through very attractive laws,[324] but the supposed economic development is not evident. Consequently, going by the equitable maxim "he who seeks equity most do equity", if the government expects development through the inflow of foreign investments and fears that a people-centred interpretation of peoples' rights will deter foreign investments, then she should give the people the expected development. Only then will she have 'equity' because she has done 'equity'. The point that has been made here is that if the government acts for the benefit of the people, then it can make concessions to MNCs for the purpose of attracting them. It does mean, though, that the kind of concessions the government can make will be constrained; but that is essential to the process.

The point which this chapter makes is that a people-centred construction should enable the people to have the opportunity to hold valid and sustainable claims in national and international law against oil companies and the government with respect to activities in the oil industry. Professor Crawford commenting in relation to this said that:

> The key criterion of a peoples' right in this respect must be whether the right avails as against decisions of the government of the territory in which the people live: that is to say, whether governmental decisions on the disposal of natural resources are subject to the principle of domestic jurisdiction, or whether they are, on the contrary, subject to international scrutiny on the basis that particular decisions are abusive.[325]

[324] For eg Law No. 99/013 of 22nd December 1999, Law No. 2002/004 of 19th April 2002 and their Decrees of application, etc.

[325] Crawford, Some Conclusions, supra note 251, at 171

Still in relation to this, but writing with reference to self-determination under the African Charter, Professor Li-Ann Thio raises the following issue touching on the rights of peoples over their governments:

> 'Peoples' could be understood to constitute all the persons within the state, an aggregate of different groups who assert a collective right against their state. The right of self-determination as a continuing right would freely entitle peoples to determine their political status and to pursue socioeconomic development, thus empowering an oppressed people against an abusive governing elite by grounding legitimacy in popular will. Distinguishing the 'state' from 'peoples' conforms with a concept of popular sovereignty providing that the right to self-determination is violated where states do not legitimately represent their people, consisting of both majority and minority groups. [326]

Emeka Duruigbo[327] while citing Nmehielle[328] rightly explains that although Thio's contention is in connection with the political aspect of self-determination, it seems reasonable to also apply this reasoning to economic self-determination, of which the principle of permanent sovereignty over natural resources is undoubtedly a component. Accordingly, actions not grounded in the peoples' interest taken by government, which involve natural resources could be open to challenge as violations of international law. Therefore, in line with Anthony Carty,[329] whether the government acts without the consent of the people, or turns out not to have acted in the interest of the people, the principle makes the action of the government subject to subsequent scrutiny.

The equitable maxim which provides that 'where there is a right there is a remedy' suggests that right holders must be capable of enforcing their rights. Consequently, arguing that Cameroonians have a right to sovereignty over

---

[326] See Li-ann Thio, "Battling Balkanization: Regional Approaches Toward Minority Protection Beyond Europe", (2002), 43 Harv. Int'l L.J. 409, 464.

[327] cf note 297 supra.

[328] Vincent O. Orlu Nmehielle, The African Human Rights System: Its Laws, Practice and Institutions 147 (2001).

[329] Anthony Carty, The Third World Claim to Economic Self-Determination: Economic Rights of Peoples: Theoretical Aspects, in The Right to Development in International Law 43, 44 (Subrata Roy Chowdhury et al. eds., 1992).

petroleum oil equally suggests that a duty attaches to some person or entity. In this connection, a cause of action will lie both under international law as well as under domestic legislation. Here, the government or oil companies, as moral persons, are the bearers of that duty. Also, if people have a right to permanent sovereignty over petroleum oil, then they equally have a right to develop. The next chapter discusses the peoples' right to development.

4

THE PEOPLES' RIGHT TO DEVELOPMENT

4.0. Introduction

The right to development (RTD) has been part of the international debate on human rights for close to forty years. However, this has not yet entered the practical realm of development planning and implementation in Cameroon. For example, Cameroon has tended to express rhetorical support for this right but neglected its basic precepts in development practice. The purpose of this chapter is to show that the RTD is one of the rights available to Cameroonians as a result of oil exploitation from their land, and that the right is being violated. This chapter offers an historical overview of the right, examines its application under the African Charter and evaluates its application in Cameroon, with a view to showing that it is not being respected.

4.1. An Historical Overview of the Right To Development.

In the 1970s and 1980s, the RTD was introduced as one of several rights belonging to a third "generation" of human rights.[330] According to this view, the first generation consisted of civil and political rights conceived as freedom from state abuse. The second generation consisted of economic, social, and cultural rights, including claims made against exploiters and oppressors. The third generation consisted of solidarity rights belonging to peoples and covering global concerns like development, environment, humanitarian assistance, peace, communication, and common heritage. The cataloguing

[330] Stephen P. Marks, "Emerging Human Rights: A New Generation for the 1980's?", (1981), 33 RUTGERS L. REV. 435, 435-52.

of human rights into such neat generations is appealing in its simplicity. A general priority has been given to guaranteeing individual freedoms in the eighteenth-century revolutionary struggles of Europe and North America, to advancing social justice in the nineteenth- and twentieth-century struggles against economic exploitation, and to assigning rights and obligations to the principal agents able to advance global public goods in the late twentieth century.[331]

The right to development can be traced back to the 1944 Declaration of Philadelphia, which was incorporated into the ILO Constitution of 1946.[332] That Declaration affirmed the following principle: 'All human beings, irrespective of race, creed or sex, have the right to pursue both their material well-being and their spiritual development in conditions of freedom and dignity, of economic security and equal opportunity.'[333] The U.N. Charter requires members of the United Nations to promote, as an ensemble, 'higher standards of living, full employment, and conditions of economic and social progress and development.'[334] The Universal Declaration on Human Rights gives this idea another twist by providing that everyone 'is entitled to realization, through national effort and international co-operation and in accordance with the organization and resources of each State, of the economic, social and cultural rights indispensable for his dignity and the free development of his personality.'[335] The Universal Declaration adds: 'Everyone is entitled to a social and international order in which the rights and freedoms set forth in the Declaration can be fully realized.'[336] The right to development also has been connected with the right to life. The argument is that because everyone is entitled to a 'decent life' and not merely to the right to exist, the realization of economic, social, and cultural rights must be essential to an individual's physical and intellectual well-being. As early as 1968, the International Conference on Human Rights pointed out in the Teheran Declaration that 'the achievement of lasting progress in the achievement of human rights is

[331] Ibid. "The Human Right to Development: Between Rhetoric and Reality", (2004), 17 Harv. Hum. Rts. J. 137.

[332] International Labour Organisation Constitution annex II(a), at p.24 (1969). See 9 M. Hudson, International Legislation 124 (1950).

[333] International Labour Organisation Constitution, supra note 324; M. HUDSON, supra note 328, at 126.

[334] U.N. Charter art. 55, para. a.

[335] Universal Declaration of Human Rights, art. 22.

[336] Ibid. art. 28.

dependent upon sound and effective national and international policies of social and economic development.'[337]

The special importance of the right to development was first brought to the consciousness of governments and scholars by Judge Keba M'Baye, who was Chief Justice of the Supreme Court of Senegal, and an active member of the U.N. Commission on Human Rights,[338] and later Vice President of ICJ. In his many writings and speeches since 1972, Judge M'Baye strongly advocated the recognition of the right to development as a human right. The right to development he argued, must be a human right, because it is essential to the exercise of other human rights.[339] Due to his influence, UNESCO's 1978 Declaration on Race and Racial Prejudice,[340] included the following broad definition of the right to development: 'the right of every human being and group to full development . . . implies equal access to the means of personal and collective advancement and fulfillment in a climate of respect for the values of civilizations and cultures, both national and world-wide.'[341] After the formal articulation of the RTD in the form of texts using the human rights terminology in the late twentieth century by Judge M'Baye, the U.N. General Assembly proclaimed development as a human right in its 1986 Declaration on the Right to Development.[342]

The 1993 Vienna Declaration and Programme of Action called the RTD "a universal and inalienable right and an integral part of fundamental human

---

[337] 23 U.N. GAOR Supp. (No. 41) at 14, 16 (resolution XVII and XXI) U.N. Doc. A/Conf. 32/41 (1968).

[338] Judge Kéba M'Baye, 'Le Droit au Développement Comme un Droit de L'Homme' (The Right to Development as a Human Right), Leçon inaugurale de la Troisième Session d'enseignement de l'Institut International des Droits de L'Homme (Inaugural Address of the Third Teaching Session of the International Institute of Human Rights) (July 3, 1972), in 5 Revue Des Droits De L'Homme (Human Rights Journal), 503 (1972).

[339] Ibid.

[340] Adopted Nov. 27, 1978, by the General Conference of the United Nations Educational, Scientific and Cultural Organization at its 20th Session, Section III.C.1.

[341] Ibid. art. 3

[342] U.N. GAOR, 41st Sess., Supp. No. 53, at 183, U.N. Doc. A/RES/41/128 (1986). The Commission referred to the RTD in resolutions before the General Assembly adopted the Declaration. See, e.g., U.N. ESCOR, 33d Sess., Supp. No. 6, at 74-75, U.N. Doc. E/CN.4/1257; U.N. ESCOR, 35th Sess., Supp. No 6, at 107, U.N. Doc. E/CN.4/1347; U.N. ESCOR, 37th Sess., Supp. No 5, at 238, U.N. Doc. E/CN.4/1475. See also Commission Resolutions 4 (XXXIII) of 21 February 1977; 4 (XXXV) of 2 March 1979; 36 (XXXVII) of 11 March 1981; 985/44 of 14 March 1985.

rights."[343] The RTD has also been given prominence in the mandate of the High Commissioner for Human Rights,[344] and the General Assembly required the High Commissioner to establish "a new branch whose primary responsibilities would include the promotion and protection of the right to development."[345] The right is regularly mentioned in declarations of international conferences and summits and in the annual resolutions of the General Assembly and the Commission on Human Rights.

The United States opposed and was reluctant to recognize the right to development as an international human right and voted against its adoption. However, other countries on their part, had a strong basis for decrying the failure of half-century of decolonization and development cooperation to eliminate poverty and achieve the objectives of numerous development strategies. They took the position "that developing countries continued to face difficulties in participating in the globalization process, and that many risked being marginalized and effectively excluded from its benefits."[346] They therefore stressed the impact of international trade, access to technology, debt burden, and the like on the enjoyment of the RTD.[347] In consequence therefore, developing countries had a breakthrough on April 22, 1998, when the U.N. Commission on Human Rights adopted by consensus, a resolution on the RTD,[348] recommending to the Economic and Social Council, the establishment of a follow-up mechanism consisting of an open-ended working group, (OEWG) and an Independent Expert. The purpose of the working group was to monitor and review the progress of the Independent Expert and report back to the Commission.[349] The Independent Expert was to "present to the working group at each of its sessions, a study on the current state of progress in the implementation of the right to development as a basis for a focused discussion, taking into account, *inter alia*, the deliberations and suggestions of the working group."[350] Dr. Arjun Sengupta, a prominent Indian economist, was

[343] Vienna Declaration and Programme of Action: Note By The Secretariat, World Conference on Human Rights, Part I, 10, U.N. Doc. A/CONF.157/23 (1993).

[344] G.A. Res. 48/141, U.N. GAOR, 48th Sess., Supp. No. 49, at 261, U.N. Doc. A/48/141 (1993).

[345] G.A. Res. 50/214, U.N. GAOR, 50th Sess., Supp. No. 49, at 296, U.N. Doc. A/50/214 (1995).

[346] G.A. Res. 56/150, U.N. GAOR, 56th Sess., Supp. No. 49, at 341, U.N. Doc. A/56/150 (2001).

[347] Ibid.

[348] Commission on Human Rights Res. 72, U.N. ESCOR, 44th Sess., Supp. No. 3, at 229, U.N. Doc. E/CN.4/1998/177 (1998).

[349] cf note 343 supra.

[350] cf note 342, at p. 233.

appointed Independent Expert and by 2004 had produced eight reports, while the OEWG had held five sessions.[351] The Independent Expert was replaced by a High-Level Task Force (HLTF) on the implementation of the RTD, which was installed in pursuance of the Commission on Human Right's resolution 2004/7 within the framework of the OEWG.[352] Under the Chairperson of Professor Stephen Marks,[353] the objective of the HLTF is to provide expert support to the OEWG in fulfilling its mandate. The Task Force is composed of representatives from identified trade, finance and development institutions or organizations and additionally, of five experts from diverse backgrounds with practical experience related to the implementation of the RTD.[354]

The RTD has evolved through various resolutions to the current United Nations Commission on Human Rights resolution 63/178 of 18 December 2008, which was adopted with a striking majority in favour of the right and envisaged the elaboration of a convention on the RTD. The elaboration of a convention envisaged in this resolution, brings to mind the question of the legal status of the RTD which will be discussed in the section that follows.

4.2. The Legal Status of the Right To Development.

International commitment by governments does not necessarily translate into a legally binding right. The RTD itself is not yet a legally binding concept, but draws its legal foundation from binding human rights covenants. From a legal point of view, the RTD can be described as 'soft law',[355] generally accepted but not binding. This section examines the status of the RTD in contemporary international law. Attention here has been focused on the recognition of the right in international, regional and national legal instruments.

The Declaration on the RTD which was adopted by a GA resolution in 1986, is the most comprehensive and detailed formulation of the RTD and

351 cf note 343 supra.

352 Commission on Human Rights, resolution 2004/7, UN Doc. E/CN.4/RES/2004/7.

353 Professor Stephen Marks is a Francois-Xavier Bagnoud professor of Health and Human Rights at Harvard School of Public Health.

354 Report of the OEWG on the RTD on its fifth session, 18 March 2004, UN Doc. E/CN.4/2004/23,p. 16. By virtue of resolution 9/3, of September 2008, the HLTF and the OEWG have a mandate until 2010.

355 This term denotes a group of human rights which have been generally accepted by the world community and reaffirmed in declarations and resolutions by the members of many states, but which have not reached the status of law in those countries.

thus the basis of any discussion on the right. The Declaration defines the right as follows:

> The right to development is an inalienable human right by virtue of which every human person and all peoples are entitled to participate in, contribute to, and enjoy economic, social, cultural and political development, in which all human rights and fundamental freedoms can be fully realized.[356]

In accordance with the Declaration, the human person is the central focus of development, as well as the beneficiary and active participant. Hence, Article 2 not only indicates the human person as subject, but as a holder of responsibilities in relation to the promotion and protection of an appropriate political, social and economic order for development, both individually and collectively. States therefore, have the obligation to formulate appropriate national development policies that aim at the constant improvement of the well-being of the population on the basis of active, free and meaningful participation.[357] The report of the OEWG on the right to development in its third session[358] considers the RTD to include the principle of sovereignty over natural resources, popular participation in development, equality of opportunity, the creation of favourable conditions for the enjoyment of other rights, including civil, political, economic, social and cultural rights as well as accountability, transparency, rule of law and good governance at all levels and in all sectors.

With respect to the legal basis or recognition of the right to development in treaty law, several international as well as regional instruments have been highlighted as referring directly or indirectly to the right, or even to elements of it.

---

[356] Art 1.1 Declaration on the Right to Development.

[357] See art. 8. This article also requires states to take necessary measures for the realization of the right to development by ensuring the enjoyment of human rights, equality of opportunity and eradication of social injustices as well as promotion of popular participation in the development process.

[358] UN Doc.E/CN.4/2002/28/Rev. 1 sect.VIII. A., 11 April 2002.

4.2.1. Multilateral Treaties.

The 1966 International Covenant on Civil and Political Rights (ICCPR),[359] and the 1966 International Covenant on Economic, Social and Cultural Rights (ICESCR),[360] were adopted as an elaboration of the Universal Declaration of Human Rights (UDHR) in two legally binding human rights instruments. In as much as express reference on the right to development is not found in these Covenants, implicit reference is found in their common Article 1, which provides in relation to the right to self-determination, that all peoples shall freely pursue their economic, social and cultural development.[361] The Article further provides that 'in no case, may a people be deprived of its own means of subsistence'.[362] Equally, implicit recognition of the right to development is most glaring in Articles 2 and 11 of the ICESCR, dealing with international cooperation. Article 2(1) provides that:

> Each State Party to the present Covenant undertakes to take steps, individually and through international assistance and co-operation, especially economic and technical, to the maximum of its available resources, with a view to achieving progressively the full realization of the rights recognized in the present Covenant by all appropriate means, including particularly the adoption of legislative measures.

On its part, Article 11 on the right to an adequate standard of living provides for the duty 'to continuous improvement of the living conditions', as well as 'recognizing to this effect, the essential importance of international cooperation based on free consent'. This clearly shows similarities with the right to development in terms of the gradual character of the provision as well as the importance of international cooperation.

Traces of the right to development are also found in the 1981 Convention on the Elimination of All Forms of Discrimination Against Women,[363] the

[359] ICCPR, adopted in New York, 16 December 1966, entry into force 23 March 1976.

[360] ICESCR, adopted in New York, 16 December 1966, entry into force 3 January 1976.

[361] Article 1(1) ICCPR, ICESCR.

[362] Article 1(2) ICCPR, ICESCR.

[363] Adopted in New York 18 December 1979, entry into fore 3 September 1981.

1989 Convention on the Rights of the Child,[364] and the 2006 Convention on the Rights of Persons with Disabilities.[365]

4.2.2. Regional Instruments

The concept of the right to development finds implicit recognition in regional instruments like the 1969 American Convention on Human Rights and the 1988 Additional Protocol on economic, social and cultural rights (Protocol of San Salvador),[366] and the 1961 European Social Charter.[367] However, the only regional hard law guarantee of the right to development which exists in the realm of international human rights law, is the African Charter on Human and Peoples' Rights.[368]

The express recognition of the right to development by the African Charter in Article 22, read in conjunction with Article 21, is a plus for this work which argues that the people of Cameroon deserve to have an enhancement in the quality of their lives as a result of the flourishing oil industry.[369]

By recognizing the right to development as belonging to all peoples and encompassing economic, social, and cultural aspects, and because states have a duty to ensure the exercise of the right to development, it may be said that all peoples have a right to a general satisfactory environment favourable to their development. Although the African Charter does not define what development is, the United Nations Development Programme offered a sufficient working definition. It considers development in terms of human development and in turn views and conceives the notion of human development as the creation of 'an environment in which people can develop their full potentials and lead

364 Adopted in New York, 20 November 1989, entry into force 2 September 1990.

365 Adopted in New York, 13 December 2006, entry into force 3 May 2008.

366 Adopted in San Jose, 22 November 1969, entry into force 18 July 1978; Protocol of San Salvador, adopted on 17 November 1988, entry into force 16 November 1999.

367 Adopted in Turin, 18 October 1961, entry into force, 26 February 1965, revised in Strasbourg, 3 May 1996, entry into force, 1 July 1999.

368 Adopted in Banjul, 27 June 1981, entry into force , 21 October 1986. Article 22 of this Charter provides that: (1)All people shall have a right to their economic, social and cultural development with due regard to their freedom and identity and in the equal enjoyment of the common heritage of mankind. (2)States shall have the duty, individually or collectively to ensure the exercise of the right to development.

369 For the content of Art. 21, see supra chapter two, pp. 84 – 85.

productive, creative lives in accordance with their needs and interest'.[370] By analogy therefore, the right to development entails the creation of the stated kind of environment. Sengupta[371] sees this as touching on three main aspects, namely, the right to a means of creating that environment, the right to a process of creating that environment, and the right to the benefits that flow from the creation of such an environment.

An issue which may deserve attention is whether Article 22 of the African Charter incorporates this kind of reasoning. The Bakweri Land Claims case offers an insight.[372] This is a case which was explicitly grounded on the content of Article 22, where the complainants framed their main grievances, namely, the concentration of their historic lands in non-native hands, in terms of the violation of the right to development under Article 22.[373] This case did not go beyond the admissibility stage not because it was not properly filed but because it did not exhaust local remedies. The case is *locus classicus* for the fact that peoples can bring an action against the state to enforce the right to development. Although this case was not brought to enforce the right to development in relation to oil exploitation, it serves as an eye opener both because it refers to RTD, and has individuals suing the State.

[370] See http:// www.undp.org/humandev (last accessed on June 29 2010).

[371] Arjun Sengupta, The Human Right to Development, Oxford Development Studies, vol. 32, at 183 – 192, 2004.

[372] African Commission on Human and Peoples' Rights, Bakweri Land Claims Committee V. Cameroon, Communication No. 260/2002, African Human Rights Law Report, 2004, at 43.

[373] See Ndiva Kofele-Kale, "Asserting Permanent Sovereignty over Ancestral Lands: The Bakweri Land Litigation against Cameroon", (2007), 13 Ann. Surv. Int'l. & Comp. Law, 103.

5

THE RIGHT TO A HEALTHY ENVIRONMENT

5.0. Introduction

An era that has witnessed and is witnessing environmental destruction as a result of activities related to oil exploitation calls for more attention on the right to a healthy environment. That all other human rights depend on this right is not an overstatement, if we consider the fact that the highest right accorded a person – the right to life[374]- could become meaningless if the environment in which the person is living has so degraded that the right to life is threatened. The question whether there should be a recognized international human right to a "healthy environment", becomes relavant. Or do people possess only state-created "environmental" rights, which, however important, fall short of a standard that is both universal and fundamental in nature, as human rights are understood to be? Is it even necessary that a universal right to a healthy environment should exists or are the environmental rights expressed in national laws or found as components of other recognized human rights sufficient? If a human right to a healthy environment exists, what does the phrase "healthy environment" encompass? Can it be adequately defined to make this right useful? How does it compare to other established international human rights such as freedom from torture or the right to life?[375] Or even the RTD just discussed?

[374]See the preamble of the Cameroon Constitution of 1966.

[375]These and other fundamental rights are contained in e.g. art. 3 and art. 5 of the Universal Declaration on Human Rights, G.A. Res. 217A, U.N. Doc. A/810, at 71 (1948), and art. 6 and art.

From 1990, and especially in conjunction with the 1992 U.N. Conference on Environment and Development,[376] much ink has flowed regarding the acceptance of a right to a healthy environment as a recognized principle of international human rights law.[377] But the unanswered question was to know when an environmental violation becomes a human rights violation. John Lee,[378] proposes that an environmental violation becomes significant enough to become a human rights violation when, as a result of a specific course of state action, a degraded environment occurs with either serious health consequences for a specific group of people or a disruption of a people's way of life. While agreeing with Lee, this writer thinks that the definition is not wide enough to cover all those whose actions are capable of causing a degraded environment. He fails to recognize that non-State actors like multinational corporations have a potential of carrying out activities capable of degrading the environment. He also fails to recognize the fact that the violation could affect only an individual. According to this research therefore, an environmental violation will be considered to have risen to the status of a human rights violation if as a specific course of state or non-state actor's action, a degraded environment occurs with either serious health consequences for an individual

---

7 of the International Covenant on Civil and Political Rights, 999 U.N.T.S. 171. (1966).

[376]This Conference was held in Rio de Janeiro from June 3-14, 1992, and was attended by 178 nations and 100 heads of state. Out of this conference came the Rio Declaration on Environment and Development, U.N. Doc. A/ CONF.151/5/Rev.1 (1992) [hereinafter Rio Declaration]; the Framework Convention on Climate Change, U.N. Doc. A/AC.237/18(Part 2)/Add.1 (1992), entered into force March 21, 1994; the Convention on Biological Diversity, U.N.E.P. Doc. Bio. Div./N7-INC5/4 (1992), entered into force December 29, 1993; and Agenda 21, U.N. Doc. A/ CONF.151/26/Rev.1 (1992).

[377] Dinah Shelton, Human Rights, Environmental Rights, and the Right to Environment, 28 Stan. J. Int'l. L. 103 (1991); Iveta Hodkova, Is There a Right to a Healthy Environment in the International Legal Order?, 7 Conn. J. Int'l L. 65 (1991); James T. McClymonds, The Human Right to a Healthy Environment: An International Legal Perspective, 37 N.Y.L. Sch. L. Rev. 583 (1992); Jennifer A. Downs, Note, A Healthy and Ecologically Balanced Environment: An Argument for a Third Generation Right, 3 Duke J. Comp. & Int'l L. 351 (1993); Richard Desgagne, Integrating Environmental Values into the European Convention on Human Rights, 89 Am. J. Int'l L. 263 (1995); Neil A. F. Popovic, In Pursuit of Environmental Human Rights: Commentary on the Draft Declaration of Principles on Human Rights and the Environment, 27 Colum. Hum. Rts. L. Rev. 487 (1996); Joshua P. Eaton, The Nigerian Tragedy: Environmental Regulation of Transnational Corporations, and the Human Right to a Healthy Environment, 15 B. U. Int'l L. J. 261 (1997).

[378]The Underlying Legal Theory to Support a Well-Defined Human Right to a Healthy Environment as a Principle of Customary International Law, 25 Colum. J. Envtl L., 283, 2000.

or a specific group of people, or a disruption of an individual or people's way of life.

By virtue of this definition, people who live in environments that would be considered appalling by Western standards, for example, Briqueterie in Yaounde, Old Town in Bamenda, Haousa quarters in Kumba, etc., may not claim a right to a healthy environment on the basis of the fact that their human rights have been violated. In contrast however, the following environmental situations may be serious enough to be human rights violations for which a human right to a healthy environment might provide a remedy: the adverse environmental impact on the Atlantic coast of Cameroon;[379] the adverse impact of the Chad-Cameroon pipeline project on the local populations living along the pipeline;[380] the operations of Shell Oil in the Ogoniland region of Nigeria and the effects on the Ogoni people;[381] and the operations of Texaco and Petroecuador in the Oriente region of Ecuador, and the effects on the indigenous tribes and settlers in that region.[382]

These latter situations differ from the general situation of an overall unhealthy environment in that a government or another actor, such as a transnational corporation, has undertaken a specific course of action that has had a serious effect on the environment of a localized group of individuals. Economic or cultural factors, which in the former case might act in opposition to a right to a healthy environment, should play no role in these more limited cases.[383] This chapter sets out first or all to establish the existence of the right, and, secondly, to demonstrate that individuals have a private right of action. It then argues that since a link exists between the environment and human

---

[379] See Dieudonne Alemagi, The oil industry along the Atlantic coast of Cameroon: Assessing Impact and possible solutions, August 2007, Available online (last accessed June 30 2010).

[380] See statement made by Ron Royal, President of Esso Chad, ExxonMobil's top manager in Chad, to a parliamentary delegation from the German Bundestag in January 2007: 'We should never have called this a development project'.

[381] Joshua P. Eaton, "The Nigerian Tragedy: Environmental Regulation of Transnational Corporations, and the Human Right to a Healthy Environment", (1997), 15 B. U. Int'l L. J. 261.

[382] See Judith Kimerling, "Rights, Responsibilities and Realities: Environmental Protection Law in Ecuador's Amazon Oil Fields", 2 Sw. J.L. & Trade Am. 293 (1995). (In the wake of the Texaco operation a scene of environmental destruction was left which included drinking water which contained levels of toxic oil constituents many times greater than United States Environmental Protection Agency guidelines, gas flares fouling the air, unlined or improperly lined open toxic waste pools, and heightened levels of illness in both people and animals.).

[383] In the later case a specific, potentially reversible act has occurred, which is lacking in the general case. This involves the concepts of causation and state responsibility.

rights, an independent and comprehensive code on the human right to a healthy environment, which is narrowly and vigorously defined, is not only necessary but is imperative to be applicable in Cameroon's oil industry which is anticipating an oil boom. This will avoid flirting with documentation or pieces of legislation in order to ascertain a violation of the right to a healthy environment for the purpose of obtaining a remedy. Before developing this argument, it is necessary to have an overview of this right.

5.1. Evolution of the Right to a Healthy Environment.

The environmental movement which began in the late 1960s evolved into the adoption of the Stockholm Declaration on the Human Environment in 1972.[384] While it is not a binding instrument, it references some form of "environmental right" in Principle 1.[385] The Preamble of the Stockholm Declaration recognized the intimate relationship between environmental protection and the enjoyment of human rights and indeed noted that a healthy environment is necessary for the enjoyment of human rights.[386] Despite this recognition in 1972, the progress towards accepting a human right to a healthy environment has been slow.

The Stockholm Declaration adopted in 1972 recognized the link between environmental protection and human rights in several of its provisions. The Preamble, for example, states that both the natural and man-made environments are "essential to his (man's) well-being and to the enjoyment of basic human rights - even the right to life itself."[387] This is a clear recognition of the fact that, to enjoy human rights, a healthy natural and man-made environment is essential, although the formulation does not refer to a healthy or clean environment.[388]

Principle 1 of the Declaration also embodies similar language, although it is generally thought of as falling short of recognizing a right to a clean environment; nor does it embody the rights language employed in UN human

[384] Declaration of the United Nations Conference on the Human Environment, Pmbl. U.N. Doc. A/CONF.48/14 (1972), reprinted in 11 I.L.M. 1416 [hereinafter Stockholm Declaration].

[385] Ibid. at 1417.

[386] Ibid. at 1416.

[387] Ibid. at 1416.

[388] Ibid. at 1416.

rights instruments.[389] According to Principle 1:

> Man has the fundamental right to freedom, equality and adequate conditions of life, in an environment of a quality that permits a life of dignity and well-being and he bears a solemn responsibility to protect and improve the environment for the present and future generations.[390]

This formulation recognizes the fundamental right of man to freedom, equality, and adequate conditions of life and not a right to a healthy environment *per se*.[391] In other words, it recognizes that an environment of a particular quality is necessary for man to enjoy his fundamental rights to freedom, equality, and adequate conditions of life. This is different from recognizing an independent right to a clean environment, because it refers also to a political and social environment. This formulation falls within the second distinction made above, namely, a healthy environment being necessary to enjoying other basic human rights. Therefore, the Stockholm Declaration falls short of recognizing an independent fundamental right to a clean environment.

At the time of the Stockholm Conference, the United States, which vehemently opposed the inclusion of a similar right twenty years later in the Rio Declaration, proposed the inclusion of a specific right to a clean environment in the Stockholm Declaration.[392] The formulation proposed by the United States reads as follows: "Every human being has a right to a healthful and safe environment, including air, water and earth, and to food and other material necessities, all of which should be sufficiently free of contamination and other elements which detract from the health or well-being of man."[393] The conference participants, particularly those from developing countries, however, preferred the indirect formulation in Principle 1. Therefore, the American formulation was rejected.[394]

The next milestone in the evolution of international environmental law

---

[389] Ibid. at 1416.

[390] Ibid. at 1416.

[391] The use of the word "man" here instead of "person" has been interpreted as using non rights language

[392] See Dinah Shelton, "What Happened at Rio to Human Rights?", (1992), 3 Y.B. Int'l Envtl. L. 75, 76-77.

[393] Ibid.

[394] Ibid.

was the World Charter for Nature adopted in 1982.[395] This instrument is unique in that it is the first, and so far the only, of its kind which recognized the rights of nature, distinct from the rights of human beings.[396] Most other instruments recognize the need for environmental protection because of its utility to man, not because it needs protection in its own right. In other words, most instruments approach environmental protection in an anthropocentric manner, while the World Charter for Nature was the first instrument, albeit non binding, to adopt an ecocentric approach.[397] As such, it does not embody the rights of man in human rights parlance. On the contrary, it endorses the right of every form of life, "warranting respect regardless of its worth to man."[398]

Additionally, the World Charter for Nature embodies certain environmental rights: it provides for the right of all persons to participate in the decision-making process and to "have access to . . . redress when their environment has suffered damage."[399] It also provides for the Environmental Impact Assessment (EIA) process, which provides access to information and the right to participate in the decision-making process.

Next, came the World Commission on Environment and Development (WCED) which coined the now famous phrase "sustainable development" in a bid to reconcile the increasingly polarized debate on environmental protection and economic development.[400] There is no doubt that sustainable development is anthropocentric in nature and provides for the rights of present and future generations to develop in a sustainable manner. The draft principles on sustainable development appended to the report contained a provision on human rights; it provides that "all human beings have the fundamental right to an environment adequate for their health and well-being."[401] This formulation is clearly drafted in "rights language," although the language itself is rather ambiguous and too open. The Report of the Legal Experts accepts

---

[395] See G.A. Res. 37/7, U.N. GAOR, 37th Sess., U.N. Doc. A./RES/37/7 (1982), reprinted in 22 I.L.M. 455

[396] Ibid. at 457.

[397] Ibid.

[398] Ibid. at 456.

[399] Ibid. at 460.

[400] See World Comm'n on Env't & Dev., Our Common Future 4-5 (1989).

[401] Experts Group on Envtl. Law of the World Comm'n & Dev., Environmental Protection and Sustainable Development, Legal Principles and Recommendations 25 (R.D. Munro & J.G. Lammers eds., 1987).

this when it says that, although this formulation is better than the Stockholm formulation for several reasons, "the requirement that the environment must be 'adequate for human health and well-being' is extremely vague."[402] Apart from being endorsed by the U.N. General Assembly, along with the WCED report,[403] these draft articles have not received much attention.

The Hague Declaration on the Environment adopted in 1989 also recognized the link between human rights and the environment.It explicitly endorses the right to live in dignity and in a viable environment.[404] Its preamble provides:

> The right to live is the right from which all other rights stem. Guaranteeing this right is the paramount duty of those in charge of all States throughout the world. Today, the very conditions of life on our planet are threatened by the severe attacks to which the earth's atmosphere is subjected.

Referring to the phenomena of global warming and ozone depletion, the Declaration urges a global response to them:

> Because of the nature of the dangers involved, remedies to be sought involve not only the fundamental duty to preserve the ecosystem, but also the right to live in dignity in a viable global environment, and the consequent duty of the community of nations vis-à-vis present and future generations to do all that can be done to preserve the quality of the atmosphere.[405]

In 1990, the General Assembly, welcoming the decision of the Commission on Human Rights and of the Sub-Commission on Prevention of Discrimination and Protection of Minorities to study the problems of the environment and its relation to human rights, explicitly endorsed that "all individuals are entitled to live in an environment adequate for their health and well-being."[406] The General Assembly resolution refers to the right of everyone to an adequate standard of living for their own health and well-being as contained in the

---

[402] Ibid. at 39.

[403] See G.A. Res. 42/87, U.N. GAOR, U.N. Doc. A/Res/42/187 (1987).

[404] See Hague Declaration on the Environment, Mar. 11, 1989, 28 I.L.M. 1308.

[405] Ibid.

[406] G.A. Res. 45/94, U.N. GAOR, 45th Sess., at 2, U.N. Doc. A/RES/45/94 (1991).

UDHR and the ICESCR and points out that "a better and healthier environment can help contribute to the full enjoyment of human rights by all."[407] Moreover, it emphasizes that "environmental degradation can endanger the very basis of life."[408] Although this resolution specifically endorses the relationship between environmental degradation and the enjoyment of human rights, it does not embody rights language stricto sensu: It provides that all individuals are entitled to, rather than have the right to, live in an environment adequate for their health and well-being.[409] Thus, this resolution, while recognizing the relationship between human rights and environmental protection, does not expressly provide for a right to a healthy environment. The difference in the terminology ("entitlement" and "right") used, is a matter of preference because they convey the same meaning.

The Rio Declaration of 1992, the most recent instrument on the subject, while embodying a provision linking human beings with the environment, does not strictly contain a provision on a human right to the environment.[410] It simply provides in Principle 1 that "human beings are at the centre of concerns for sustainable development. They are entitled to a healthy and productive life in harmony with nature."[411] This formulation, which was heavily criticized for its manifestly anthropocentric nature,[412] does not recognize a human right to a healthy environment, even though policy-makers had ample opportunity to do so at the conference.[413] Instead, the Rio Declaration places human beings at the center of development, and while sustainable development underlies the entire Declaration, there is no further recognition of a fundamental right to a clean environment. The debates at the conference suggest that the omission was deliberate and not a mere oversight.[414] Marc Pallemaerts, comparing the Stockholm Declaration with the Rio Declaration, states: "By contrast, the first principle of the Rio Declaration, where it clamors that 'human beings

[407] Ibid. art. 1.

[408] Ibid. art. 2.

[409] Ibid.

[410] See U.N. Conference on Environment and Development: Rio Declaration on Environment and Development, U.N. Doc. A/CONF.151/5/Rev.1 (1992), reprinted in 31 I.L.M. 874.

[411] Ibid. at 876.

[412] Marc Pallemaerts, "The Future of Environmental Regulation: International Environmental Law in the Age of Sustainable Development: A Critical Assessment of the UNCED Process", (1996), 15 J.L. & Com. 642.

[413] See supra, note 392.

[414] Ibid. at 89.

are at the center of the concerns for sustainable development,' sounds like the triumph of a delirious anthropocentrism."[415]

5.2. Recognition of the Right

Several international instruments and judicial decisions recognize the right to a healthy environment as a customary norm.[416] This further illustrates the readiness of the international community to accept an explicit human right to a healthy environment.

5.2.1. International Recognition of the Right

The Stockholm Declaration and the Rio Declaration recognize the principle of environmental protection. Principle 1 of the Stockholm Convention holds that a "man has the fundamental right to . . . adequate conditions of life, in an environment of a quality that permits a life of dignity and well-being, and he bears a solemn responsibility to protect and improve the environment for present and future generations."[417] The Rio Declaration was also an effort to reflect growing international consensus of the importance of environmental protection and espoused the need for state involvement in achieving sustainable development.[418] Although these declarations are non-binding law, they may establish a growing opinio juris towards environmental protection, which, if coupled with widespread state practice of environmental protection, can lead to the development of a new customary international norm. For now, these declarations simply establish growing principles of environmental protection and state obligation that can be later incorporated into treaties.

Conventions on international humanitarian law lead to the development of historical norms which recognize the fundamental nature of environmental protection.[419] Protocol I of the Geneva Conventions bans "methods or means of warfare which are intended, or may be expected, to cause widespread, long-

[415] See Pallemaerts, supra note 408 at p. 642.

[416] Lynn Berat, "Defending the Right to a Healthy Environment: Toward a Crime of Genocide in International Law", (1993), 11 B.U. Int'l L.J. 327, 338.

[417] United Nations Conference on Human Environment, June 3-14, 1972, Stockholm Declaration, P 1, U.N. Doc. A/.CONF.48/14/Rev.1 (June 5-16, 1972).

[418] See United Nations Conference on Environment and Development, June 3-14, 1992, Rio Declaration on Environment and Development, P 7, U.N. Doc. A/CONF.151/26 (Aug. 12, 1992).

[419] David Hunter et al., International Environmental Law and Policy, at 316 (3d ed. 2007).

term and severe damage to the natural environment."[420] A similar provision is mirrored in the 1977 Convention on the Prohibition of Military or Any Other Hostile Use of Environmental Modification Techniques, which prohibits each state from engaging in such techniques "having widespread, long-lasting or severe effects as the means of destruction, damage or injury to any other State Party."[421] In addition, the 1980 Convention on Prohibitions or Restrictions on the Use of Certain Conventional Weapons Which May be Deemed to be Excessively Injurious or to Have Indiscriminate Effects prohibits incendiary attacks on forests and plant cover unless the forest is part of a military objective or the military requires use of natural elements to cover, conceal, or camouflage combatants.[422]

5.2.2. National Recognition of the Right to a Healthy Environment

National legislation and constitutions also show universal consensus in environmental rights. The Angolan constitution holds that "all citizens shall have the right to live in a healthy and unpolluted environment,"[423] and the Argentina constitution holds that "all residents enjoy the right to a healthy, balanced environment which is fit for human development . . . ."[424] Brazil's constitution holds that "everyone has the right to an ecologically balanced environment, which is a public good for the people's use and is essential for a healthy life."[425] Turkey and Portugal have similar provisions for environmental health.[426] South Africa more poignantly established that "everyone has the right to an environment that is not harmful to their health or well-being."[427]

[420] Protocol Additional to the Geneva Conventions Relating to the Protection of Victims of International Armed Conflicts (Protocol I), art. 35(3), Dec. 12, 1977, 1125 U.N.T.S. 3.

[421] Convention on the Prohibition of Military or Any Other Hostile Use of Environmental Modification Techniques, art. 1.1, Dec. 19, 1976, 31 U.S.T. 333, 1108 U.N.T.S. 152.

[422] See Convention on Prohibitions or Restrictions on the Use of Certain Conventional Weapons Which May Be Deemed to Be Excessively Injurious or to Have Indiscriminate Effects, art. 2(4), Oct. 10, 1980, 1342 U.N.T.S. 137.

[423] Angolan Constitution [Angl.] art. 24(1).

[424] Constitución Argentina [Const. Arg.] [Constitution] art. 41.

[425] Constituicão Federal [C.F.] [Constitution] art. 225 (Braz.).

[426] Constitution of Turkey [Turk.] art. 56 provides: "Everyone has the right to live in a healthy, balanced environment." Id. Constitution of the Portuguese Republic art. 66 provides: "Everyone has the right to a healthy and ecologically balanced human environment and the duty to defend it."

[427] S. Afr. Const. 1996 cl. 24(a).

In *Juan Antonio Oposa v. Factoran*, the Philippine Supreme Court held that the right to a healthy environment is a basic human right and lawmakers need not write in the constitution and the fact that it is codified, underscores its importance and requirement of state compliance.[428] The Cameroon Constitution on its part provides that "every person shall have a right to a healthy environment. The protection of the environment shall be the duty of every citizen. The State shall ensure the protection and improvement of the environment".[429] A question which deserves attention at this juncture is whether the Cameroonian Constitution creates an enforceable right or whether the right needs to be embodied in another legislation or decree before providing a right enforceable by Cameroonians against each other and against the State or non-State actors? It is important to point out that the preamble of the Cameroonian Constitution is not merely a declaration of aspirations, but is an integral part of the Constitution which creates enforceable rights. In spite of the fact that the Cameroonian Constitution creates enforceable rights, this work still argues in favour of a separate legislation or decree which will articulate in a more detailed manner, the right to a healthy environment.

5.2.3. Regional Recognition of the Link Between Human Rights and the Environment

Regional human rights treaties also recognize the right to a healthy environment. The first regional instrument to do so was the African Charter on Human and Peoples' Rights in 1981, which recognized the right of all people to a "satisfactory environment favourable to their development."[430] In 1988, the Additional Protocol to the American Convention on Human Rights in the area of Economic, Social, and Cultural Rights, created by the Organization of American States, initiated a right to a healthy environment through the following provision: "(1) everyone shall have the right to live in a healthy environment and to have access to basic public services and (2) The State Parties shall promote the protection, preservation and improvement of the environment."[431] The protocol also includes state action guidelines, such

---

[428] Ibid.

[429] See preamble of the 1996 Constitution of the Republic of Cameroon.

[430] African Charter on Human and Peoples' Rights art. 24, June 27, 1981, 21 I.L.M. 58.

[431] Additional Protocol to the American Convention on Human Rights in the Area of Economic, Social, and Cultural Rights "Protocol of San Salvador," art. 11, Nov. 17, 1988, O.A.S.T.S. No. 69,

as requiring states to cooperate at international level and adopt all necessary measures to protect environmental rights, depending on the available resources and degree of development of the state.[432] Moreover, the Organization of Economic Cooperation and Development ("OECD") propounded that the right to a healthy environment is a fundamental human right.

Furthermore, regional human rights bodies have successfully filed suit for inadequate environmental conditions.[433] Although there is no explicit right to a healthy environment in the European Convention on Human Rights, the European Court recognizes environmental rights under other rights made explicit by the convention, namely, the rights to life and property.[434] Besides *Lopez Ostra v. Spain*, the European Court of Human Rights presided over numerous human rights cases involving environmental harm. For example, in *Guerra v. Italy*, the European Court held that Italy violated the applicants' right to privacy and family life under Article 8 of the European Convention on Human Rights, when Italy failed to protect applicants from the severe environmental pollution imposed upon the town of Manfredonia by the Enichem Agricoltura factory.[435] The court found that the toxic emissions affected the individuals' well-being and prevented them from enjoying their Manfredonia homes, thereby affecting their private and family lives and giving a private cause of action.

Similarly, the African Commission of Human and Peoples' Rights in *Social and Economic Rights Action Centre (SERAC) and the Centre for Economic and Social Rights (CESR) v. Nigeria*, relying upon, inter alia, Article 24 of the African Charter on Human and Peoples' Rights, found Nigeria in violation of the right to a satisfactory environment by permitting Shell Corporation to disregard the health and environment of communities when exploiting oil in Ogoni land.[436]

---

reprinted in Basic Documents Pertaining to Human Rights in the Inter-American System 79 (San Jose, Costa Rica, Secretariat of the Inter-American Court of Human Rights 2003), available at http://www.oas.org/juridico/English/treaties/a-52.html.

432 Ibid. art.1.

433 Hari M. Osofsky, Learning from Environmental Justice: A New Model for International Environmental Rights, (2005), 24 Stan. Envtl. L.J. 71, 109.

434 Jennifer Cassel, Enforcing Environmental Human Rights: Selected Strategies of US NGOs, (2007), 6 Nw. U. J. Int'l Hum. Rts. 104, 106, 123, 126.

435 Guerra v. Italy, 26 Eur. Ct. H.R. 211, 228 (1998).

436 See Justice C. Nwobike, The African Commission on Human and Peoples' Rights and the Demystification of Second and Third Generation Rights Under the African Charter: Social and Economic Rights Action Center (SERAC) and the Center for Economic and Social Rights

The Commission held that the Nigerian government condoned the violation of international environmental standards by (1) providing military support to oil companies; (2) failing to provide environmental impact studies; and (3) refusing an independent assessment of environmental harm.[437] Although the Commission only made non-binding recommendations, the newly enacted African Court on Human and Peoples' Rights is authorized to give advisory opinions, order payment of compensation, and can hear cases brought directly by individuals.[438]

In *Maya Indigenous Communities of the Toledo District v. Belize*, the Inter-American Court of Human Rights found that Belize violated the rights of the Mayan communities when it permitted the exploitation of natural resources within Mayan lands without the community's informed consent, and permitted logging and oil drilling that caused irreversible environmental harm to the land relied upon for subsistence by the Mayan communities.[439] While recognizing the State's concerns for economic growth, the Commission held that development activities must be accompanied by appropriate and effective measures to ensure that they do not proceed at the expense of the fundamental rights of persons, who may be particularly and negatively affected, including indigenous communities and the environment upon which they depend for their physical, cultural and spiritual well-being.[440] The court through this decision, indicated its recognition of the connection between human rights and the environment.

5.3. Theoretical Basis for the Right to a Healthy Environment

The right to a healthy environment is a prerequisite for other international human rights, such as the rights to life and health, thereby requiring environmental protection as part of the protection of human rights. In 2001, Klaus Toepfer expressed this notion in his statement to the 57th Session of the Commission on Human Rights:

(CESR) v. Nigeria, 1 Afr. J. Legal Stud. 129, 137-38 (2005).

[437] Ibid.

[438] Hunter et al. supra, at 1406.

[439] Maya Indigenous Cmtys. of the Toledo Dist. v. Belize, Case 12.053, Inter-Am. C.H.R., Report No. 40/04, OE/Ser.L/V/II.122, doc. 5 rev. 1 P 153 (2004), available at http:// www.cidh.org/annualrep/2004eng/Belize.12053eng.htm. (Last accessed on June 10th 2010)

[440] Ibid. at 194.

> Environmental conditions clearly help to determine the extent to which people enjoy their basic rights to life, health, adequate food and housing, and traditional livelihood and culture. It is time to recognize that those who pollute or destroy the natural environment are not just committing a crime against nature, but are violating human rights as well. Thus, a healthy environment is a precondition for the protection of other inherent rights.[441]

Various adjudicative bodies affirm the link between environmental harm and the right to life. For example, the United Nations Human Rights Committee recognized this connection in *Port Hope Environmental Group v. Canada*, stating that environmental harm may also violate the right to life in Article 6(1) of the ICCPR.[442] In his opinion in the *Gabcikovo-Nagymaros Case*, Judge Weeramantry stated that:

> the protection of the environment is . . . a vital part of contemporary human rights doctrine, for it is a *sine qua non* for numerous human rights such as the right to health and the right to life itself. Damage to the environment can impair and undermine all the human rights spoken of in the Universal Declaration and other human rights instruments.[443]

It was said in that case that actual death is not necessary to present a right to life claim in international law. One needs only to show that the environmental harm presents a grave risk to human life.[444] The Human Rights Committee ("Committee") in Port Hope acknowledged that the plaintiff was able to argue a right to life claim based on the threat to life created by toxic waste. [445]

---

[441] Klaus Toepfer is the Former Executive Director of the United Nations Environment Programme. His statement is quoted in Press Release, United Nations Environment Programme, Living in a Pollution-Free World a Basic Human Right (Apr. 27, 2001), available at http:// www.unep.org/Documents.

[442] Port Hope Envtl. Group v. Canada, Communication No. 67/ 1980, 2 Selected Decisions of the Human Rights Committee Under the Optional Protocol 22, UN Doc. CCPR/C/OP/2, UN Sales No. E.89.XIV.1 (1990).

[443] Gabcikovo-Nagymaros Project (Hung. v. Slovk.), 1997 I.C.J. 7, 92 (Sept. 25) (separate opinion of Vice-President Weeramantry).

[444] cf note 417 supra, at 22.

[445] Ibid.

The ideal human right to a healthy environment should be both universal (as a human right it is possessed by all people) and useful (it should be of benefit to those who possess the right),[446] by providing a remedy for an environmental violation that is also a human rights violation. The right can be useful either indirectly (defined broadly in an idealized form and used solely as a basis, or catalyst for national laws which address the environmental situation) or directly (defined as invocable by individual holders of the right). The aim of this section is to establish a basis for a directly useful right.

It has been suggested earlier on at the beginning of this work, that an environmental violation is also a human rights violation when "as a result of a specific course of action, a degraded environment occurs, with either serious health consequences for a specific group of people or a disruption of a people's way of life." This suggestion can now be seen to find support in the manner in which a right to a healthy environment is developing as a principle of customary international law.

Principle 1 of the Rio Declaration, which has set the standard for a pattern of consistent and widespread state practice, provides that "Human beings . . . are entitled to a healthy and productive life in harmony with nature." Considering Principle 1 in conjunction with the contextual development of a right to a healthy environment, a right to sustainable development, and the rights of future generations, it follows that effects on health and a continuation of an established way of life are integral components of any right to a healthy environment.

A right that is directly useful in the sense used here must be justiciable. There are four general components, as expressed by the European Court of Human Rights that can be used to determine the justiciability of a right. These components are of a sufficiently broad nature, so that they should apply to nearly every judicial system of appropriate jurisdiction and therefore provide a common standard of justiciability. In the absence of a multilateral treaty or convention regarding a right to a healthy environment, the development of the right as a principle of customary law can be compared against this standard to judge the direct usefulness of the right.

5.3.1. The Right Must Benefit Recognized Individuals

Human rights are not only universal but also individual rights; even in a group context, the individual is the beneficiary of the right. In the context of

[446] For the Universality of Human Rights, see the UDHR.

a right to a healthy environment, the fact that the right benefits individuals is reflected in Principle 1 of the Rio Declaration and many national constitutions, as well as in several national and international court cases.[447]

While all individuals are beneficiaries of the right, determining who among this group can benefit from the right in a particular environmental situation invokes the concept of 'standing'. The concept of standing provides that the individual must show that the challenged conduct has caused him individual "injury in fact."[448] This principle of standing is reflected in *Balmer-Schafroth and Others v. Switzerland*,[449] a European Court of Human Rights case in which the Court stated that applicants had failed to show that the operation of the power station at issue exposed them "personally to a danger that was not only serious but also specific and, above all, imminent."

An important analogy can also be drawn from the concept of "direct effects," as used in the law of the European Union. A provision of Community law is "directly effective" if it creates rights for individuals, and not merely obligations for states, without any legislative action on the part of the states required.[450] A key requirement for a directly effective provision is that of precise definition.[451] While the rights are granted to all individuals in a Member State, the individual must be "individually concerned" by a violation of that right in order to state a claim.[452] This requirement was recently addressed in the context of environmental rights in *Stichting Greenpeace Council*

---

[447] See note 378, supra.

[448] See Black's Law Dictionary 590 (Pocket ed. 1996).

[449] Balmer-Schafroth v. Switzerland (Application No. 22110/93) (1998) 25 E.H.R.R. 598, August 26, 1997, Applicants requested that a nuclear power station be closed down because it did not satisfy the applicable technical and safety requirements and was a threat to the region's environment.

[450] See, e.g., Case 26/62, Van Gend en Loos v. Nederlandse Administratie der Belastingen, E.C.R. 1 (1963). This landmark decision by the European Court of Justice, described direct effects as "an obligation, ... not qualified by any reservation on the part of states which would make its implementation conditional upon a positive legislative measure enacted under national law."

[451] See, Case 41/74, Van Duyn v. Home Office, E.C.R. 1337 (1974). The Court of Justice, in a case concerning whether art. 48 of the European Economic Community Treaty was directly effective, stated at P 6, "These provisions impose upon Member States a precise obligation which does not require the adoption of any further measure on the part either of the Community institutions or of the Member States and which leaves them, in relation to its implementation, no discretionary power."

[452] Treaty of European Union at art., P 4, "Any natural or legal person may, under the same conditions, institute proceedings against a decision addressed to that person or against a decision which, although... addressed to another person, is of direct or individual concern to the former."

(Greenpeace International) and Others v. EC Commission.[453] In this ECJ case, Greenpeace appealed from a decision by the Court of First Instance declaring Greenpeace's action inadmissible because it was not individually concerned in the controversy.[454] In the appeal, Greenpeace alleged that the Court of First Instance did not take into account the specific nature and character of the "environmental legal interest."[455] Greenpeace argued that because its interest in environmental protection was shared by all Community citizens, requiring that an act should harm an individual, will effectively bar individuals from challenging Community measures that affect their environmental interests.[456] The construction project was commenced before an environmental impact assessment had been obtained, in violation of Directive 85/337, which had been determined by the Court of Justice to be "of a clear and unconditional nature, thus producing direct effects in the domestic legal order."[457]

The Court in its decision stated that while "environmental protection is one of the fundamental objectives of the Community," this recognition does not confer on a natural or legal person a right or legal interest that is automatically enforceable. It said that this is true regardless of the specific nature of the legal interest in environment protection or the modern developments in international law concerning environmental protection, as exemplified by the Rio Declaration and Agenda 21.

While the Stitching case was concerned with a procedural matter, it is applicable to the issue of justiciability for a right to a healthy environment. A well-defined human right to a healthy environment as a principle of customary international law provides the human right in a universal manner to all people, in essence making it directly effective. But to be useful, the right must also be justiciable. The concepts of standing and "individual concern" are similar in nature, and are linked as a general principle of law with regard to the procedural requirements concerning the justiciability of a right. As illustrated by *Balmer-Schafroth* and *Greenpeace,* the recognized individuals (or group of similarly

[453] Case C-321/95P, Stichting Greenpeace Council (Greenpeace International) and Others v. E.C. Commission, 3 C.M.L.R. 1 (1998).

[454] Ibid. at p 1. (Greenpeace brought an action seeking annulment under art. 173 of the TEC, of the decision taken by the Commission to disburse to the Spanish government funds in reimbursement of expenses incurred in the construction of the two power stations on the Canary Islands.).

[455] Ibid. at p 23.

[456] Ibid. at p 24.

[457] Ibid. at pp 20- 21.

situated individuals) whose rights have been violated must claim the beneficial remedy, as they alone have suffered the violation. Similarly, the affected group must be limited and definable in order for the right to sustainable development and the rights of future generations to be recognized.

5.3.2. *The Right Must Impose Duties Upon a Recognizable Group.*

At common law, a duty can arise in tort or in contract.[458] For a universal human right to a healthy environment, the duties must arise in tort, as a tort is a breach of a duty the law imposes universally.[459] The duty established by a human right to a healthy environment is narrower than that established by a tort, as the former is limited by the applicability of international and human rights law.[460] Despite its relative narrowness, there is a duty imposed by law to provide a healthy environment. In general, for every duty there is a corresponding right.

In a tort situation, a duty is a legal relationship arising from a standard of care, the violation of which subjects the responsible party to liability.[461] The legal relationship, in the absence of a multilateral treaty or convention, is supplied by customary international law, which binds the states to uphold a right to a healthy environment as a principle of customary law. But there is also a secondary legal relationship between the state and the individual, who would be the possessor of any right to a healthy environment. Under human rights law, the state accepts an obligation to ensure the protection of the rights of the individuals[462] and becomes the "responsible party" or "recognized group" upon whom the duty is imposed.[463] But a secondary party, such as a

---

[458] See Black's Law Dictionary 134 (Pocket Edition, 1996) (a contract is defined as "any legal duty not imposed by the law of tort; esp. a duty created by decree or declaration of a court."). See also Trietel, The Law of Contract, 10th Ed. London: Sweet and Maxwell, 1999, at p. 1.

[459] Ibid.

[460] In general, international law imposes duties between states, while human rights law imposes a duty upon the state to protect the rights of individuals under its jurisdiction. These duties are not imposed upon individuals.

[461] Ibid.

[462] See Donna Gomien et al., Law and Practice of the European Convention for Human Rights and the European Social Charter 17 (1996) (describing the relationship between the State and individual in human rights law).

[463] For example, the duty of the state to protect the environment is explicitly recognized in 61 national constitutions. It is also recognized in the European Court of Justice case Diego Cali & Figli Srl v. Servizi Ecologici Porto Di Genova SpA (SEPG), supra note 230. The court used this case, which involved the competition rules of the TEC, supra note 213, to clarify to what extent

transnational corporation, could also be a responsible party.[464]

5.3.3. There Must Be a Causal Link Between the Duties and the Right.

This component involves a standard of care, the violation of which subjects the responsible party to liability. A case has been made here that the standard for a human right to a healthy environment should be: As a result of a specific course of action; a degraded environment occurs, with either serious health consequences for a specific group of people or a disruption of a people's way of life. The nature of this violation includes causation and liability.

The state or a party (such as a TNC) acting within a legal relationship with the state, should be subject to liability. It is thus proposed that acts of commission and only certain acts of omission by the responsible party should satisfy the causation requirement.

There are two ways an "environmental violation of such serious magnitude so as to be also a breach of one's fundamental human rights" could occur. There can either be a violation on the part of a state of an international obligation, or an internationally lawful activity that acts as the cause of the violation.[465] In general, a state is responsible for any violation of its obligations under international law resulting from action or inaction by the government of the state or any political

---

protection of the environment constitutes a state responsibility. Id. at P 3. It stated that based on an analysis of the TEC, as well as princs. 4, 7 and 11 of the Rio Declaration, and Agenda 21, "protection of the environment, particularly when based on prevention, constitutes a public authority activity." Id. at P 56.

[464] See Lugano Convention, June 21, 1993, Europ. T.S. No. 150, ch. III, arts. art. 8, which exempts liability if the responsible party was acting on specific orders of a public authority.

[465] See Catherine Tinker, State Responsibility and the Precautionary Principle, in The Precautionary Principle and International Law 58-60, 66-67 (David Freestone et al. eds., 1996). A distinction has been drawn in the Brundtland Report (World Commission on Environment and Development, Our Common Future (1986)) and by the International Law Commission (Report of the International Law Commission on the Work of its Twenty-eighth Session, (1976) 2 Yearbook of the International Law Commission, U.N. Doc.A/CN.4/Ser.A/1976/Add.1 (pt. 2)) for purposes of state responsibility, between violations of international law and acts that are not unlawful under international law. In a comment to art. 21, the Brundtland Report states "The notion of state responsibility must not be confused with the notion of strict liability under international law... While the rules and principles of international law regarding state responsibility ... deal with the occurrence and consequences of internationally wrongful acts, ... strict liability involves the financial accountability of States under international law for the harmful consequences of acts which are not unlawful under international law."

subdivisions of the state.[466] This responsibility occurs only for official acts, or official inaction when there was a duty to act.[467] A state's duties are the obligations imposed upon it by international law as well as by its own constitution. In general, inaction results when the state fails to carry out an international obligation to act imposed by agreement or customary law. Similarly, customary international human rights law is violated only if the violation is practised, encouraged or condoned by the state as official state policy.[468]

A state, therefore, violates an obligation either through commission or omission. Defined as either a neglect of a duty or a failure to do something, omissions can take various forms.[469] One form of omission results when there is a deliberate inaction as a matter of state policy. As seen above, this triggers state responsibility for the inaction. Next, an omission can result due to a measure of uncertainty as to the risk of a violation. Here, while there has been no violation of the obligation, it remains a possibility. Finally, there may be an unintentional omission. This omission results when economic or cultural factors infringe upon a state's ability to address an environmental situation. Both the second and third types of omission may include lawful activity which is responsible for the environmental situation.

The precautionary principle, and its relationship to state responsibility and human rights law, sheds light on the second and third types of omissions. The precautionary principle is an anticipatory response used in situations of uncertainty where a violation has not yet occurred and no harm has been done, but where a strong risk of such a violation exists.[470] A remedy is provided in anticipation of a violation. In human rights situations, the precautionary principle is followed where there is uncertainty in the face of imminent, serious and irreparable harm.[471]

There are two problems with the use of the precautionary principle in a human rights context. First, no one has yet suffered a violation of his or her human rights. However, this absence is not a serious obstacle to the justiciability of a right. The requirement for standing can still be satisfied, as there exists a well-defined group

[466] See note 378 supra.

[467] Ibid.

[468] Ibid.

[469] See Black's Law Dictionary 455 (Pocket ed. 1996).

[470] See Menno T. Kamminga, The Precautionary Approach in International Human Rights Law: How It Can Benefit the Environment, in The Precautionary Principle and International Law (David Freestone et al., eds., 1996).

[471] See Ibid. at 181, 184 (The Human Rights Committee requires the risk to be imminent.).

of individuals, who risk a violation of their rights.

Of greater concern is the relationship between the precautionary principle and state responsibility. Before the precautionary principle is used to trigger state responsibility, there must be a clearly defined legal obligation that the state has a duty to uphold. Additionally, a question has been asked as to whether there exists a legal obligation to follow the precautionary principle in an environmental context.[472]

Despite these uncertainties, it remains well-established that a well-defined human right to a healthy environment as a principle of customary law is necessary to set a clear standard for state conduct. Acts or omissions that, as a matter of state policy, violate a clearly defined right to a healthy environment would trigger state responsibility. In an uncertainty case, only those state omissions that risk imminent and serious violation of the well-defined standard would invoke the precautionary principle and state responsibility. A similar result is obtained in the unintentional omission case, thereby eliminating cases of general inaction due to economic or cultural factors, though general inaction could create an imminent and serious risk. Through this standard, the linkage between the state duties and the right exists.

5.3.4. The Duties Must Be of a Kind that the Court Can Recognize and Enforce.

Duties of the state that have been well-defined through a clear standard, which will eventually constitute part of the right to a healthy environment, should be enforceable in any court of proper jurisdiction as a recognized principle of customary international law.[473]

After discussing the underlying legal support for the right to a healthy environment, the question which begs for an answer is whether a rigorous and narrow definition of this right, to make it useful and justiciable is necessary for Cameroon. In other words, are the activities of the oil industry threatening or harmful enough to justify such a definition?

---

[472] See Tinker, supra note 465, at 57. ("If the first step of establishing the existence of a legal obligation or duty to observe the precautionary principle fails, then it is difficult, if not impossible, to imagine moving to the second step of the state responsibility analysis, that of demonstrating a breach of a legal duty or obligation; ... At this stage the failure of a state to follow the precautionary principle is not an 'internationally-wrongful' act triggering state responsibility for its breach.").

[473] See note 373 supra.

6

RIGHTS-BASED DEVELOPMENT/ ENVIRONMENTAL LEGISLATION FOR CAMEROON

6.0. Introduction

The RTD and the right to a healthy environment have been established and clearly indicated as rights to which Cameroonians are entitled. They are in fact inalienable rights of Cameroonians. An issue which deserves attention at this juncture is whether the violations of these rights by the activities of the oil industry have reached a crisis proportion as to merit separate legislation aimed at enhancing their enjoyment. Results of field work carried out during this research and which are incorporated in this chapter indicate that the violations are rife and serious enough to deserve particular attention. This chapter therefore highlights the impact of oil exploitation on development and on the environment in Cameroon, concluding that the need for a rights-based development/environmental legislation for Cameroon is not only necessary but urgent.

6.1. Oil Exploitation and the Right To Development in Cameroon.

The Declaration on the Right to Development in Article 1 defines such a right as an inalienable human right by virtue of which every human person and all peoples are entitled to participate in, contribute to, and enjoy economic, social, cultural and political development in which all human rights and fundamental freedoms can be fully realized. This right includes full sovereignty over natural resources, self-determination, popular participation in development, equality of opportunity and the creation of favourable conditions for the enjoyment of other civil, political, social, economic and cultural rights.

The exploitation of oil creates the illusion of a changed life, life without work or a life for free. This seems to have been the expectations of Cameroonians but the reality is far different. Cameroon still remains a country with poor social indicators. A household survey conducted in 2001 showed that 40.2% of the population lived below the poverty line.[474] Mortality rate was also shown to stand at 75.8 per 1000 live births.[475] Road infrastructure is deplorable. For example, in Ndian Division of the South West Region which produces about 75% of the Country's crude oil, the roads are near impassable in some seasons. What is more, the whole division does not have a single filling station.

The question which this research sought to investigate first was whether the oil industry was not making any contribution to the government budget. The result of the investigation was that the industry makes a huge contribution. For example in 2008, TOTAL E&P alone paid its usual taxes which amounted to US $143million (approximatly 64 billion Francs CFA), in addition to making available to SNH a percentage of its total production as provided for by its oil contract.[476] It is important to point out that the oil industry in Cameroon is directly under the control of SNH. In this connection, for any company to be allowed to exploit oil in Cameroon, such a company must set up a subsidiary in the country and give 20% of its shares to SNH. According to the official,[477] if Cameroonians did not benefit from oil money, it was as a result of mismanagement. In answer to a question on the contribution of the oil industry in the enhancement of the standard of living of Cameroonians, the official pointed out that the industry was "doing a lot - together with companies like PECTEN and PERENCO; we are trying for example, in the Kribi region, we have a programme on renovating schools, upgrading fishermen's equipment, granting scholarships and providing health care."[478]

[474] Katz, M., Lifting the oil curse: Improving Petroleum Revenue Management in Sub-Saharan Africa, IMF, Washington DC, 2004.

[475] Ibid.

[476] Informal interview of a TOTAL E&P top official who claimed anonymity in Douala on May 9th 2010. This company was chosen for this interview because it is the biggest oil company in Cameroon in terms of operated production.

[477] Ibid

[478] Ibid.

The official also pointed out that in 2003, a cooperation project was launched, referred to as "DEVELOPPEMENT DURABLE des zones riveraines des sites d'exploitation pétrolieres" (SUSTAINABLE DEVELOPMENT in zones neighbouring to petroleum extraction activities).[479] The project members were: TOTAL E&P, PECTEN, PERENCO and SNH, The Ministry of Industry, Mines and Technological Development; Ministry of Finance and the Ministry Territorial Administration and Decentalisation. The aim of this project was to enhance an enjoyment of the right to development. The official was, however, unable to assess the current status of the project.

From the foregoing, it could be submitted that companies exploiting petroleum in Cameroon at least make a contribution to the national treasury, sufficient enough to stimulate an enhancement of the RTD. However, if the benefits do not trickle down to the owners of the oil, then it is as a result of poor governance. Priority is given to other projects. Hence in 2004, David Tchinou said that:[480]

> It is true that transparency around public budgets, revenue and expenses is poor in general in Cameroon. But this is a priority of the international community in Cameroon to do something about. IMF, the WB, the EU, and others are working under a large programme for improved fiscal governance. It is however a daunting task, and involves much more than just a publication in the news paper every year. They are making progress, but it is slow, especially because of the low know-how in the relavant bodies of public administration. The WB does not prioritise tracking revenues from source (oil) to specific expenses. Once the money is in the treasury, it has no colour *and can therefore be put to any use including starching it in foreign accounts.*[481]

However, the road to transparent management of oil revenue began in 2005 with Cameroon's adhesion to EITI principles. This adhesion to EITI may just be a cosmetic to drum up support from international financial institutions. This makes the need for a rights - based development legislation for Cameroon imperitive.

---

479 Ibid.

480 See WB ECON Analysis, West Africa's Oil Resource – Curse or Blessing, Report No.2004-065.

481 Emphasis is mine.

6.2. Does Oil Exploitation in Cameroon Pose a Real Threat to the Environment?

Potential environmental problems can arise at several junctures during the life of an oil production activity. The life cycle of an oil production activity may include site preparation, well drilling and completion, hydrocarbon production, service and workover, and site abandonment.

After seismic studies are completed whereby geologists and geophysicists have identified a prospective exploration site and a permit is obtained, the operator must prepare the site to accommodate the drilling rig and equipment. Wells are often located in remote areas, and special arrangements must be made for access to the site. In marshy areas, the operator may dredge channels to facilitate barge transportation of the drilling rig and other equipment to the site. At a land location, the operator usually clears the site and builds access roads. At a land location also, the operator may also excavate an earthen pit, known as a reserve pit. This pit is designed to serve as a place for the disposal of used drilling mud, cuttings from the hole, and accumulated rainwater, all of which are normally considered Nonhazardous Oil field Waste (NOW). However, other hazardous wastes that accumulate at the site could be placed in the reserve pit.

Drilling equipment gets dirty. Soil, fluids and other drilling materials may interfere with the equipment's proper operations. In addition, hydraulic oils, grease, or other lubricants may be present on the rig surfaces. As a result, the equipment must be periodically washed with water and sometimes mild detergents. This rigwash may contain various contaminants and is a potential source of contamination if proper disposal is overlooked.[482] Specialized crews usually perform the casing and cementing jobs. Casing is simply large-diameter pipe assembled and lowered down the hole much like the drill string. Proper casing of the hole is necessary to prevent cross-contamination of the different reservoirs that the well traverses. Cementing operations also involve certain environmental risks. First, mixing operations may be performed at the drill site. Improper handling could result in soil contamination from chemical additives or other sources. Often, excess cement is pumped up through to the surface and must be disposed of properly. Further, cement trucks must wash out any excess cement before leaving the location to avoid hardening

---

[482] See Berry St. John & Craig Wyman, Restoration of Oil Field Sites, American Bar Association, 1999.

of the cement in the truck. This washout must be properly managed. Where drilling data from the targeted formation indicate the presence of oil in commercial quantities, the operator will decide to complete the well. During well completion activities, well control is maintained by drilling fluid or by completion fluid which is pumped in and out of the well. All such fluids must be handled properly and in a closed system to avoid contaminating the fluid and the formation, and because of cost and environmental considerations. Certain wells require stimulation to initiate production. This may be done by fracturing using explosives or hydraulic methods. Stimulation is often done by acidizing or solvent-treating the formation. When the well is placed in production, well stimulation and completion fluids are trucked away for treatment and reuse or for disposal at commercial disposal sites. Improper handling or disposal of these materials can result in contamination of the well site. When the well is completed, the production phase begins. This is the phase where the oil is brought out to the surface and prepared for transportation to a refinery or processing plant. Drilling and production are not the only activities performed at a well site. Before a new well is put into production, completion operations are performed. During production, the complex operations and equipment associated with oil extraction necessitates frequent maintenance and overhaul activities. When the useful life of a well is over, plugging and abandonment (P&A) normally takes place.

This brief survey of the life cycle of an oil extraction activity gives a birds-eye view of the kind of adverse impact that the environment will face as a result thereof.[483]

The areas in Cameroon that are vulnerable to environmental degradation as a result of oil production are the three major oil fields and the track along the Chad-Cameroon pipeline project. To be able to determine whether this activity is a real threat to the environment in these areas, it is relevant to highlight the various environmental challenges facing the oil industry. These challenges range from oil spills, to gas flaring, abandonment of wells, only to mention a few. These are challenges that seriously damage or have a potential to seriously damage the environment, with their attendant consequences on human life. Whether these issues are serious enough in Cameroon to rise to the status of human rights violations, is an issue of grave concern.

---

[483] The life cycle of an oil extraction activity was obtained through an informal discussion with Mr Forgwe George of the Direction de Mine et Geologie in the Ministry of Industry, Mines and Technological Development.

Oil production in Cameroon is currently taking place mainly along the coastline. There are two significant hydrocarbon basins along the coastline of Cameroon, namely, the offshore Rio del Rey Basin on the Niger Delta and the offshore Douala/Kribi Campo Basin.[484]

The offshore Rio del Rey basin is situated on the Niger Delta. From the Eocene to the present, the delta has prograded southwestward through the process of sedimentation, forming oil-rich depobelts that represent the most active portion of the delta at each stage of its development.[485] These petroleum-rich depobelts form one of the largest regressive deltas in the world.

6.2.1. Environmental impacts

A recent study,[486] sampled stranded tar balls emanating from the oil industry, on beaches, West and South East of Douala on the Cameroon coast. The study points out that tar-ball loads obtained from these beaches are higher than in other beaches in West and Central African countries, except for Côte d'Ivoire and Nigeria. Since Cameroon's oil production is relatively small, this is a worrying signal, especially taking into consideration recent developments in the Gulf of Guinea. Tar balls are formed due to oil spillage in the sea. They are fragments or lumps of oil weathered to a semi solid or solid consistency, sticky to the touch and difficult to be separated from contaminated surfaces.[487] According to Barbosa[488] the analysis of tar balls revealed the presence of 16 polyaromatic hydrocarbons of which benzo(*a*)pyrene and naphthalene are highly carcinogenic to humans and animals. Furthermore, tar balls washed onto land are biodegradable and can percolate into ground and surface water, and if consumed by humans, adverse effects like nervous and endocrine systems disorders are likely to occur.[489] These concentrations for now may

---

[484] Dieudonne Alemagi, supra note 370.

[485] Doust, H., and Omatsola, E., 1990, Niger Delta, in, Edwards, J. D., and Santogrossi, P.A., eds., Divergent/passive Margin Basins, AAPG Memoir 48: Tulsa, American Association of Petroleum Geologists, p. 239-248.

[486] Oben P. M., A Survey of Environmental Management System initiatives in Industries along the Atlantic coast of Cameroon, (2006), Int'l J. of Sustainable Business.

[487] Ibid.

[488] Barbosa 2003 http://www...

[489] Gabche, C. E; Folack, J Cameroon Coastal River Network and its Impact in the Coastal and Maritime Environment. Paper presented at the 27th International Liege Colloquim on the Ocean Hydrodynamics, Processes in Regions of Fresh Influence. Liege, Belgium, 1995.

not create a substantial risk, but are indicative of the fact that a continuing accumulation will at one point constitute a substantial risk. Hence, there is the need for a narrow definition of the right to a healthy environment to make it usefull in Cameroon.

One notable example of an oil spill on the Cameroon coast occurred on the 7th of September 2004. According to Akum,[490] this took place at the Cameroon National Oil Refinery (SONARA). The spill occurred when oil was being pumped from a tanker to storage tanks onshore. Mile Six beach, close to the oil refinery was covered with spilled oil decolorising the black volcanic sand of the beach to brown, and a thick dark-brown crude oil slick was found floating on tidal water with wave action. Akum further notes that the predominated brown appearance of oil slick at Mile Six beach revealed that the quantity of spilled oil was enormous.[491] Crude oil is made up of hydrocarbons which are carcinogenic. In addition, oil spill on water prevents oxygen in the air from dissolving in water. Oxygen deficiency in the aquatic milieu is lethal to marine life. Crude oil inhibits germination of seeds of Zea mays and Capsicum frutescens. It also acts as a potent contact herbicide on these two plants and on Abelmoschus esculentus.[492] Some ecosystems, such as mangroves, and salt marshes which characterise the coast of Cameroon, are particularly sensitive to oil spills and can take years to recover.[493]

Salter and Ford[494] contend that world carbon dioxide emissions have increased nearly four-fold since 1950. According to the Intergovernmental Panel on Climate Change (2001), approximately three-quarters of the anthropogenic emissions of carbon dioxide to the atmosphere that is believed to be the principal cause of global warming have their origin from the combustion of fossil fuels. Gas flaring, a process of combusting fossil fuels, is a major source of carbon dioxide pollution from the oil industry. It has been a common practice for gas to be flared on a continuing basis from the oil refinery (SONARA). Gas flaring inflicts several impacts on health and environmental quality. The United Kingdom Offshore Operation Association in 1997[495] observed that apart from carbon dioxide, gas flaring from oil refineries emits

490 Akum, Z. E. 2005 http://www.postnewsline.com/2005/07/limbe_industrial.html.

491 Ibid.

492 Amakiri and Onofeghara, 1983.

493 IMO et al., 1993.

494 Salter and Ford, 2000.

495 See supra note 486.

atmospheric ozone damaging gases like CFCs (chlorofluorocarbons), HCFCs (hydro fluorocarbons), ozone-forming smog gases—VOCs (volatile organic compounds) and acidifying gases—NO_x (nitrogen oxides) and SO_x (sulphur oxides). These are bad because they contaminate the environment thus depriving the inhabitants of the right to a healthy environment. This means that although Cameroon has only one oil refinary, it poses a danger especially to the local communities hosting it. A bulk of the production waste from oil drilling and extraction is made up of hazardous and toxic effluents called *produced water*. Extracted from the ground with oil, produced water is often discharged into surface waters. Doyle[496] argues that produced water is at least four times saltier than ocean water and often contains 'industrial strength' quantities of toxins such as benzene, xylene, toluene, and ethylbenzene. All produced water and other drilling waste emanating from the operations of an oil extraction company along the coastline of Cameroon are treated for hydrocarbon content and disposed of into the sea. Although treated, produced water and drilling waste could still contain quantities of heavy metals and other naturally occurring material that are of major concerns to the environment, safety and health[497]

The development and extraction of petroleum deposits in southern Chad and the transportation of this resource via a cross-country pipeline to Cameroon's coast is currently operational and represents one of the largest development projects ever implemented in Sub-Sahara Africa.[498] However, the Environmental Management Plan (EMP) of this project did not consider in sufficient depth its impact on the surrounding communities in both countries.[499] The plan placed strong emphasis on the occupational health impacts of the workers but neglected the impacts on the host communities. The project had a larger effect on the host communities in both countries than on the construction workers who were usually employed for between a few days and a few months.

Equally, while the environmental assessment (EA) covered the expected 20- to 30-year life span of the project, it did not make an explicit attempt to define

[496] T.W. Doyle, Decision-based model of habitat establishment in salt basin wetlands of western North America. National Biological Survey Research Information Bulletin 47, 1994.

[497] The life cycle of oil: a new report analyzes health and environmental impacts. (Petroleum). (Statistical Data Included): An article from: Energy by Paul R. Epstein, Jesse Selber, 2002-03-22.

[498] See Dieudonne Alemagi, citing Guyer, 2002.

[499] Ibid., citing Utzinger et al., 2005.

the potential geographic area affected by the project. Coastal communities that accommodate this project expressed concerns about its impacts on fishing activities. Their citizens also argued that they had received little information about emergency prevention and response procedures (International Advisory Group, 2004). In a recent report, the African Forum and Network on Debt and Development (2007) argued that the construction and operation of the Chad–Cameroon petroleum pipeline project has led to the destruction of a major community of coral reefs, which serve as a natural habitat for several hundred fish species. Several of these species[500] have apparently disappeared, and the fishing activity of the local populations around the coastal city of Kribi has declined. The pipeline project also failed to prepare an oil-spill response plan. Responding to an oil spill like the one experienced by the Gulf of Mexico from April through August of 2010 is a massive and complex undertaking requiring numerous ships and equipment, effective institutions and trained personnel.[501] Cameroon is a poor country with limited resources to respond to a major oil spill. Therefore, a gigantic project like the one in question ought not to have even taken off without a site-specific oil-spill response plan. It is tempting to argue that the negative impacts of the Chad—Cameroon petroleum development and pipeline project stem from a lack of public participation during the planning phase of the project. Jobin[502] notes that public consultation of affected groups during the planning phase of the project was conducted in the presence of armed security forces. An approach of this nature reduces the civil liberties of the affected communities and this could have influenced their expressed opinion during such consultations.

From the foregoing discussion, it is evident that the presence of, and exploitation of oil in Cameroon necessitates the enactment of a rights-based environmental regulation for the country. If an oil spill like the one which recently occured in the Gulf of Mexico occurs in the Gulf of Guinea, Cameroonians in the absence of a rights - based environmental regulation will not have a basis for holding the violators accountable. BP, which was involved in the oil spill in the Gulf of Mexico, was held responsible on the basis of an Oil Spill legislation which exists in the USA.[503]

[500] Dieudonne Alemagi supra.

[501] See President Obama's speech to the American People in response to the oil spill in the Gulf of Mexico.

[502] Jobin, 2003.

[503] See American Oil Pollution Act of 1990.

6.3. The Need for a Rights-Based Environmental Regulation for Cameroon' Oil Industry.

The right to a healthy environment is a developing legal standard that is currently implemented in evolving international customary law, in regional human rights conventions, and in national constitutions and legislation. Recognizing the right to a healthy/clean environment as a human right will change the adjudication of environmental cases, mechanisms, and remedies available for environmental rights claims. Due to the inadequacy of international environmental law in providing a means for individuals to file a claim against polluters for damages and injunctive relief, a rights-based approach provides a mechanism for victims of environmental disasters to enforce state environmental obligations and hold multinational corporations liable for environmental harm. The case between Bhopal and Union Carbide is an example of how a human-rights approach would provide a more efficient means of achieving compensation and deterring environmental law violations. Environmental law seeks to protect natural resources and ecology; yet, it provides little or pays little premium to the means of redress for the individual.[504] When a state jurisdiction proves inadequate to resolve the harm caused to a victim of environmental abuse, there is little redress available for the victim.[505] Furthermore, international law proves inadequate because environmental matters are governed by treaties in which states are parties. Thus, only states, and not individuals, can bring claims when there is a problem of trans-boundary harm. A human rights approach will shift matters of environmental harm from a state concern to the realm of the individual, thus providing access to the many regional and international human rights bodies for individual environmental claims when state law is insufficient.

Recognizing a right as a human right invokes strong moral sensibilities and emphasizes the inalienable nature of this right. Human rights law underscores the importance of the issue and establishes a non-derogation principle of that right. The recognition of environmental rights as fundamental can stimulate political activism and involvement in environmental protection. Author and environmental rights activist, Michael R. Anderson notes that "concerned citizens and NGOs are more likely to rally around a general statement of right

---

[504] See David Hunter et al., International Environmental Law and Policy, (3d ed. 2007), at 1367.

[505] Ibid. at 1425, 1429.

than a highly technical bureaucratic regulation expressed in legalese."[506] A right is a clear protection that provides a moral incentive to foster environmental concern, whereas a regulatory law, which is inundated with legal and scientific terminology, is more impersonal and may not induce the same level of activism. Thus, human rights law provides a means for hearing individual as well as state complaints and shifts the focus of environmental law as a purely state concern to a concern of the state and the individual.

However, critics argue that in recognizing new human rights claims, such as the right to a healthy environment, there is a possibility of diminishing the value of previously established human rights.[507] That is, extending the scope of human rights may effectively weaken human rights claims generally and detract from their fundamental nature.[508] The criteria for establishing human rights should remain rigorous and new rights should be implemented only if they "have a clearly defined object and an identifiable subject and can be reasonably expected to be enforced."[509] Critics claim that modern rights, such as the right to a healthy environment, are social policy constructs and have no legal basis for enforcement.[510] Critics instead argue that such moral rights remain speculative; they act only as an incentive to create new law, and do not have the same legal basis as rights established in Human Rights Covenants.[511]

In November 2006, the Republic of Cameroon signed a production sharing contract with KOSMOS ENERGY[512], designating it as the lead operator of the Ndian River Block[513] in the Rio del Rey Basin. During the two dimensional (2D) seismic study carried out by Kosmos Energy, the expectations of the

[506] Michael R. Anderson, Human Rights Approaches to Environmental Protection: An Overview, in Hunter et al., supra note 386, at 1368.

[507] Stephen P. Marks, Emerging Human Rights; A New Generation for the 1980's, (1981), 33 Rutgers L. Rev. 435, 451.

[508] Ibid.

[509] Ibid.

[510] See A.H. Robertson, Human Rights in the World 296 (4th ed. 1996) ("Advocates of ' new human rights' tend to confuse objectives of social policy with rights in the lawyers' sense. If one wishes to see some objective achieved, a clean and healthy environment, for example, it is tempting to say that this is a right to which we are all entitled. But it is not a good idea to take wishes for reality.").

[511] Ibid.

[512] Kosmos Energy HC is a branch of Kosmos Energy LLC, a US based independent international oil and gas Exploration and Production Company.

[513] Ndian River Block is located in the extreme north-east of the Gulf of guinea in the South West Region of the Republic of Cameroon.

villages located on the Ndian River Block were varied. The expectations included compensation for damage to crops and property; sharing in the benefits of petroleum operations; recruitment of local labour; transparent recruitment mechanisms; and the need to train youths of the area to meet expectations of petroleum operations.[514] These expectations are based on the need to enhance an enjoyment of the peoples' inalienable rights to development and to a healthy environment. An elite[515] of one of the villages on the Ndian River Block intimated that they were bent on making sure that Cameroonians benefit from the operations of Kosmos Energy. He pointed out that the committee was going to ensure that the 260 job opportunities available be distributed equitably, paying particular attention to the villages directly concerned with the operations of the company.[516] Kosmos Energy on its part has as one of its policies, the respect of environmental regulation for the effective management of the environment. Although environmental policy implementation remains the responsibility of the Ministry of Environment and Protection of Nature (MINEP), the Ministry of Industry, Mines and Technological Development (ministry incharge of hydrocarbons) and the National Hydrocarbons Corporation (SNH) are expected to participate in decision-making within the oil industry.

The Environmental Framework Law[517] together with its decree[518] of implementation, outlines the regulatory procedure for carrying out and approving Environmental and Social Impact Accessment (ESIA) studies in Cameroon which includes the submission of an application file and terms

[514]Discussion with Chief Anje Micheal, traditional ruler of Mbongo village, one of the villages located on the Ndian River Block. "God has given us our thing, something that fetches a lot of money, but look at my village. Have you seen any cable in the air? We still use bush lamps. Have you seen any tap (referring to pipe-bourne water)? I am sure you have a car, but look at what brought you here (pointing to the motor byke which was taking me around). This people who have come (KOSMOS) seem to be serious. They are holding some good meetings. I think my people may smile one day".

[515]Misori Ule Joseph H., a representative from Mbonge in the Steering Committee for the 2D Seismic project recruitment exercise, between 22/10/09 to 04/11/09

[516]Ibid., In a discussion, he indicated that the following proposals were made: Illoani Zone – 10%; Mbongo Zone – 15%; Mofako Zone – 15%; Mbonge Zone – 10%; Bokosso Zone – 15%; and the rest of Cameroon – 35%.

[517]Law No. 96/12 of 5th August 1996 laying down the Procedure for carrying out ESIA; Chapter 3, Art. 7 – 17.

[518]Decree No. 2005/0577/PM of 23rd february 2005 to implement Law No. 96/12 of 5th August 1996.

of reference of the ESIA for approval, conducting the ESIA which includes stakeholder consultations, submission of the ESIA Report resulting in the issuance of a Certificate of Environmental Conformity (CEC) by the Minister incharge of the environment. The government of Cameroon has also devised a number of guidelines for use in the oil industry. These guidelines include: the Development and Application of Health, Safety and Environmental Systems (1994); Environmental Management in oil and Gas Exploration and Production (1997); and Waste Management Guidelines (1993).

Man in his natural self is a product of nature, and some one who talks of nature, talks of the environment. This means that the right to a healthy environment is supposed to be the bedrock of all other rights. To have 'a clearly defined object...', is not a monopoly for other rights. The same considerations used to define objectives for other rights go too well with the right to a healthy environment. The language used in the right to a healthy environment, does not seem to be different from the language used for other rights like the right to development. Thus, critics have an arduous task of making a distinction between the language used in the various rights. There is no gainsaying the fact that a dog may be given a bad name, so as to justify its being taken to the guillotine. A rights-based environmental regulation for the oil industry in Cameroon will make Cameroonians live in a real healthy environment.

7

MANAGING CAMEROON'S OIL INDUSTRY

7.0. Introduction

The right of Cameroonians to sovereignty over their petroleum, necessarily imports an entitlement to demand that government should manage this oil revenue for the maximum benefit of the people. It equally demands that the exploitation of oil should be carried out with due consideration for the environment. This chapter argues that the existence of rights means that corresponding duties also attach. The chapter therefore examines the demonstrably inadequate efforts that are being made by the government and oil companies to discharge their various duties. In this connection, the chapter discusses the Extractive Industries Transparency Initiative (EITI) and the Global Reporting Initiative (GRI), which are multi-sectorial and multi-stakeholder initiatives aimed at fulfilling, protecting and promoting the human right to development and the human right to a healthy environment.

7.1. Operationalizing the Rights

It has been correctly observed that "if the phrase 'rights of peoples' has any independent meaning, it must confer rights on peoples against their own governments."[519] In line with the Hohfeldian conception of legal relationships and obligations, the peoples' right translates to government's correlative duties.[520] Indeed, "it is a deeply rooted presumption of international law

[519] See James Crawford, Some Conclusions, in The Rights of Peoples (James Crawford ed., 1988) at 56. See also Gillian Triggs, The Rights of 'Peoples' and Individual Rights: Conflict or Harmony?, in The Rights of Peoples, ("If peoples' rights are to have any meaning beyond States' rights, they must include the right of a 'people' against its own government.").

[520] See Wesley Newcomb Hohfeld, Fundamental Legal Conceptions as Applied in Judicial

that rights and duties are correlative."[521] Therefore, the right of peoples is transformed into a duty of states.[522] Primarily, this duty would restrain irresponsible use and management of resources by public officials and obligate them, as agents of the state, to utilize positively, the resources for peoples' benefit.[523]

Even if one were to assume a situation where the right to sovereignty over natural resources resides in the state and does not attach to peoples, it will not necessarily follow that the state is without responsibility in how it chooses to manage the resources. States' rights over natural resources are accompanied by a corresponding responsibility that cannot be easily shirked. In a report on the Spanish Zone of Morocco Claims, President Huber of the Permanent Court of International Justice stated, "Responsibility is the necessary corollary of a right. All rights of an international character involve international responsibility."[524] By the same strand of reasoning, all rights of a national character involve national responsibility. Similarly, in the *Barcelona Traction case*, the International Court of Justice emphasized that "responsibility is the necessary corollary of a right."[525]

A simple way of describing the responsibility of a state here is to view it as obligating the government to administer public assets in the interest

---

Reasoning and Other Legal Essays 38 (1923). Examples of the extensive corpus of legal commentary and critique of Hohfeld's work in this area include Walter Wheeler Cook, Hohfeld's Contributions to the Science of Law, 28 Yale L.J. 721 (1919); A.K.W. Halpin, Hohfeld's Conceptions: From Eight to Two, 44 Cambridge L.J. 435 (1985); Isaac Husik, Hohfeld's Jurisprudence, 72 U. Pa. L. Rev. 263 (1923-1924); Peter Jaffey, Hohfeld's Power-Liability/Right-Duty Distinction in the Law of Restitution, 17 Can. J.L. & Jurisprudence 295 (2004); Max Radin, A Restatement of Hohfeld, 51 Harv. L. Rev. 1141 (1938); Roy L. Stone, An Analysis of Hohfeld, 48 Minn. L. Rev. 313 (1963-1964). Hohfeld was not the first to espouse the notion of the correlativeness of rights and duties. For earlier works on this issue, see H.J. Randall, Hohfeld on Jurisprudence, 41 L.Q. Rev. 86 (1925).

[521] See Nico Schrijver, Sovereignty over Natural Resources, supra, note 223, at 29.

[522] See Paul Peters et al., Permanent Sovereignty, Foreign Investment and State Practice, in Permanent Sovereignty Over Natural Resources in International Law, at 88, 95-96.

[523] Ibid. at 259 (suggesting, however, that there is not always a clear concurrence between rights and duties in international law: "Legal rights generally denote benefits conferred on its holder and the ability to enforce the correlative duties of another subject although sometimes (especially in international law) there is a lack of correspondence between rights of one subject and duties of another.").

[524] See G.A. Res. 626 (VII), U.N. Doc. A/2361 (Dec. 21, 1952); Ian Brownlie, Principles of Public International Law (6th ed. 2003). At 437.

[525] Barcelona Traction, Light & Power Co., Ltd. (Belg. v. Spain), 1970 I.C.J. 3, P 36 (Feb. 5).

of the people and for national development. In the 1952 debates on a draft resolution regarding the right over natural resources, the representative from Iran premised the argument in support of the concept on the interests of the people.[526] According to Professor W. Michael Reisman, the central idea relating to the declaration on permanent sovereignty over natural resources is that "the national community in which the resources are found is to be a significant beneficiary of their exploitation."[527]

In 2003, the British Government announced its position on this matter in its Principles and Agreed Actions on the Extractive Industries Transparency Initiative,[528] affirming that the "management of natural resource wealth for the benefit of a country's citizens is in the domain of sovereign governments to be exercised in the interests of their national development."[529] The statement continued to posit that not only should governments proactively use resources for the benefit of people, they were also prevented from exercising permanent sovereignty in a way that would cause substantial harm to their peoples.[530]

In Africa, the shift from past emphasis on states' rights aspects of PSNR, started in the case of *Social and Economic Rights Action Centre (SERAC) v. Nigeria.*[531] In that case, the African Commission on Human and Peoples' Rights interpreted Article 21 of the African Charter to encompass a duty on

---

[526] He stated that "certain industrialized countries would have to realize that in the modern world a policy of exploiting the resources of another country against the interests of that country's inhabitants could not be justified." Kofele-Kale, Patrimonicide.

[527] See W. Michael Reisman, Harnessing International Law to Restrain and Recapture Indigenous Spoliations, 83 Am. J. Int'l L. 56, 56 (1989) at 57. See also Hossain, Introduction, in Legal Aspects, ("At the core of the concept of permanent sovereignty is the inherent and overriding right of a state to control and dispose of the natural wealth and resources in its territory for the benefit of its own people.").

[528] For a discussion on this initiative, See Cynthia A. Williams, "Civil Society Initiatives and "Soft Law" in the Oil and Gas Industry", 36 N.Y.U. J. Int'l L. & Pol. 457, 487 (2004). Cameroon adhered to this initiative in 2005, see infra.

[529] Ibid. (citing Extractive Industries Transparency Initiative, Statement of Principles and Agreed Actions (2003), at http:// www.dfid.gov.uk/pubs/files/eitidraftreportstatement.pdf (last visited July 12, 2010)).

[530] See Subrata Roy Chowdhury & Paul J.I.M. de Waart, Significance of the Right to Development: An Introductory View, in The Right to Development in International Law, at 7, 15.

[531] Soc. & Econ. Rights Action Ctr. & Ctr. for Econ. & Soc. Rights v. Nigeria, African Comm'n Hum. & Peoples' Rights, Comm. No. 15/96 (2001) at http://www1.umn.edu/humanrts/africa/comcases/155-96.html (last visited July 12, 2010).

governments.[532] This interpretation can be viewed as setting an important precedent on the African Continent and a great eye-opener for Cameroonians.

The issue under discussion could also be analyzed from the perspective of the government occupying the position of a trustee or an agent in relation to the country's natural resources. As a trustee or an agent, the government has a responsibility to discharge its obligations in good faith. She is in a fiduciary relationship with the citizens, such that she cannot be permitted to abuse the relationship. Implicit in this trust or agency relationship, is the expectation that the political leadership will not divert the national wealth they hold on trust for their personal use[533] and that they will not allow their duty as an agent to conflict with their personal interest.[534] The numerous duties of trustees and agents would apply to the extent possible.[535] It is imperative to institute appropriate mechanisms in international law by which nationals can enforce their rights under this trust and agency relationships.

In carrying out her duty, the government has to take positive steps after drawing from other experiences on the continent so as to come up with a paradigm specific and legally consistent with the legal rights of Cameroonians. This work has earlier on argued in favour of the Cameroon citizenry's ownership of their petroleum. The government therefore has to involve them in the transparent management of the revenue generated from its exploitation as well as to set up arrangements that will enable the generated revenue to reach the masses, so as to uplift them from the economic doldrums. The fact that the government is making quite some progress towards transparent management of the oil revenue is her recognition of the duty it owes to Cameroonians, to enable them enjoy the right to development and the right to live in a healthy environment. Yet, much still has to be done to achieve the desired goal.

---

[532] For detailed discussion of this issue, see generally Dinah Shelton, International Decisions: Decision Regarding Communication 155/96 (Social and Economic Rights Action Centre/ Centre for Economic and Social Rights v. Nigeria), (2002), 96 Am. J. Int'l L. 937; Nsongurua J. Udombana, "Between Promise and Performance: Revisiting States' Obligations Under the African Human Rights Charter", (2004), 40 Stan. J. Int'l L. 105.

[533] Kofele-Kale, Patrimonicide, at 98.

[534] See G.H.L Friedmann, The law of Agency (Agents duties arising from the fiduciary nature of the relationship).

[535] For an explanation of the powers and duties of a trustee in the administration of a trust, see L.A. Sheridan & George W. Keeton, The Law of Trusts 250-338 (11th ed. 1983).

7.2. Importance of the Transparency in the Management of Oil Revenue.

There has been a growing recognition over the last two decades of the importance of transparency and strong governance for economic growth and social development, particularly in oil-producing economies. The rise in international oil prices over the last six years, resulting in large windfall profits for oil-producing countries, has also strengthened calls from the civil society and a broader range of stakeholders for greater transparency and accountability. The International Monetary Fund has recently published a *Guide on Resource Revenue Transparency*,[536] while the U.K.-led Extractive Industries Transparency Initiative (EITI)[537] has garnered increasing international support in both oil-producing and consumer countries.[538] The EITI aims at fostering voluntary cooperation between governments, private oil companies, and civil society to enhance transparency in the oil and mining sectors. While substantial efforts have already been undertaken to strengthen transparency, continued and sustained action is necessary to address the remaining gaps in this area. In the early 1990s, the Cameroon government enhanced its supervision of the national oil company (Société Nationale des Hydrocarbures, SNH), including the transfer of oil revenue to the budget. Some argued that there is an association between resource riches and poor economic performance (the "paradox of plenty" or "resource curse"), and a significant body of literature has sought to explain the relationships between resource abundance and economic performance.[539] But the resource curse is

[536] The Guide was issued first in June 2005 and revised in April 2007.

[537] See infra for a discussion of the EITI.

[538] More than 20 countries have endorsed EITI, including the eight sub-Saharan African oil producing countries (see www.eitransparency.org). The Cameroonian authorities announced in March 2005 that they would adhere to the EITI principles and work with other stakeholders in the oil sector to improve transparency.

[539] Auty (1997), for instance, examines the relationship between broadly defined resource-rich groups of countries over the period between 1960-90. Sachs and Warner (2000) show a robust inverse relationship between growth and resource riches for a sample of 97 countries over the period 1970-1989. However, the above mentioned view has not remained unchallenged. Hausman and Rigobon (2003), while supporting the generally inverse relationship, point out that oil-rich countries performed well economically in the 1980s when oil was doing well—contrary to what would be expected under the "Dutch disease" hypothesis. Lederman and Maloney (2003), raised doubts about the robustness of the Sachs and Warner findings, and subsequently in *Natural Resources: Neither Curse nor Destiny* (2007) argue, on the

not inevitable: a range of countries with prudent and transparent management practices (including Botswana, Canada, Chile, and Norway) have benefited from resource wealth.[540] The key question for a large number of countries is how they can ensure that their abundance in resources remains a blessing. The answer lies, at least in part, in the transparent management of oil revenue.

Empirical work, particularly in the last decade, has demonstrated the importance of transparency and good governance to effective policymaking, economic growth, and poverty reduction.[541] The prevalence of weak transparency and corruption in public management is not limited to oil-producing countries, but oil-rich economies appear to be in this respect particularly vulnerable. The oil sector is prone to mismanagement and abuse because of the magnitude of the revenues at stake and its enclaved-sector nature with few people involved.[542]

Strengthened effort to enhance transparency in the oil sector can therefore be instrumental in changing the overall perceptions about governance in the country.[543] Furthermore, specific attention needs to be given to the exhaustible nature of oil. Because oil constitutes nonrenewable national wealth, the principle of an intergenerational distribution of government income flows should apply.[544] Currently, assuming the accuracy of figures reflecting a

---

basis of case studies, that resource wealth combined with appropriate policies and institutions can contribute significantly to long-term growth.

[540] The importance of institutions as an explanatory variable is stressed by Sala-i-Martin and Subramanian (2003), who provide evidence to show (both in a cross-section study and in the case of Nigeria) that the impact of resource wealth is strongly linked to its impairment of institutional quality, and that little of the effect arises from natural resource endowments per se.

[541] See, for example, Kaufmann, Kraay, and Zoido-Lobaton (1999) and subsequent surveys carried out by the World Bank (www.worldbank.org/wbi/governance).

[542] A World Bank staff while preparing the Report on the Observance of Standards and Codes in 2000, commented that while Cameroon has a legal framework that meets a number of transparency criteria, "the complexity and cumbersomeness of the system (and enforcement thereof) are such that Cameroon is at present unable to fulfill the various principles set out in the Code of Good Practices on Fiscal Transparency".

[543] Cameroon was ranked 137th out of 159 countries in Transparency International's 2005 Corruption Perception Index.

[544] According to Davis, Ossowski, and Fedelino (2003) and Katz and others (2004), national wealth can be approximated by the present value of the rent earned in its production (essentially, proceeds from projected future sales after deduction of the relevant costs). Using the principle of intergenerational equity, this national wealth should be used in a manner that will leave future generations at least as well off as the current one.

relatively modest level of government revenues from oil, Cameroon's ability to ensure quality spending is deemed sufficient to make immediate use of oil revenue. Quality spending, i.e., productivity-enhancing expenditures, is essential to ensure that future generations benefit in a manner consistent with their rights from the oil wealth (which would take the form of a man-made wealth).

7.3. Loopholes in Cameroon's Oil Sector Transparency Initiative.

Cameroon has continued to be cited as a small oil producer, and at times often forgotten as being among the great producer nations in the Gulf of Guinea. Sometimes, officials in charge of the petroleum sector in the country speak only of little productions here and there, with particular focus on the Bakassi and Logone areas, which are emerging as fresh reserves. This may be deliberate so as not to create an awareness of Cameroon's potentials. Yet, it remains factual that Cameroon is among the great producers of oil in Africa. Cameroon has been a member of the Extractive Industries Transparency Initiative, EITI, since March 2005 but the oil industry in the country remains near opaque in violation of the principles of the initiative. A few factors, however, are identified as accounting for the lack of transparency in Cameroon's oil industry:

Firstly, transparency is perceived to be lacking as a result of the complexity of the production-sharing contracts (PSCs), which limits the understanding of institutional arrangements in the sector. The publication of basic information regarding these contracts would support better public understanding of the oil sector flows. For instance, it could usefully be explained that oil companies receive between 13 and 22 percent of the oil profit,[545] with the remaining portion accruing to the government either through corporate taxes paid by the private oil companies or through transfer by SNH of the oil profit generated by the sales of the government's share of oil output.

Secondly, there is a lack of well-specified and transparent rules for the transfer of the government's oil revenue. As a basic principle of fiscal transparency, all government revenues, including those deriving from oil,

[545] Oil profit is defined here as production minus operating costs. The oil profit percentage per field will be higher for fields that are more difficult to access and carry higher exploration risks (which are not reimbursed if unsuccessful). See Stephane Cosse, Strengthening Transparency in the Oil Sector in Cameroon: Why Does It Matter?, IMF Policy Discussion Paper, 2005 at 12.

should be accounted for in the budget, unless well-specified and alternative arrangements capable of being monitored are in place.[546] This is essential because fully accounting for revenue facilitates the allocation and monitoring of budgetary resources consistent with spending priorities. In the same vein, spending must be fully accounted for even when funded through the use of oil revenue. If oil revenue and spending are only partly recorded, policymakers and the public cannot assess the amount of available budgetary resources that can potentially be directed toward poverty-reducing expenditure.

Thirdly, limited dissemination of information undermines public scrutiny and accountability. Publication of data on the oil sector has been very limited in Cameroon, thus preventing effective public scrutiny and an active debate on the use of oil resources. In order to hold policymakers accountable and to strengthen governance, the public (particularly parliament and civil society organizations) needs information on how oil resources are generated and spent (or saved). Involving directly experts and/or nongovernmental organizations can also contribute to promote the public debate as these actors can help explain the often complex issues involved in this sector. Furthermore, encouraging active parliamentary engagement, particularly at the time of the discussion of the budget law can support a more effective oversight.

7.4. Current Struggles.

Within the past five years, considering the shortcomings of the transparency initiative, and recognizing the need for greater transparency, the government is taking steps to strengthen transparency in the budgetary process,[547] as well

[546] On the specificities of these alternative arrangements, see the Fund's Guide on Resource Revenue *Transparency* (IMF, 2007).

[547] Under the programs agreed with the IMF, the authorities have committed to (i) limiting the level of SNH'sadditional costs related to oil production activities to a fixed annual amount; (ii) limiting SNH's cash advances only to sovereign spending sector in the second half of 2005 and eliminating them in 2006; and (iii) undertaking cash advances only after prior approval by the minister of finance and within remaining budgetary allocations. Also, in September 2005, the prime minister signed a decree that increased the budgetary allocations for ministries that had relied on these advances above existing authorization levels (e.g.the ministry of defense) in order to reflect SNH's advances in the proper expenditure categories. This decreewas to serve as a benchmark for the authorities in setting budgetary allocations in the 2006 budget law.Overall, these measures, if fully implemented, represent a major advance toward budgetary transparency and should enable better monitoring of the composition of spending, including poverty-reducing expenditures.

as encouraging public scrutiny and debate.[548] The most significant of these efforts has been the adherence to the EITI in March 2005.

7.5. The Extractive Industries Transparency Initiative (EITI)

7.5.1. Background.

The EITI is a multi-stakeholder dialogue, involving governments, oil companies, and NGOs, motivated by the Publish What You Pay coalition of 120 NGOs, led by Global Witness, an NGO in the U.K., and several other founding members.[549] The aim of this initiative was to redress the huge distributional disparities in resource-rich-yet-poor countries, where government corruption and lack of concern for the country's people could so often lead to enormous wealth for a very few people in the host countries, combined with a populace that is, on the whole, desperately poor.[550] On its part, the driving force behind the Publish What You Pay campaign was to instigate changes in international stock market and accounting rules so that oil, gas, and mining companies would be required to disclose, on a country-by-country basis, their net payments to governments in each country from which they extract natural resources.[551] The basis of this was that revenue transparency will help to promote government accountability and reduce

[548]Oil sector data are now published on the website of SNH (www.snh.cm) and of the prime minister's office(www.spm.gov.cm). They include quarterly production and revenues, as well as SNH's annual audits up to2003, both for SNH's activities on account of the government and for its own activities. This also illustrates the attention that Cameroon gives to its participation to the worldwide Joint Oil Data Initiative (JODI) to raise the awareness of all oil market players of the need for more transparency in oil market data.

Civil society and other stakeholders in the oil sector have since July 2005 been increasingly involved in the sector as a result of the establishment of the committee (and its technical secretariat) in charge of monitoring implementation of EITI principles in Cameroon. In October 2005, a draft EITI action plan was sent for discussions with civil society and oil companies with a view to finalizing it in early 2006.

[549]See Global Witness, Global Witness Statement to the Extractive Industries Transparency Initiative (June 2003), at http:// www.globalwitness.org/reports/show.php/en.00043.html. (Last visited on July 13th 2010)

[550]Ibid.

[551]See Publish What You Pay, Publish What You Pay, at http:// www.publishwhatyoupay.org (last visited July 13, 2010).

corruption in many resource-rich-yet-poor-countries.[552] From the onset of this initiative, Cameroon erroneously was not considered as falling among these countries. Erroneous because Cameroon is a resource-rich-yet-poor-country. So one would find no justification for not including it among such a category of countries. This may be attributed to the lack of information on the issue. Officials in charge of the petroleum sector in the country sometimes speak only of little productions here and there,[553] giving the impression that the amount of oil produced by the country is insignificant. For example, in 2008 in Yaounde, a workshop was organized to discuss issues concerning the EITI. In the workshop, emphasis was laid on prospects and hope in the future. Simon Tamfu, Director of Exploration at the National Hydrocarbons Corporation (SNH), said that "prospects in the oil sector in Cameroon are very good. There are also prospects that we are planning to drill in the deeper horizon in the Douala basin as well as in the Rio del Rey surrounding, particularly Idabato, where most of the oil exploitation activities are presently undertaken even though only in the shallow zone".[554]

This EITI initiative actually began in June 2002 with conversations between Global Witness and major British oil companies, such as BP and Shell, asking them to voluntarily disclose their net payments to host governments.[555] The companies responded by agreeing in principle with the concept of disclosure and readily recognized that their economic interests would be promoted by stable political conditions in the countries in which they do business. This stability could be promoted by greater disclosure and a resulting increase in public accountability.[556] Yet, there were a number of practical concerns that

---

[552] See Press Release, Bank, Fund Fail the Test Over Missing Oil Billions (Sept. 19, 2003), at http://www.globalwitness.org/press_ releases/display2.php?id=217. such countries include Algeria, Angola, Azerbaijan, Cambodia, Chad, Colombia, Congo-Brazzaville, Democratic Republic of the Congo, Equatorial Guinea, Gabon, Guinea Bissau, Indonesia, Iraq, Kazakhstan, Nigeria, Papua New Guinea, Sudan, Turkmenistan, and Venezuela.

[553] See Frank Garriba, How Transparent is Oil Management in Cameroon? Available at http://edennewspaper.net/index.php? (last visited on July 13, 2010).

[554] Ibid.

[555] See Human Rights Watch, World Report 2002, 566-68 (discussing IMF efforts to promote oil revenue transparency and address corruption in Angola), available at http://www.hrw.org/wr2k2/pdf/business.pdf.

[556] See Howard Carter, CEO, ISIS Asset Management, Address at the Extractive Industries Transparency Initiative (EITI) London Conference (June 17, 2003) (transcript available at http://www.dfid.gov.uk/news/news/files/eiti_draft_report_isis.htmtop). ISIS is a $100 billion asset management company that uses corporate governance and corporate social responsibility

prevented BP and Shell from agreeing to take the lead on this issue. First, many of their contracts had confidentiality provisions that prohibited the companies from disclosing this information without the host governments' consent. Second, each had a concern about competitive disadvantages if only a few companies participated. That is, if Shell and BP insisted on disclosure, to the host government's perceived disadvantage, there would still be a number of other large companies prepared to negotiate for the same concessions to extract resources without requiring disclosure. Thus, this was an area that Global Witness quickly recognized would need government intervention, such that there would be a level playing field among competitors.[557]

The campaign got a serious boost when billionaire investor and social activist George Soros became interested in the issue and wrote to Prime Minister Tony Blair asking him to promote government regulation to require extractive industry transparency.[558] Using a soft law approach, Prime Minister Blair and the British Government then took the lead in 2002 in pulling together oil companies, international organizations, such as the IMF and the World Bank, investors, and NGOs to address revenue transparency through what became the EITI. The EITI was launched by Prime Minister Blair at the World Summit on Sustainable Development in Johannesburg, South Africa, in September 2002, where he encouraged all oil companies (public, private, and state owned), international organizations, investors, and NGOs to work together to develop a framework for reporting extractive revenues and payments.[559] At Evian, in early June 2003, the effort got another boost from the G-8 countries' growing concern about fighting corruption, which is coming to be understood as "one of the key obstacles to social and economic development," and their parallel concern about economic mismanagement.[560]

---

measures and engagement across its entire portfolio. It was one of the first institutional investors to support the Publish What You Pay Campaign. Ultimately, ISIS spoke in support of the EITI on behalf of institutional investors from the U.K., United States, Continental Europe, and Canada who, together with ISIS, manage about $3 trillion of client funds.

[557] See Global Witness, supra note 31 (noting that it was "highly concerned" that the voluntary approach proposed by the EITI would "not work where it was most needed").

[558] Cynthia A. Williams, Civil Society Initiatives and soft law in the Oil and Gas Industry, (2004), 36 N. Y. U. J. Int'l L. & Pol. 457.

[559] See http:// www.dfid.gov.uk/News/News/files/eiti_guide_b.pdf (last visited July 12, 2010).

[560] See Extractive Industries Transparency Initiative, Statement of Principles and Agreed Actions, § II (June 17, 2003), at http:// www.dfid.gov.uk/pubs/files/eitidraftreportstatement.pdf (last visited July 12, 2010).

The G-8 agreed on an action plan that included intensified, yet still voluntary, attention to transparency and accountability issues in countries where extractive industry revenues are important.[561]

On June 17th, 2003, the British Government held a conference on the EITI where its Principles and Agreed Actions were publicly announced.[562] Among the Principles are:

- A shared "belief that the prudent use of natural resource wealth should be an important engine for sustainable economic growth that contributes to sustainable development and poverty reduction, but if not managed properly, can create negative economic and social impacts;"[563]
- An affirmation that the "management of natural resource wealth for the benefit of a country's citizens is in the domain of sovereign governments to be exercised in the interests of their national development;"[561]
- A recognition that "public understanding of government revenues and expenditure over time could help public debate and inform the choice of appropriate and realistic options for sustainable development;"[565]
- An emphasis on "the importance of transparency by governments and companies in the extractive industries and the need to enhance public financial management and accountability;"[566]
- A belief that "payments disclosure in a given country should involve all extractive industry companies operating in that country;" [567]
- An affirmation that in "seeking solutions, we believe that all stakeholders have important and relevant contributions to make-including governments and their agencies, extractive industry companies, service companies, multilateral organisations, financial organisations, investors and non-governmental organisations."[568]

---

[561] See Fighting Corruption and Improving Transparency: A G8 Declaration (June 2003), available at http://www.g8.fr/evian/extras/506.pdf.

[562] cf supra, note 558.

[563] Extractive Industries Transparency Initiative, supra note 560, at III.

[564] Ibid.

[565] Ibid.

[566] Ibid

[567] Ibid.

[568] Ibid

Among the agreed actions were the following:

- That participants would work to develop and test "methods of payment disclosure, revenue disclosure and publication in the extractive industries in countries heavily dependent on natural resources;"[569]
- That participants would work at the country level "to implement reporting guidelines consistent with EITI principles, agreed between each host government and companies working in its country, along with support from the civil society, international institutions and other relevant players."[570]

A striking feature of the initiative perhaps, is the broad range of countries, companies, NGOs and investors that signed the Statement of Principles and Agreed Actions and are participating in the EITI.[571] In addition, institutional investors with $3 trillion of funds under management signed onto the Principles, representing a broad spectrum of U.K., U.S., Continental European, and Canadian investors, led by U.K. investors.[572]

---

[569]Ibid. at IV.

[570]Ibid. at IV.

[571]Cynthia A. Wiliams, The companies include AngloAmerican plc., Areva, BG Group, BHP Billiton, BP, ChevronTexaco, ConocoPhillips, DeBeers, ExxonMobil, Newmont Mining, NNPC, Repsol YPF, Rio Tinto, Shell, SOCAR, Sonangol, Statoil, and Total. The Governments, convened by the United Kingdom, include those of Azerbaijan, Belgium, the Democratic Republic of Congo, Equatorial Guinea, France, Germany, Ghana, Indonesia, Italy, Japan, Kazakhstan, Mozambique, Netherlands, Nigeria, Norway, Sierra Leone, Timor-Leste, Trinidad and Tobago, the United Kingdom, and the United States. International organizations include the IMF, the OECD, the U.N. Development Program, and the World Bank. A broad range of NGOs initiated and supported the EITI, including the following signatories: The African Network for Environmental and Economic Justice, CAFOD, CARE International, Global Witness, Human Rights Watch, Open Society Institute, Publish What You Pay coalition (which includes 120 organizations and individuals), Save the Children Fund, Transparency International, and Transparency Kazakhstan.

[572]See Extractive Industries Transparency Initiative, supra note 42, Part V. The signatories that joined the investor statement in support were Banco Fonder, Boston Common Asset Management, Calpers, Calvert Group Ltd., CCLA, Central Finance Board of the Methodist Church, Christian Brothers Investment Services, Co-operative Insurance Society, Deutsche Asset Management U.K., Dresdner RCM Global Investors, Domini Social Investments, Ethical Funds, ethos Investment Foundation, F&C Management Ltd., Fidelity Investments, Frater Asset Management, Henderson Global Investors, Hermes Investment Management Ltd., Insight Investment Management, ISIS Asset Management, Jupiter Asset Management, Legal &

The rapid growth of this idea promoted by NGOs and today broadly supported and sponsored by governments can be explained on three counts. Firstly, companies, developing countries, and investors recognized that the initiative served their economic interests. Companies that are recognized as leaders in corporate social responsibility, such as BP and Shell, have adopted Codes of Conduct that do not permit paying bribes, and, therefore, want a level playing field, including broadly applicable bans on bribery. This will permit them to compete effectively. Thus, disclosure rules that discourage the payment of bribes by requiring their disclosure (at least in theory) are in the economic self-interest of responsible companies.[573] Secondly, many host governments now recognize that being perceived as corrupt, as insufficiently serious about the rule of law, or as mismanagers of their economies, lowers foreign direct investment and can, therefore, reduce important sources of support, economic development, and revenue.[574] So, measures that support good government are increasingly welcome, again, at least in theory. Lastly, institutional investors in the United Kingdom, where the campaign began, recognized that the extractive industry entails long-term infrastructural investment and, as a result, is subject to significant financial risk where corruption, conflict, and desperate poverty intersect.[575] Thus, the political and social stability of countries in which companies invest is understood by these investors to be a paramount concern.

General Investment Management, Local Authority Pension Fund Forum, M&G, Merrill Lynch Investment Managers, Morley Fund Management, New York State Common Retirement Fund, Nottinghamshire County Council, Progressive Asset Management, Railpen, Sarasin, Schroders Investment Management, SNS, State Street Global Advisors Ltd., Storebrand, Trillium Asset Management, University Superannuation Scheme, and Walden Asset Management.

[573] A recent World Bank survey indicated that 40% of 3600 companies surveyed paid bribes. David Hess & Thomas W. Dunfee, Fighting Corruption: A Principled Approach: The C2 Principles (Combating Corruption), 33 Cornell Int'l L.J. 593, 596 (2000), citing Thomas Omestad, Bye-Bye to Bribes: The Industrial World Takes Aim at Official Corruption, U.S. News & World Rep., Dec. 22, 1997, at 39, 42. Yet, public opinion is turning against this practice, even as international development organizations and NGOs are recognizing the hugely corrosive effects on sustainable development and poverty reduction of corruption.

[574] Ibid. See Hess and Dunfee.

[575] Cynthia A. Williams, says that Nigeria, which has been the locus of continuing violence and conflict for a decade at least, has received over $300 billion in oil revenues over the past 25 years, and is the world's sixth largest oil producer, and, yet, per capita income is less than $1 per day. See Charlotte Denny, Scramble for Africa: Corruption and Chaos: True Cost of New Oil Rush, Guardian (Manchester), June 17, 2003, at 1.

This initiative was developed without high-level involvement from the U.S. State Department, and without serious support from the U.S. government. To keep the U.S. companies and the U.S. government involved, the British government was pressured into backing away from supporting mandatory EITI disclosure. Thus, the EITI is currently a voluntary disclosure initiative, and the support of important U.S. players such as ChevronTexaco was explicitly premised on the initiative remaining voluntary.[576] Moreover, for this reason, campaigners from Global Witness and Catholic Relief Services, do not expect the EITI to work. According to one Global Witness spokesperson, "The purely voluntary approach will not work in the countries where it is most needed because many political and business elites have major vested interests in avoiding transparency".[577] Cameroon, like most developing countries, seems to be paying lip service to the initiative so as to buy favours from multilateral financial institutions like the World Bank and the International Monetary Fund. According to a member of the Cameroonian Publish What You Pay coalition, "there is a perception that the government is using EITI to gain Heavily Indebted Poor Country (HIPC) status, but is not really committed to implementation."[578]

7.5.2. EITI Status in Cameroon.

Convinced by the advantages of the EITI, namely, the fight against corruption, the promotion of good governance, the promotion of transparency and accountability, and the improvement of the investment climate, Cameroon announced its intention to join the initiative in March

[576] In its 2002 Corporate Responsibility Report, ChevronTexaco had the following to say about voluntary initiatives like the EITI.

"Transparency is one of the fundamental values that guide ChevronTexaco's business conduct, and we have participated in the dialogue associated with many recent revenue transparency initiatives. A consistent message from ChevronTexaco has been that for any of these initiatives to be meaningful and achievable, they must honor the sanctity of contracts; be inclusive of governments, nongovernmental organizations and companies, without a unilateral focus on any one; and remain voluntary".

ChevronTexaco, 2002 CR Report: Revenue Transparency 13 (2003), at http:// www.chevrontexaco.com/cr_report/social_issues/ethics/revenue_transparency.asp (last visited July 13, 2010).

[577] See Charlotte Denny, Scramble for Africa: Corruption and Chaos: True Cost of New Oil Rush, Guardian (Manchester), June 17, 2003, at 1 (quoting Simon Taylor of Global Witness).

[578] See Eye On EITI, Civil Society Perspectives and Recommendations on the EITI, Publish What You Pay, 2006, at p. 8.

2005 in the EITI conference in London. This announcement was followed in June 2005 by a decree[579] creating the Monitoring and Implementation Committee for EITI Principles. The Committee which reports to the Minister of Finance as chair, is the steering and decision-making body for EITI issues. The Monitoring Committee Technical Secretariat was created in September 2005,[580] to coordinate, plan and monitor initiatives to implement the EITI. Its mandate also included the production and publication of reconciliation statements. To date, two reports have been published, the first covering the period from 2001-2004 which was published in 2006, and the second covering 2005 which was published in 2007. The reports covering the years 2006, 2007 and 2008 are currently being prepared.

The Monitoring and Implementing Committee is composed of the following members:

A Chairperson in the person of the Minister of Finance;

Members representing the Public and Para-public sectors:

- A representative of the Presidency of the Republic;
- A representative of the Prime Ministry;
- The Minister in charge of hydrocarbons or his representative;
- The Minister of Justice or his representative;
- The General Manager of the National Hydrocarbons Corporation (SNH);
- The President of the National Anti Corruption Commission.

Members representing the Private Sector:

- The General Manager of TOTAL E&P Cameroon;
- The General Manager of PECTEN Cameroon;
- The General Manager of PERENCO Cameroon;
- The General Manager of GEOVIC Cameroon;
- The President of the Chamber of Commerce, Industry and Mines.

Members representing the Civil Society:

- Two members of Parliament, one from the ruling party and one from the opposition;
- The President of Transparency International Cameroon;
- Three representatives of Non Governmental Organizations;
- Three representatives of Decentralized Local Collectivities;

579 Prime Ministerial Decree No. 2005/2176/PM of June 16, 2005.

580 Ministerial Decision No. 002328/MINEFI/CAB of September 15, 2005.

- The President of the Union of Journalists in Cameroon;
- Two representatives of the Religious Communities.

The Committee meets at least once every semester on the convocation of the President, who may on his own accord, or at the instance of other members invite any other persons to take part in the deliberations by virtue of their competences, related to the subject being discussed. Invitations for meetings, which are supposed to be addressed to members at least seven days before the meeting indicating the time, date, venue and agenda of the meeting, must be accompanied by working documents. A quorum of the Committee is formed when at least half of the members are present. Its resolutions are adopted by a three-quarter vote of the members present.

The mission[581] of the Monitoring Committee consists in:

- Ensuring the follow-up of the implantation of the principles and measures developed within the framework of the EITI;
- Elaborating a governmental action plan for the implantation of the EITI principles and to ensure their application;
- Identifying any obstacles constraining the smooth application of the EITI principles and proposing to the government, appropriate solutions for eliminating these obstacles;
- Ensuring the auditing of extractive industries by international auditors and also making sure that extractive industries show proof of payments made to the government and that the government show proof of sums effectively registered as coming from extractive industries;
- Ensuring the publication on the government website and in the media of comprehensive and exhaustive information on the payments received by the State from extractive industries, as well as EITI international reports showing the conformity of such payments;
- Searching on behalf of the government for technical and financial assistance necessary for the putting in place of the EITI principles, as well as participating in EITI international meetings.

When a country intends to adhere to the EITI principles, it has to go through three different stages. It must first of all acquire the status of an

[581] See http://www.eiticameroon.org (last visited on June 29, 2010).

engaging country, when it officially declares its intention to adhere. Cameroon acquired this status in March 2005. Secondly, the status of a *candidate country* is acquired when the country concerned has fulfilled the four conditions or requirements put in place, namely, that there has been an official declaration to that effect, and that there has been the designation of a national Monitoring and Implementation Committee; that the country has committed itself to work with civil society organizations, and that the country has elaborated a plan of action. Cameroon acquired this status in March 2008. Lastly, a country acquires the *compliant country* status when the EITI board issues a favourable report after examining the level of implementation of the initiative's principles. A country has a maximum of two years to become a compliant country after acquiring the status of a candidate country. Cameroon was supposed to go through the validation exercise in view of acquiring the compliant country status in March 2010. However, at her request, this date was changed to September 2010. At the time this thesis was submited, it was not clear whether Cameroon had already acquired this status or not.

7.5.3. The Monitoring and Implementation Committee.

The overall objective of the EITI is to ensure a transparent management of natural resource (oil) revenue so as to ensure socio-economic development and enable the citizens to enjoy the human right to development. The success of this initiative in Cameroon will depend on how committed the Monitoring and Implementation Committee is to the principles of the initiative. The principles demand among others that each country should appoint a leader with the time, bureaucratic skills, and political influence to drive EITI implementation. The appointment in Cameroon of the Minister of Finance to lead this initiative seems problematic. This is in the sense that the Minister of Finance already has a very busy schedule to be given such a demanding assignment. This definitely has an effect on the execution of the programme of action of the initiative. One of the principles also demands that each State should recognize the fact that genuine civil society participation is a requirement of EITI. Hence, States should support their active engagement in each critical step of the EITI process. The Cameroon government has not been very committed to this principle. EITI meetings at times are organized hastily and as such, documents are not circulated as required, making it impossible for members to participate effectively in deliberations. A member of the

Publish What You Pay coalition from Cameroon pointed out that: "the civil society did not get a chance to make contributions on the working plan. The government came with the documents to the meeting and went through them at the meeting… the civil society representatives did not have the chance to prepare because the documents were not made available before the meeting. As a result, there was no basis for an informed decision on the part of the civil society."[582] With respect to the membership of the monitoring committee, one of the EITI principles demands that every state should ensure that the civil society representatives be genuine members of that sector and not chosen from representatives of the interest of political parties, companies, or the like. While appointing members of the civil society in Cameroon, two members of parliament are considered as representing the civil society, knowing ful well that they are politicians. The legislature is supposed to occupy a prominent position in the monitoring of the transparency process in the oil industry.[583] In constituting the membership of the Committee, the executive (representatives of the Presidency and the Prime Ministry) and the judiciary (Minister of Justice) are placed as members of the public or para-public sectors, and the legislature is placed as a member of the civil society. A call from the EITI for the institutionalization of EITI into statutory law to help ensure continuity and sustainability, demands a greater role for the legislature than the one accorded by the government.

The government's adherence to the EITI is an attempt to discharge a duty incumbent on her to manage oil revenue in a way that will permit the citizenry to enjoy the human right to development. This EITI is being supported by the Publish What You Pay (PWYP) coalition of civil society organizations. On the other hand, the right to a healthy environment imposes a duty on oil companies to conduct their extractive activities having regard for socio-economic and environmental issues. The Global Reporting Initiative makes the monitoring of the discharge of this duty easier. Before examining this initiative, it is necessary to take a look at the role of the PWYP coalition in the transparency framework.

---

[582] See supra note 469, at 12

[583] See infra chapter eight for a discussion on the role of the legislature in the process of transparency and accountability in the oil industry.

7.6. Publis What You Pay

7.6.1. Origin

In December 1999, Global Witness published a report called A Crude Awakening; an exposé of the apparent complicity of the oil and banking industries in the plundering of state assets during Angola's 40-year civil war. It became clear that the refusal to release financial information by major multinational oil companies aided and abetted the mismanagement and embezzlement of oil revenues by the elite in the country. The report concluded with a public call on the oil companies operating in Angola to 'publish what you pay'.

It was clear, however, that the lack of transparency in the extractive industries was also a significant concern in other resource-rich but poor countries. In June 2002 therefore, Global Witness along with other founding members,[584] launched the worldwide PWYP campaign, calling for all natural-resource companies to disclose their payments to governments for every country of operation. From a few, mostly UK-based groups at its launch, PWYP members today span nearly 60 countries, with PWYP national affiliated coalitions in 31 of these. The rise in civil society participation can be attributed primarily to the great thirst for change in resource-rich developing countries among civil society groups, given the devastating impact of the resource curse. The campaign is largely consistent with ongoing local priorities regarding good governance, corporate accountability and poverty reduction and thus has served as a useful vehicle for local groups to continue to push for greater access to information and accountability.

PWYP's call for companies to "publish what you pay" and for governments to "publish what you earn" is a necessary first step towards a more accountable system for the management of natural resource revenues. However, it is impossible to ensure proper management of natural resource wealth by looking exclusively at revenues. PWYP members therefore also call for transparent and accountable management and expenditure of public funds as an essential way to addressing the poverty, corruption and autocracy that too

[584] They include CAFOD, Open Society Institute, Oxfam GB, Save the Children UK, and Transparency International UK. This small founding coalition of NGOs was soon joined by others such as Catholic Relief Services, Human Rights Watch, Partnership Africa Canada, Pax Christi Netherlands and Secours Catholique/CARITAS France, along with an increasing number of groups from developing countries.

often plague resource rich countries. This is, the campaign's "publish what you spend" objective.

A further call of PWYP is for the public disclosure of extractive industry contracts and for licensing procedures to be carried out transparently in line with best international practices. This is central to any effort to trace revenues and expenditures in the extractive industries as contracts determine the benefits, obligations and indeed, the transparency of the agreements between countries and industry. This is the campaign's "publish what you don't pay/ should pay" objective. Since the launch of the Publish What You Pay campaign in 2002, the coalition has grown in both scope and geographical presence and has established itself as the global civil society platform working on the extractive industry transparency issues. From its inception, PWYP's objectives have been for companies to "publish what you pay" and for governments to "publish what you earn" as a necessary first step towards a more accountable system for the management of natural resource revenues.

7.6.2. Transparency of Contracts and Licensing Procedures

Publish What You Pay (PWYP) members promote the public disclosure of extractive industry contracts and call for licensing procedures to be carried out transparently and in line with best international practice. The contracts between governments and oil companies are central to any effort to trace revenues and expenditures in the extractive industries. Extractive industries contracts determine the benefits, obligations and indeed the transparency of the agreements between countries and the industry. The anticipated oil boom will result in high profits for many oil companies. But if there is no transparency of contracts and licensing procedures, the government budget will remain meager, while the high poverty level will persist and development indicators will remain dismal. If citizens are to know whether payments and receipts from extractive companies reflect a fair deal for the country, the contracts on which they are based must be made transparent as well. Unfortunately, the use of the confidentiality clause protects oil contracts from this much-needed disclosure. Companies typically claim that payment information is proprietary and would either cause commercial harm if made public or would lead citizens who lack an understanding of industry dynamics and investment risks to demand overly generous terms. Likewise, policymakers who commit their countries to bad deals based on poor information, advice or outright corruption fear a political backlash if they make these contracts public.

7.6.3. Transparency of government expenditure

Publish What You Pay (PWYP) members work towards open, participatory and transparent budget processes at national, regional and local levels, in order to ensure the effective allocation and management of oil revenues. It is impossible to ensure the proper management of natural resource wealth by looking exclusively at revenues. Transparent and accountable management and expenditure of public funds is essential to addressing the poverty and corruption that plague the country. Citizens must have the data and the tools to assess the revenues flowing into the government's coffers. But the revenue information produced from exercises like the Extractive Industries Transparency Initiative (EITI) is useful only insofar as citizens and policymakers can use it to analyze the management, prioritization and spending of these funds for economic growth and human development. The adoption of revenue transparency standards has resulted in more data being produced and disclosed, and more demand for attention to government spending and development outcomes. Thus, PWYP members promote not only transparency in resource revenue payments and government receipts, but also the accountable and transparent management and expenditure of those revenues.

7.6.4. Transparency of company payments and government revenues

Publish What You Pay (PWYP) members work to achieve transparency of oil company payments to governments where they extract, and of government revenues earned from the extractive industry including payments to local authorities, as a necessary first step towards a more accountable system for the management of oil revenue.

Two thirds of the world's poorest people live in countries rich in natural resources. In most countries, sub-soil minerals belong to the state. But in many countries, there is an inverse relationship between this public resource and public welfare. The links between resource wealth, poverty, conflict and corruption – the so called "resource curse"– are well documented. Effective and responsible governance of natural resources can generate revenues that foster economic growth and reduce poverty. Public information and public accountability are the best guarantees that a country's resource wealth will translate into lasting benefits for its citizens.

Oil, companies make payments directly to governments in the form of royalties, bonus payments and taxes, providing the state with an autonomous flow of funds that is independent of its citizens. These windfalls reduce the need for additional taxation and thereby eliminate a key motivator for citizens' scrutiny of public finances. Extractive income gives governments ample resources to buy political support through patronage, and legislatures often have little or no budget oversight. Thus, the connection between citizens and the public purse is weakest in resource-rich countries where the need for well-informed, vocal and active public oversight of government funds is greatest.

Citizens have little or no access to information about these payments, because resource contracts customarily are shrouded in mutual confidentiality clauses forbidding either party from disclosing information without prior permission of the other. In the absence of public awareness or participation in government processes for revenue collection and distribution, corruption and mismanagement of public finances are free to thrive.

Today, the global community can see a coalescing movement to promote transparency and accountability in the oil industries. Worldwide public awareness of this industry's impact on governance, human development, the economy and the environment has never been higher, and leaders and communities now understand that progress is possible if the extractive sector can be opened to public scrutiny.

PWYP-Cameroon adopted a new communication strategy in April 2010. As part of this, the NGO (PWYP-Cameroon) planned to publish a bi-annual magazine. The first issue (May 2010), entitled "Industries Extractives en Toute Transparence", aimed at generating discussion and debate on the extractive industries among a wider public audience. The primary focus of the PWYP-Cameroon coalition is to play an effective role as a watch dog of EITI implementation in Cameroon. The country was recently granted an extension to submit its final validation report by 9th September 2010. In response to this, the coalition issued a press release,[585] calling on the government to demonstrate stronger political will by making sure that it respects the new deadline.[586]

[585] PWYP-Cameroon Press Release of 22nd April 2010.

[586] PWYP Coalition Members in Cameroon include the following: - Centre pour l'Environnement et le Développement ; Service National Justice et Paix; Fondation Camerounaise d'Actions Rationalisees et de Formation sur l'Environnement; Service œcuménique pour la Paix; Réseau de Lutte contre la Faim; Transparency International Cameroon; Environnement Recherche Action-Cameroun; Groupe AGAGES Management Consultants; Réseau National Anti Corruption (RENAC); and Dynamique Mondiale des Jeunes.

7.7. Global Reporting Initiative

The Global Reporting Initiative (GRI) is a multi-sector, multi-stakeholder partnership that is working to create and refine a consistent, comparable format for companies to report voluntarily on the economic, environmental, and social impact of their actions, that is, to produce a sustainability report.[587] It was established in 1997 by an NGO in the United States, the Coalition for Environmentally Responsive Economies (CERES), an organization which uses shareholder activism to get commitments by companies to produce environmental reports and implement environmental management systems.[588] The GRI reporting format has been developed for the most part by companies around the world, NGOs, accounting firms, institutional investors, and labour, with the involvement of some government agencies (such as the U.S. Department of Labour, International Labour Affairs Bureau, and the French Ministry of the Environment) and the U.N. Environment Programme (UNEP).[589] GRI is in fact an official collaborating partner of the UNEP. This affiliation with the U.N. Environmental Programme, brings an international standing and close partnership with the UN that is a priority for a global institution such as GRI. UNEP ensures the involvement of fellow UN agencies as appropriate, depending on the relevant sustainability issue addressed. The continued partnership with UNEP includes collaboration on technical, outreach and regional development activities associated with GRI's Sustainability Reporting Guidelines.[590] Moreover, it has been endorsed by the U.N. World Summit on Sustainable Development, and the reporting format has been endorsed by securities regulators in countries as diverse as Australia, France, and South Africa. As of late 2002, the GRI was established as an independent organization, with headquarters in Amsterdam, the Netherlands.[591]

As of March 4th, 2004, 416 companies in the automotive, utility, consumer products, pharmaceuticals, financial, telecommunications, transport, energy, and chemical sectors, in addition to public entities and non-profits, have

---

[587] Global Reporting Initiative, GRI at a Glance, at http:// www.globalreporting.org/about/brief.asp (last visited May 1, 2004).

[588] Ibid., at http://www.globalreporting.org/about/faq.asp (last visited July15, 2010).

[589] Ibid.

[590] See http www.globalreporting.org (last visited July 15, 2010).

[591] See Press Release, Global Reporting Initiative Update, October 2002, available at http://www.globalreporting.org/news.

published reports that adopt part or all of the Guidelines.[592] Since the effort is voluntary, companies can adapt the GRI reporting guidelines as they wish. Thus, there is a range of adaptations of the GRI Guidelines, as well as some companies that follow them in all particulars. If a report is prepared "in accordance with" the GRI, meaning that every indicator to disclose the specified economic, environmental, or social information has been set out, or its absence explained, then the company can include the following statement in its report, signed by the CEO or Board: "This report has been prepared in accordance with the 2002 GRI Guidelines. It represents a balanced and reasonable presentation of our organization's economic, environmental, and social performance."[593] Most reporters are "following" the GRI, or "using it," or "basing their reports on it," but are not reporting "in accordance with" its guidelines.

The reporting format on environmental matters is the most highly developed of the GRI indicators and seeks to provide a picture of a company's "impacts on living and non-living natural systems, including ecosystems, land, air and water."[594] Environmental reporting using the GRI format requires a company to produce and disclose specific information on its global usage of energy, water, and materials per million dollars of sales, its emissions to air and water, its waste management profile, the environmental profile of its products and services, its suppliers' environmental performance, and its effects on land use and biodiversity. [595]

A good number of oil companies including those operating in Cameroon, are participants in the GRI process and are reporting on the economic, environmental, and social consequences of their actions, services, and products using the GRI reporting format to various degrees.[596] However, while in 2002 ExxonMobil was not listed as a GRI reporter, its citizenship report,

---

592 See http://www.globalreporting.org.

593 See Global Reporting Initiative, Sustainability Reporting Guidelines 2007, Reporting Expectations and Design (2007), at http:// www.globalreporting.org/guidelines/ (last visited July 15, 2010).

594 Ibid.

595 Ibid.

596 These include, among others, British Petroleum (BP)(U.K.), Chevron/Texaco (U.S.), Cosmo Oil (Japan), Marathon Oil (U.S.), Petro-Canada (Canada), Premier Oil (U.K.), Shell International (Netherlands), Statoil (Norway), Suncor Energy (Canada), Total (France), and Bowleven (U.K.) Global Reporting Initiative, GRI Reporters per Sector, at http:// www.globalreporting.org/guidelines/rep_sector.asp?sector=47&SeaCou2=Search (last visited May 1, 2004).

dated 2009, discusses the same triple bottom-line types of issues, advocated for by the specific GRI format.[597] ExxonMobil is the world's largest publicly traded integrated petroleum company which operates facilities and market products globally, and explores for oil on six continents.[598] In a letter to its stakeholders in 2009, the Chief Executive Officer (CEO) intimated that:

> There is a wide diversity of views on the role of a company such as ExxonMobil in today's society. We know that we will never satisfy everyone. But we can, and do set clear expectations for ourselves that underpin our approach to corporate citizenship and the challenge of sustainability. For example, we will remain committed to safe operations and environmental protection in every aspect of what we do, every day. At the time of writing, ExxonMobil is providing assistance to BP and the authorities in responding to the tragic incident in the Gulf of Mexico involving the Deepwater Horizon drilling rig. The events in the Gulf are a reminder to the entire industry of the need to be ever vigilant in protecting people, local communities and the environment.[599]

He further pointed out that meeting the challenge of sustainability demands that they should effectively address the complex environmental, economic and social issues, while delivering on their primary responsibility which is finding and providing the reliable supplies of energy needed by future generations for progress and development.[600] This oil company operates in Cameroon and is involved in both upstream and downstream operations.

Companies, particularly large global companies, participate in GRI and produce citizenship reports outside the GRI framework because many NGOs, and civil society organizations generally in Europe, the United Kingdom, the United States and Africa are demanding transparency by global companies about their economic, environmental, and social impacts and are calling for more corporate attention to social responsibility issues such as sustainability and growing global inequality. In the United States, environmental issues and

[597] See ExxonMobil, Corporate Citizenship Report, available at http:// www.exxonmobil.com/corporate (last visited on July 16, 2010).

[598] Ibid.

[599] Ibid.

[600] Ibid.

concerns in the oil industry have been predominant; most of the participating U.S. companies are from industries likely to have a high environmental impact such as energy production.[601]

8

[601] See Global Reporting Initiative, GRI Reporters per Countries: United States of America, at http://www.globalreporting.org/guidelines (last visited July 18, 2010).

COMPLIANCE AND ENFORCEMENT MECHANISMS

8.0. Introduction

Cameroon is not free from the 'oil curse'. The benefits that go with the exploitation of oil do not accrue to Cameroonians in the same way as Norwegians benefit from its exploitation. Local communities hosting oil production facilities have nothing to show for this. For example, it has been indicated earlier that Ndian Division from which about 75% of oil produced by Cameroon comes, does not have a single kilometre of tarred road nor even a single filling station. The roads are near impassable during some seasons. Social amenities which permit people to lead dignified lives, are near absent or where they exist, they are in a rudimentary state. There is equally a steady environmental degradation. For example, Cameroonians living along the Chad-Cameroon pipeline project suffer the adverse environmental effects of the project.[602] Even at the terminal in Kribi, inhabitants have lost their means of livelihood as a result of the pipeline. Deep-water horizon drilling in the Gulf of Guinea is a potential danger to aquatic life and coastal inhabitants. This notwithstanding, some measure of legal control of the industry exists. The government and oil companies are engaged in a wide range of initiatives aimed at enhancing the quality of life and the quality of the environment. But Cameroon still remains a country with poor social indicators.

This chapter argues that the problem lies in the monitoring of compliance

[602] The Washington based NGO – the Environmental Defence Fund (EDF), a fierce critic of the project predicted: "The 600 mile underground pipeline through Cameroon will pass through ecologically fragile rainforest areas ... As a result, deforestation, wildlife poaching and the loss of farmland of the local villages to the construction activities will create a destructive environmental legacy. The pipeline itself even with state of the art technology, poses the danger of groundwater contamination and pollution of important regional water systems as crude oil containing heavy metals leaks into the environment" see http://www.edf.org/pubs/reports/c_chadcam.

with, and the enforcement of the rights. Cameroon is a country with a weak and unreliable judiciary. Also, the legislature is largely captured by the executive, rendering it incapable of performing its roles which consists of representing constituent interests, making or shaping public policy and overseeing policy implementation by executive branch agencies.[603] The inability of the legislature to legislate appropriately and to oversee effectively, is at the root of the mismatch between oil industry activities and their inability to enhance the human right to development and the right to a healthy environment. This mismatch is at the base of the disparity between normative expectations and observed outcomes. This chapter therefore examines the roles of the legislature and the judiciary in the oversight of the industry's activity.

8.1. The Role of the Legislator

Cameroon's natural resources have for many decades been a source of power and wealth for the country's ruling elites and for multinational corporations, and less often for ordinary Cameroonians. Tragically and repeatedly, competition for control of revenues from natural resources has fueled cycles of corruption and poverty, forestalling opportunities to spur economic growth and social development. As global mineral and petroleum resources grow scarcer in other countries and on other continents, and new African sources come into production, resource-rich African nations like Cameroon are earning rising profits from their natural wealth. If these resources are to be used effectively and harnessed for development, more accountable and transparent mechanisms must be developed and supported by the government, multinational corporations, the legislature, political parties, civic organizations and the media. This section discusses the place of elected political officials – particularly those in the legislative branch of government – in serving as constructive leaders in improving the oversight and management of the country's oil resources so as to achieve economic development. Democratic governance requires legislatures to serve three purposes: represent citizen interests; make or shape laws and policies; and oversee the executive.[604] In the management and control of the activities of the oil industry, legislators bear responsibility for ensuring that policy and

[603] Shari B, & Barrie H, Transparency and accountability in Africa's Extractive Industry: The Role of the Legislature, NDI, 2007.

[604] Ibid., at p. 10.

regulatory frameworks support their sustainable use and exploitation, and that government agencies appropriately allocate and account for revenues.[605] This section identifies the challenges that Cameroonian legislators face in overseeing the country's oil industry.

In Cameroon, while current efforts to increase transparency and accountability in the management of oil resources emphasize the roles and responsibilities of a broad range of actors, relatively little attention has been paid to the potential contribution of elected legislators. Yet, the three core functions of the legislative body – representing constituent interests, making or shaping public policy, and overseeing policy implementation by executive branch agencies – are central to any effort in this area.

The recognition of the need to improve the management of the extractive industry in Cameroon presents a unique opening for legislators to establish themselves as relevant and credible actors in the movement towards greater transparency, accountability and responsiveness in government. Initiatives like the Extractive Industries Transparency Initiative (EITI) and Publish What You Pay (PWYP) Coalition have drawn worldwide attention to the need for increased transparency and accountability in the management of extractive industries. The result is unprecedented international political will, information and tools for reforming the management of the extractive industries. Similarly, the window of opportunity for legislators to prove themselves as relevant and capable actors in the debate over extractive industry management closed firmly in a country like Cameroon where the legislature has limited credibility in the eyes of citizens.

8.1.1. Factors Militating Against the Legislator.

The Cameroonian legislators face many constraints in fulfilling their roles and responsibilities, including weak individual and institutional capacity, little independence from the more powerful executive and ruling political party, and limited political will.[606] Oversight of the extractive industries is further

---

[605] The National Democratic Institute for International Affairs (NDI) believes that African legislatures could play more robust roles in creating viable oversight mechanisms to monitor the collection and use of revenues from extractive industry revenues, and in ensuring that the interests of civil society and citizens are taken into account, from community-level environmental concerns to the allocation and disbursement of revenues collected by central governments.

[606] cf supra, note 603.

complicated by a common perception held by many legislators themselves that the industry's technical complexity is beyond their comprehension.[607] Shari and Barrie[608] do not make particular reference to Cameroon. However, the study was carried out in Africa not excluding Cameroon. Therefore, the results hold true for Cameroon. Faced with proposals from well-informed or connected executive branch agencies or officials, legislators often lack both the information and the confidence to influence legislation, policy or the management of the extractive industry.

A weak legislature cannot serve as a counterweight to a more powerful executive branch. In Cameroon, the concept of party loyalty is so strong that the legislature is marginalized from the decision-making process and dissuaded from conducting oversight activities. The ruling party control is pervasive, and the legislature is often used to rubber-stamp executive policy after little or no debate.[609] Constitutions, legislation and other rules of procedure often vest significant legal authority in the executive, thereby diminishing the ability of legislatures to oversee the oil sector.[610]

In a large number of the countries surveyed by the National Democratic Institute for International Affairs,[611] legislators are sidelined by more powerful executives, and often lack the information and skills to fulfill their core functions. When the role of the legislative branch as a counterbalance to executive power is not fully developed, customary practice frequently gives the executive disproportionate power and authority.[612] The complex environment in which oil exploitation frequently occurs, makes it particularly difficult for legislators to exercise effective oversight. Cameroonian law does not grant the National Assembly the power to investigate state-owned companies.[613] Legislators are often under pressure to pass budgets within timeframes that do not allow for diligent review.[614]

Regulation and oversight of the extractive industries requires an understanding of complex technical and financial issues. In Cameroon, the

---

[607] Ibid.

[608] Ibid.

[609] Ibid.

[610] Ibid.

[611] Shari, B & Barrie H. Transparency and Accountability in Africa's Extractive Industries, National Democratic Institute for International Affairs (NDI) 2007

[612] Ibid.

[613] See Part III, Chapter I of the Constotution of Cameroon.

[614] Mbah Kenaston, 'Parliament Brushes Finance Bill With the Speed of Light', The Post, No. 0267, March 8th 2002.

ability of individual legislators to understand and contribute to extractive sector management and oversight is worrisomely weak. The lack of formal education among certain legislators accounts for the lack of understanding.[615] Equally, high turnover in the legislature makes it difficult for legislators to build up specific areas of expertise over time.[616]

The ultimate responsibility for the management of a country's oil resource wealth lies with that country's elected government. The principal means of ensuring a sound management at all stages of oil resource exploitation – from extraction to the collection and expenditure of revenues – is through the adoption of practices that adhere to and reinforce agreed-upon standards of accountability and transparency. Countries that have successfully used proceeds from the extractive industries for national development purposes, like Australia, Canada and Norway, have such practices in common.[617] According to a study commissioned by the World Bank,

> Our findings stress the importance of strong (or at least strengthened) institutions in the wake of natural resource discoveries as a way to curb the negative growth effects of corruption. This is especially true in less developed countries where natural resource discoveries have a much higher relative impact on both the capital stock and the extent of corruption, and are confronted with generally weaker and less adaptable institutions.[618]

Accountable governments face two principal challenges in determining the policy framework for the exploitation of oil and minerals in their countries. First, they must create a business climate that attracts private investment, a necessary precondition for the development of the extractive industries. Second, they must address relevant domestic policy issues, such as the environmental impact on communities affected by extractive activities, and ensure the equitable distribution of profits from the industry.

---

[615] Some MPs do not have above the First School Leaving Certificate, and so deliberations do not interest them. See Venegho Fon, 'MPs sleeping during deliberations in the Hemicircle at Ngoa-ekele', The Post News Paper, No. 0356, February 2003.

[616] http://en.wikipedia.org/cameroonian_parliamentary_elections_2002

[617] Cf supra, note 611.

[618] Leite and Weidman, quoted in Marshall, Ian, A Survey of Corruption Issues in the Mining & Mineral Sector. England: International Institute for Environment and Development,2001. Availableonlineat:http://www.iied.org/mmsd/mmsd_pdfs/marshall_corruption.pdf

Policy or regulatory frameworks and laws governing the exploitation and management of natural resources are often spread across different pieces of legislation and other government instruments. In most cases, constitutions vest natural resources in the people but grant the government the authority to manage those resources on their behalf. In some cases, constitutions specify formulae for revenue sharing between national and state or provincial levels of government. Mining or oil codes specify procedures and parameters for the granting of concessions and other rights of access, general conditions for exploitation, royalties, taxes, and other incentives specific to the extractive industries. Corporate tax structures and laws governing employment, the environment, and occupational health and safety also have implications for extractive industry management. Through their lawmaking functions, legislators can support the passage of laws or other instruments that create an enabling environment for sustainable and accountable management of oil and minerals. Recommendations made by the Norwegian Parliament helped determine the appropriate management systems when large offshore oil and gas deposits were discovered in the late 1960s. The Norwegian legislature continues to play a central role in overseeing the management of the extractive industries. Regrettably, legislators from a number of African countries described situations in which they were under pressure to move legislation forward quickly, often without amendment, because funding from international development partners depended on the passage of legislation.[619] Confidentiality clauses are also often used to prevent public scrutiny of contract details.[620]

> In the most successful economies, the state's role as facilitator of investment is balanced by its role, for example, as regulator – establishing laws and policies that provide for regional land use planning, ameliorate environment and social impacts, or take advantage of the opportunity to develop roads, schools, and better health care.[621]

[619] See note 602 supra.

[620] cf supra note 603, p. 11.

[621] The Mining, Minerals and Sustainable Development Project. Breaking New Ground: Mining Minerals and Sustainable Development. London: Earthscan Publications Ltd, 2002. Report for the International Institute for Environment and Development and the World Business Council for Sustainable Development.

The Cameroon legislator's inability to monitor and oversee the activities of the oil industry so as to guarantee the rights to development and a healthy environment, is clearly portrayed in the Chad-Cameroon pipeline project.

8.1.2. Legislative Oversight of the Chad–Cameroon Pipeline Project

In Cameroon where efforts to improve transparency and accountability are underway, there is doubt about the sincerity of government, and a general perception that reforms were only being undertaken in response to international pressure. The legislature's weakness in overseeing the activities of the oil sector can be explained by the legal framework of the Chad – Cameroon pipeline project.

8.1.2.1. An Overview of the Chad–Cameroon Pipeline Project.

The objective of the Chad-Cameroon oil and pipeline project was to develop oil resources that were discovered in the Doba region of southern Chad. The project included the construction of an approximately 1070 km underground pipeline to carry the crude oil from landlocked Chad across Cameroon to a proposed marine terminal near Kribi, a coastal town on the Atlantic coast of Cameroon, for delivery to the world markets. The project was realized in two phases. The first phase – the extraction of oil – included the development of oilfields in the Doba region of southern Chad, the drilling of about 300 wells and the construction of associated transport and storage facilities and infrastructure including the 1070 km pipeline which was completed in mid-2003. The second phase is the exportation phase, which includes the transportation of oil along the pipeline onto offshore floating storage for delivery to the world markets.[622] The project is now in its second phase following the completion of construction work in 2003. An estimated one billion barrels of oil is expected to be produced over the 25-year life of the project. The project construction cost was estimated at US $ 3.5 billion (2,100 billion francs CFA).[623] The project is being executed by two joint-venture companies established by a consortium of multinational oil companies with the governments of Chad and Cameroon respectively. They are; the Tchad Oil

[622] Contracting out of Human Rights: The Chad-Cameroon Pipeline Project, Amnesty International Report, September 2005, www.amnesty.org.uk, p. 13.

[623] www.worldbank.org/pics/pidcm51059.txt, p. 3. See also www.edf.org/pubs/Reports/c chadcam. html.

Transportation Company (TOTCO), which is responsible for operations from the oil fields in Chad up to the border with Cameroon, and the Cameroon Oil Transportation Company (COTCO), which is responsible for operations from the Chad border right up to the marine terminal off the coast of Cameroon in Kribi. TOTCO is owned by a consortium of three multinational oil companies (which owns 80%) and the government of Chad which owns 20% of its equity shares. The consortium comprises ExxonMobil, the project leader that owns 32% of TOTCO, Petronas 32% and Chevron 16%.[624] COTCO on its part is owned by the consortium - 80%, the government of Cameroon 15% and the government of Chad 5%. The World Bank estimated that both countries would benefit significantly from the project during its 25-year life span. Cameroon would receive an estimated $500 million in revenue from the project over the 25-year operational period. In addition, Cameroon would benefit from substantial improvements in her infrastructure, and witness increased employment. The Bank also claimed that the objectives of the project included the promotion of the economic growth of Cameroon. Despite the estimated benefits to be derived from the project, it has been plagued with criticisms from the early stages by organisations, institutions and individuals that are concerned about the adverse social, environmental and political effects of the project. The criticisms made against the project, call for an examination of the legal framework for the project.

8.1.2.2. The Legal Framework for the Project

The main legal framework for the Cameroon portion of the project is a 1998 document entitled 'the COTCO Convention of Establishment between the Republic of Cameroon and Cameroon Oil Transportation Company, S.A. (COTCO)', generally referred to as the 'COTCO Convention of Establishment' or simply as the 'COTCO Convention'. This is supplemented by applicable Cameroonian legislation, which includes: the constitution; international treaties, conventions and agreements that are signed and ratified by the government, namely, laws that are voted by the National Assembly

[624] ExxonMobil, the project leader owns 40% of the private equity, Petronas 35% and Chevron 25%. SeeWorld Bank, Chad-Cameroon Petroleum Development and Pipeline Project, Project Overview webpage:http://www.worldbank.org/afr/ccproj/project/pro_overview.htm. The companies that were originally involved in the project were ExxonMobil, Shell and Elf, but Shell and Elf withdrew suddenly in 1999, apparently as a result of intense criticisms of the project. They were replaced by Petronas and Chevron.

and signed by the President; decrees that are issued by the President or the Prime Minister. Indeed, Article 41 of the Convention entitled 'Applicable Law' provides: 'Cameroon law,[625] the general principles of international law and common practices widely used in the international petroleum industry, shall apply within the scope of this Convention.'

The legal foundations of the whole project were laid down in 1988 in a Convention between Chad and the Consortium granting the Consortium an exploration permit, valid until 2004. The permit was renewed in an additional Convention signed in 2004.[626] In 1996, Chad and Cameroon signed a bilateral treaty that provided for the construction and operation of the pipeline and other oil transportation facilities. In 1998, Cameroon's National Assembly enacted the Convention of Establishment setting out the relationship between COTCO and the Republic of Cameroon. The COTCO Convention[627] is the main contractual document which outlines the rights and obligations of the parties to the Cameroon portion of the project. The Convention itself was established pursuant to Cameroon Law No 96 – 14 of 5 August 1996 governing the Transportation by Pipeline of Hydrocarbons from other Countries. Section 7(b) provides that Companies wishing to engage in the construction, operation and maintenance of a System of Transportation by Pipeline cannot have a right to an Authorization for Transportation by Pipeline and carry out their activities in Cameroon except by virtue of a Convention of Establishment entered into with the State. Section 2(b) of the Law on its part provides that the laws governing the activities of such companies shall be 'the provision of this law, its implementation instruments and Conventions of Establishment'. Thus, it is clear that the applicable laws for

[625]Other Cameroonian laws which apply to activities undertaken under the Convention include: Law No 96/12 of 05 August 1996 relating to Environmental Management, the General Tax Code in force as of 31 December 1994, the Customs Code in force as of 31 December 1994, the Registration, Stamp Duty and Trusteeship Code in force as of 31 December 1994, and all such Cameroonian laws contemplated by article 41 of the Convention. It should, however, be noted that these pieces of legislation apply only to the extent that they are not contrary to or inconsistent with the provisions of the Convention under article 30.1.

[626]Contracting out of Human Rights: The Chad-Cameroon Pipeline Project, Amnesty International Report, September 2005, www.amnesty.org.uk, p. 20.

[627]The COTCO Convention of Establishment is a bilateral agreement between the Republic of Cameroon on the one hand and COTCO on the other hand. It defines the rights and obligations of the parties concerning the operation and maintenance of the pipeline system and oil installations from the border with Chad to the marine terminal off the coast of Cameroon. (One ambiguity of the COTCO Convention is that the Republic of Cameroon which is a party to the contract is also a member of COTCO).

the Cameroon portion of the project are Cameroon Law No 96 – 14 of 5 August 1996 and its applicable instruments as well as the COTCO Convention, which is the main legal framework for the project.

8.1.2.3. Ambiguities in the COTCO Convevtion

A stark ambiguity of the COTCO Convention is that the Republic of Cameroon which is a party to the contract is also a member of COTCO. A perusal of the Convention reveals an imbalance in the rights and obligations of the parties. The COTCO Convention relieves COTCO and more precisely the oil companies from almost all liability for environmental or social damage resulting from the project. The oil companies have employed different methods to avoid liability arising from the project.

Firstly, they have contracted indirectly by setting up the new joint-venture company – COTCO with the government of Cameroon. This means that they are not direct parties to the contract and may escape direct liability for damage they cause during the construction and operation of the pipeline.[628] Thus, liability is ultimately placed disproportionately on Cameroon, while the oil companies enjoy more rights than liability under the Convention. As observed by Horta[629]:

> The proposed arrangement appears to largely free COTCO and more precisely, the oil consortium, of responsibility from environmental damage and social disturbances related to the construction and operation of the pipeline. Ultimately, responsibility is placed squarely on the governments of Chad and Cameroon. The World Bank's explanation is that these are sovereign countries and therefore it is natural that the governments be responsible for projects within their borders.

While agreeing with Horta that governments should be responsible

[628] Furthermore, much of the work on the project is carried out not by the multinational oil companies themselves but by their subsidiaries. For example, Esso Chad, Exxonmobil's subsidiary, is responsible for the exploration, extraction and development of the oil as well as the building of the pipeline. See Contracting out of Human Rights: The Chad-Cameroon Pipeline Project, Amnesty International Report, September 2005, www.amnesty.org.uk, p. 13.

[629] K. Horta, 'The Chad-Cameroon Oil and Pipeline Plans for Environmental Monitoring: Multilayered Conflict of Interest', in S. A. Bronkhorst (ed.), Liability for Environmental Damage and the World Bank's Chad-Cameroon Oil and Pipeline Project, Netherlands Committee for IUCN, The Hague, July 2000, pp. 17–23, at 19.

for projects within their boarders, it may be unacceptable that the entities executing such projects, and who derive a lot of benefits from them, should be allowed to operate in disregard of the national legislation.

A second method used by the oil companies to avoid liability and ensure a minimum of regulation is by including exclusion provisions in the COTCO Convention. Under Article 30.1 of the COTCO Convention, the companies excluded certain relevant national legislation of Cameroon as well as international legislation applicable in the country. Article 30.1 which refers to Cameroon Law No. 96-14[630] and its implementing instruments excludes the above law where there is inconsistency. It states: ' Pursuant to Sections 8 and 73 of Law No 96-14, the parties acknowledge that the provisions of this Convention which are contrary to or inconsistent with Law No 96-14... prevail over the provisions of the said law and its implementing instruments, which are contrary to or inconsistent therewith'. Article 30.2 provides further that, all ordinary law provisions of the Republic of Cameroon which are not contrary to or inconsistent with the provisions of this Convention apply to activities undertaken under this Convention. This provision implicitly excludes all national legislation that conflicts with the provisions of the Convention. The effect of this is to place the Convention above the national laws of Cameroon despite the fact that the former is a private contract.

On its part, Article 30.3 provides that, notwithstanding Article 30.2, the following laws and instruments as well as their implementing instruments do not apply to activities undertaken under this Convention, unless otherwise provided by the Convention or by Law No. 96-14. A list of ten pieces of legislation dealing with mining fees, investment, the storage and distribution of petroleum products and the obligations of companies is then outlined. In addition to national laws, the Convention, under Article 28.4, also excludes relevant international laws to which Cameroon is signatory.

A further imbalance in the Convention relates to the right of automatic renewal by COTCO. The initial duration of the Convention is 25 years from the date of commencement of operations as provided under Article 3.1. This Article states that:

> Upon notification by COTCO to the Republic of Cameroon at least 5 years before the expiry date of its initial period, subject to the right of renunciation referred to in article 39, this Convention shall

[630] Law No 96 – 14 of 5 August 1996 governing the Transportation by Pipeline of Hydrocarbons from other Countries.

> be renewed automatically under the same terms and conditions for a second (25) years.

This right of automatic and unilateral renewal of the Convention by COTCO is clearly unfair. This is further compounded by the parallel and exclusive right of renunciation accorded COTCO under Article 39. The Republic of Cameroon is not given any corresponding rights in the Convention except those under Article 38 which are grossly inadequate and disproportionate. Criticizing COTCO's automatic right of renewal under Article 3, Leubuscher observed that:[631]

> There will be no consultation with affected groups prior to this renewal . . . Thus, if the Cameroon pipeline creates the social disturbance, health problems and environmental degradation that is expected given the potential impacts set out in the Environmental Assessment for the project, it will be extremely difficult for successive Cameroon governments to deal with those problems by modifying the Convention during the next 50 years.

The imbalance in the rights and obligations of the parties in the COTCO Convention, which is the main legal framework for the project, visibly demonstrates the inability or unwillingness of the Cameroon legislature to impose high levels of social responsibility on the multinational oil companies in bilateral arrangements. An examination of the sources of international law can help in determining the acceptability and legality of the exclusion by the oil companies of the national laws of Cameroon. It shows that this act is not concomitant with any internationally recognized practice or principle[632]. Indeed, the general principles of law and custom form part of the applicable law under Article 41 of the COTCO Convention. With regard to treaties, these are a fundamental source of international law and may be multilateral treaties, regional treaties or bilateral investment treaties. It follows therefore that the

---

[631] S. Leubuscher, 'Obligations and possible Liabilities resulting from the COTCO Convention of Establishment', in S. A. Bronkhorst (ed.), Liability for Environmental Damage and the World Bank's Chad-Cameroon Oil and Pipeline Project, Netherlands Committee for IUCN, The Hague, July 2000, pp. 35–41, at 36.

[632] Professor Sornarajah, in his seminal book, The International Law on Foreign Investment, Cambridge University Press, Cambridge, 2004, pp. 87– 96, identifies four sources of international law: treaties, custom, general principles of law and judicial decisions.

relevant multilateral and regional treaties to which Cameroon is a signatory would, *prima facie*, be applicable to the project as sources of law and cannot effectively be excluded by the oil companies.

The absence of an effective legal mechanism in the host countries to control the oil companies in bilateral arrangements means that we must look elsewhere – multilateral legal instruments in public international law and regulation by the home country. The COTCO Convention has revealed the Cameroon legislature as an institution void of any authority, empty of any iota of independence and incapable as a peoples' representative, to oversee and shape the activities of the oil industry. The Cameroon legislature, in any event but also because of the convention, therefore is an ineffective, inefficient and inadequate guarantor of the right to development and right to a healthy environment, which belongs to Cameroonians. In the face of this abandonment by the legislature, the question which deserves attention is whether the judiciary can provide a solution.

8.2. The Role of the Judiciary

It is common knowledge that where there is a right, there should be a remedy capable of enforcement by judicial means. This means that Cameroonians should be capable of enforcing the rights to a healthy environment and to development. For this to be possible, the credibility, predictability and reliability of Cameroon's judiciary system must be detained for questioning. This section argues that the judiciary does not enhance the enjoyment of such rights because of its unpredictable and unreliable nature.

8.2.1. Weaknesses of the Cameroon Judiciary.

It is a settled and well-established rule of international law that before resorting to an international tribunal to redress a grievance against a state for injury on its national(s), that person(s) must first exhaust all available domestic remedies, unless, of course, such remedies are clearly inadequate or their application is unreasonably prolonged.[633] Support for this rule was provided by the Permanent Court of International Justice in the *Interhandel Case (Switzerland v. United States)*, where the Court noted that the "rule that

[633] See generally Restatement of the Foreign Relations Law of the United States, 713, Comment and Reporters' Notes (1987).

local remedies must be exhausted before international proceedings may be instituted is a well-established rule of customary international law."[634] This rule is also recognized by the Banjul Charter and the jurisprudence of the African Commission. Article 56(5) of the Banjul Charter requires the pursuit and exhaustion of domestic remedies before instituting any proceedings before the African Commission.[635] The African Commission recognizes the fact that the requirement to exhaust domestic remedies is a necessary first step before the institution of international proceedings. In this connection, it has advanced three practical reasons.[636] The first of these is the need to "give domestic courts an opportunity to decide upon cases before they are brought to an international forum, thus avoiding contradictory judgments of law at the national and international level."[637] Secondly, that a government against whom a complaint has been brought "should have notice of a human rights violation in order to have an opportunity to remedy such violation, before being called to account by an international tribunal ... The exhaustion of domestic remedies requirement should be properly understood as ensuring that the State concerned has ample opportunity to remedy the situation of which applicants complain."[638] Finally, the requirement of prior exhaustion of domestic remedies before knocking at the door of the African Commission is intended to ensure that the African Commission does not become a "tribunal of first instance for cases which an effective domestic remedy exists."[639]

The International Law Commission's Draft Articles on Diplomatic Protection,[640] which deals with the exceptions to the local remedies rule in its Article 15, outlines five different situations in which local courts offer no prospect of redress. Article 15(a) provides that "local remedies do not need to be

---

[634] See Interhandel (Switz. v. U.S.), 1959 I.C.J. Rep. 6, 26-27 (March 21). For a recent discussion by the World Court of the local remedies rule, see Elettronica Sicula, S.p.A (ELSI) (United States v. Italy), 1989 I.C.J. 15, 28 I.L.M. 1111 (July 20).

[635] See African Charter on Human and Peoples' Rights, June 27, 1981, OAU Doc. CAB/LEG/67/3/Rev.5, reprinted at 21 I.L.M. 58 (1982). The Charter was adopted by the Organization of African Unity on June 27, 1981 and entered into force October 21, 1986. See precisely art. 56(5).

[636] See The Social and Economic Rights Action Center for Economic and Social Rights v. Nigeria, African Commission on Human and Peoples' Rights, Communication No. 155/96, 37-39.

[637] Ibid.

[638] Ibid.

[639] Ibid.

[640] See I.L.C., Draft Articles On Diplomatic Protection, Report Of The I.L.C., 55th Sess. GAOR, 58th Sess., Supp. 10, U.N. Doc. A/58/10, at 76 (May 5-9, 2003).

exhausted where (a) there are no reasonably available local remedies to provide effective redress, or the local remedies provide no reasonable possibility of such remedies."[641] In Commenting on this article, the drafter suggests instances when the requirement of exhaustion of local remedies may be dispensed with: (i) local courts are notoriously lacking in independence; (ii) there is consistent and well-established line of precedents adverse to the claimant; and (iii) the respondent State does not have an adequate system of judicial protection.[642] This draftsman could be focusing on the Cameroon judiciary system in making the comments. This is because the three points highlighted in the comment vividly capture the situation of Cameroon's judiciary system. The Cameroonian courts are notoriously lacking in independence, as there is no real separation of power between the executive and judicial branches of government. In addition, the system of judicial protection is inadequate, given that the courts are over-burdened and corrupt.[643]

8.2.1.1. The Lack of Judicial Independence.

The legal and political context in which justice is administered in Cameroon allows the President of the Republic to wield extraordinary powers at the expense of the judiciary. This subordination of the judicial branch to the will of the presidency goes back to the origins of the Republic. In promulgating the basic law of the land, the constitutional drafters set out to create an "*imperial presidency*"[644] by making this institution the font of a vast array of judicial and non-judicial powers.[645] As a result of this deliberate constitutional engineering, the appointment to and removal from high office under this scheme is by Presidential decree.[646] The President appoints the Prime Minister and other

[641] Ibid.

[642] Ibid.

[643] Ndiva Kofele-Kale, "Asserting Permanent Sovereignty Over Ancestral Lands: The Bakweri Land Litigation Against Cameroon", (2007), Annual Survey of International and Comparative Law.

[644] See e.g., Mbu Etonga, An Imperial Presidency: A Study of Presidential Power in Cameroon, in An African Experiment in Nation Building: The Bilingual Cameroon Republic Since Reunification, 133-158 (Ndiva Kofele-Kale, ed., 1980).

[645] Ndiva Kofele-Kale, "Asserting Permanent Sovereignty Over Ancestral Lands: The Bakweri Land Litigation Against Cameroon", (2007), Annual Survey of International and Comparative Law, at p. 15.

[646] See the 1996 constitution of the Republic of Cameroon as amended.

members of Government (Article 10).[647] None of these executive officers exercise any independent authority since their authority is merely delegated. For example, the prime minister, who is the head of government, is someone who functions only as a "subordinate to assist the President in the exercise of his executive power. He is not a co-beneficiary with the President and his appointment in charge of any departments does not imply an abdication by the President of his power over those departments."[648] Under this kind of system, the final say on domestic remedies, whether of an administrative or legal nature, in the Cameroonian context, is in the hands of the President of the Republic. Although the Constitution provides for a separation of powers among the three branches of government, in reality the Executive overshadows the other two branches. The U.S. State Department describes Executive power in Cameroon as follows:

> The 1972 constitution as modified by 1996 reforms provides for a strong central government dominated by the executive. The president is empowered to name and dismiss cabinet members, judges, generals, provincial governors, prefects, sub-prefects, and heads of Cameroon's parastatal firms, obligate or disburse expenditures, approve or veto regulations, declare states of emergency, and appropriate and spend profits of parastatal firms. The president is not required to consult the National Assembly. The judiciary is subordinate to the executive branch's Ministry of Justice. The Supreme Court may review the constitutionality of a law only at the president's request. [649]

Presidential decisions therefore carry a kind of *res judicata* effect on other state institutions and organs. The doctrine of *res judicata* holds that a matter which has received a final judgment by a court of final jurisdiction, such as the Supreme Court, cannot be opened again for hearing on its merits. This scenario epitomizes the fact that Cameroon's judiciary totally lacks independence,

---

[647] Article 10(1) provides: "The President of the Republic shall appoint the Prime Minister and, on the proposal of the latter, the other members of Government. He shall define their duties. He shall terminate their appointment. He shall preside over the Council of Ministers."

[648] Mbu Etonga, note 638 supra, at 136.

[649] U.S. Dep't of State, Background Notes: Cameroon (Oct. 2006), available at http://www.state.gov/r/pa/ei/bgn/26431.htm.

since it is largely captured by the President of the Republic. In its 1999 Human Rights Report on Cameroon, the United States Department of State described Cameroon's judiciary as one that "cannot act independently and impartially, since all judges and magistrates are directly nominated by the President." The Report goes on to observe that "politically sensitive cases are never heard."[650] Judicial officers owe their appointments to the President (Article 37(3))[651] and serve at his pleasure. This power of appointment and removal is like a sword of Damocles dangling over the heads of judges, ready to descend the moment one of them steps out of line. In theory though, the President is assisted by a Higher Judicial Council in the appointment of members of the bench and officials of the legal department.[652] It is this body, sitting in council, that decides the fate of all judicial officers from judges, magistrates, prosecutors of the Republic, down to senior court registrars. However, this organ, which is responsible for all appointments, promotions and dismissals in the judiciary, is completely under the control of the President, who appoints the majority of its members and presides over all its meetings.[653] The United Nations Human Rights Committee had earlier in 1994 observed that Cameroon's judiciary fails to meet internationally accepted norms of independence. After reviewing Cameroon's 1994 periodic report on the state of human rights in the country, the United Nations Human Rights Committee questioned "the independence of the judiciary. In particular, the composition of the Supreme Council of Magistracy is not such as to guarantee respect for this principle."[654] Five years later in 1999, when considering Cameroon's third periodic report, the United Nations Human Rights Committee again observed that Respondent (Cameroon) still had not addressed all the concerns it had previously expressed in its concluding observations on the second report of 1994.[655]

---

[650] U.S. State Department, 1999 Country Reports on Human Rights: Cameroon (Feb. 23, 2000), available at http://www.state.gov/g/drl/rls/hrrpt/1999/231.htm.

[651] "The President of the Republic shall guarantee the independence of judicial power. He shall appoint members of the bench and of the legal department. He shall be assisted in this task by the Higher Judicial Council which shall give him its opinion on all nominations for the bench and on disciplinary action against judicial and legal officers ...." See Law No. 65 of 96-06 of 18 January 1996 to amend the Constitution of 2 June 1972, Article 37(3).

[652] Ndiva Kofele-Kale, note 603, supra.

[653] Ibid.

[654] U.N. H.R. Comm., Concluding Observations of the Human Rights Committee: Cameroon. 18/04/94, U.N. Doc. CCPR/C/79/Add.33, at 14 (Apr. 18, 1994).

[655] See U.N. H.R. Comm., Concluding Observations of the Human Rights Committee: Cameroon.

The lack of an independent or impartial judiciary severely compromises the competence of any domestic court in handling a case before it. It is therefore very unlikely that any action brought before a court in Cameroon to vindicate the RTD or the right to a healthy environment will succeed. Perhaps the better option may be to seize an international tribunal for example the African Commission on Human and Peoples Rights. However, the African Commission will require the exhaustion of local remedies by the claimant before accepting to entertain the matter.

Arguments presented by the BLCC in the Bakweri Land Litigation against Cameroon,[656] provide an insight on the issue of the supremacy of the Presidency and its dominance over the judiciary in Cameroon.[657] It argued that this supremacy and dominance has given rise to a peculiar form of *de facto* Executive 'preemption' of decision-making by subordinate state organs, regardless of whether there is an actual conflict between them or not. This *de facto* preemptive authority is peculiar for two reasons. First, it is *implied* since the Constitution is noticeably silent on the exercise of such authority. Second, because the underlying constitutional objective of the preemption doctrine is to avoid conflicting regulation of conduct by various official bodies that might have some authority over the same subject matter. In the Cameroon scheme, however, presidential 'occupation' of the judiciary and the legislature has nothing to do with jurisdictional conflicts. Rather, it reflects the wide range of powers, legislative as well as judicial, that the Constitution confers on the President.[658] Presidential 'preemption' of decision-making at all levels and in all areas, judicial as well as non-judicial, operates in much the same way as an ouster clause which bars "the ordinary courts from taking up cases placed

04/11/99., U.N. Doc. CCPR.C.79.Add.116, at 2 (Nov. 4, 1999).

[656] It should be noted that complainants were seeking a declaration from the Government of Cameroon that lands registered in the Imperial German land registers (Grundbuch), occupied by CDC since 1947, and defined as Private Property under Cameroon's 1974 Land Law belong to the Bakweri. However, such an acknowledgment that would bind Respondent State could only come from the authority that issued the 1994 CDC Privatization Decree in the first place, or given on its instructions. That authority being none other than the President and Head of State. Although the President chose not to make such a declaration between 1994 and the filing of the complaint before the Commission, he could have, in theory, been compelled by court order to do so. But such an order, BLCC submitted, was not likely to come from a court system that is under the President's total control and whose judges are personally appointed, promoted or removed, by him. See Ndiva Kofele-Kale, supra, note 603.

[657] Ndiva Kofele-Kale, note 603, supra.

[658] Ibid

before the special tribunals or entertaining any appeals from the decisions of the special tribunals."[659] An examination of the legal effect of "ouster" decrees as was the case in Nigeria's *Ken Saro-Wiwa et al.*, indicate that they tend to "render local remedies non-existent, ineffective or illusory" because they create a "legal situation in which the judiciary can provide no check on the executive branch of government."[660] In practice, presidential preemption ousts the jurisdiction of the ordinary courts thus depriving complainants of effective domestic relief. The involvement of Executive branch officials in *Ken Saro-Wiwa*, illustrates what can happen in Cameroon, where the judiciary has been reduced to impotence, incapable of playing its traditional role of providing a check on the executive branch.

8.2.1.2. The Inadequacy of Judicial Protection

Cameroon does not have an adequate system of judicial protection. On the contrary, there is an implied power of discretion built into the judicial system. Justice, under this discretionary regime is exercised by non-judicial power in a discretionary manner through a process of *de facto* ousting of the jurisdiction of courts. This procedure manifests itself through legal decisions made by ministers and law enforcement officials completely by-passing the courts.[661] In theory as in practice, the President is the Supreme Magistrate

---

[659] See International Pen, Constitutional Rights Project Interights on behalf of Ken Saro-Wiwa Jr. and Civil Liberties Organization v. Nigeria. African Commission on Human and Peoples' Rights, Communication No. 137/94, 139/94, 154/96 and 161/97.

[660] Ibid.

[661] See Ndiva Kofele-Kale, supra, note 603. Hardly a week goes by that the popular press fails to report on this "annoying interference." In an article entitled Criminal Law: A conflict of systems, Asong Ndifor, senior editor of The Herald, offers these examples: "During the trial of SCNC activists in Bamenda in 2001 the legal department wrote to magistrate Abenego Bea instructing him on how to handle the case. He repudiated the instruction and passed his judgement according to the evidence he had. He was later given a punitive transfer to the legal department in Buea. There is also the recent case where a Buea high court ruled that John Niba Ngu should be reinstated as general manager of the Cameroon Tea Estate but the South West legal department rejected the ruling and refused to order execution of the judgement." Asong Ndifor, Criminal Law: A Conflict of Systems, THE HERALD, June 16-17 2003, at 8 (Cameroon). In the Monday, August 11, 2003 edition of The Post newspaper, the Minister of Justice and Keeper of the Seals is reported to have "ordered that all pending matters concerning Beneficial Life Insurance Company be withdrawn from court. This order is contained in a submission filed by the Southwest Attorney General .... The Attorney-General stated in his submission that 'we have instructions from the Hon. Minister of State in Charge of Justice and Keeper of the Seals,

with the power to delegate some of his executive and, by extension, his judicial powers to subordinate officials who act in his name.[662] For instance, sometime in February 2002, the Minister of External Relations represented before another international body that the Government was favourably disposed towards a friendly settlement of the Bakweri matter. This undertaking was clearly meant to signal the Government's preference for a non-judicial resolution. Complainants in good faith relied on this stated preference for a resolution through dialogue to their own detriment. The Minister of External Relations, an official with no independent authority and whose authority is merely delegated, could not have taken such a binding obligation without explicit directives from the presidency. However, the effect of this executive branch official's decision was to preempt other organs of government, including the courts, from looking into the Bakweri land question.[663] The African Commission had the opportunity to pronounce on the discretionary nature of justice, when it described a Governor's power as a "discretionary extraordinary remedy of a non-judicial nature" and ruled that "it would be improper to insist on the complainants seeking remedies from sources which do not operate impartially and have no obligation to decide according to legal principles."[664] It goes without saying that any remedy provided through this source is likely to be neither adequate nor effective.

In Cameroon, courts are overburdened with cases that will take years to clear. For instance, in 1996 the World Bank reported that the number of cases pending before the Cameroon Supreme Court stood at 3,000.[665]

---

that all pending matters in court, whether criminal or civil, touching and concerning the parties in this case be withdrawn from court.'" See Minister Orders Withdrawal of All Beneficial Life Cases, THE POST, No. 0495, Aug. 11, 2003, at p. 2 (Cameroon).

662 Article 10(2) of the 1996 Constitution provides: "The President of the Republic may delegate some of his powers to the Prime Minister, other members of Government and any senior administrative officials of the State, within the framework of their respective duties." See Law No. 65 of 96-06 of 18 January 1996 to amend the Constitution of 2 June 1972, Article 10(2).

663 See note 599, supra.

664 See Constitutional Rights Project v. Nigeria, African Commission on Human and Peoples' Rights, Communication No.60/91

665 See World Bank, Technical Annex To The Memorandum And Recommendation (Report No. P-6928-CM) On A Proposed Credit In The Amount Equivalent To Sdr 8.8 Million To The Republic Of Cameroon For A Privatization And Private Sector Technical Assistance Project, World Bank Rpt No. T-6928-CM, at 6, 25 (May 22, 1996) (commenting on the slowness of the judicial process and observed that in 1996 3000 cases were pending at the Supreme Court).

Unofficial sources however put the number at 4,343 as of June 2003.[666] As an example, in October 1996, a representative of Cameroon appeared before the African Commission, at its 20th Session, urging the Commission to overturn its decision on admissibility in the case of *Annette Pagnoulle (on behalf of Abdoulaye Mazou) v. Cameroon*[667] on the ground that Mazou had not exhausted his domestic remedies, whereas the case had been pending in Cameroon's Supreme Court for four years. Also, before petitioning the African Commission, the case of the *Victims of Post-Electoral Violence in the North West Province v. Cameroon* had languished in the Supreme Court for five years with no relief in sight.[668]

Corruption also contributes to the inadequacy and unpredictability of judicial protection offered by Cameroonian courts. Cameroonian courts have been routinely dismissed by expert observers as well as the general public as corrupt ; they are institutions where justice is for sale,[669] usually to the highest bidder or to barons of the regime. These observations have been made by the highest ranking state official responsible for the judiciary.[670] Even the President

---

[666] See note 603, supra.

[667] See Annette Pagnoulle (on behalf of Abdoulaye Mazou) v. Cameroon, African Commission on Human and Peoples' Rights, Communication No. 39/90.

[668] See Victims of Post-Electoral Violence in the North West Province v. Cameroon, African Commission on Human and Peoples' Rights, Communication No. 272/2003.

[669] For instance, three out of ten Cameroonians polled by Gallup International for Transparency International's 2003 Global Corruption Barometer, singled out the judiciary as the institution from which they would like to eliminate corruption if they were given the opportunity. The July 2002 Gallup survey polled 30,487 people in 44 countries on the following question: "If you had a magic wand and could eliminate corruption from one of the following institutions, what would your first choice be?" The institutions enumerated including among others, the courts, the customs, educational system, medical services, police, etc. Thirty-one percent of the Cameroonian respondents picked out the courts as their first choice with the police coming in a distant second being singled out by only 13.7 per cent of the respondents. The Transparency International Global Corruption Barometer: A 2002 Pilot Survey of International Attitudes, Expectations and Priorities on Corruption, at 29 (July 2003), available at http:// www.transparency.org/content/download/1566/8095/file/barometer2003.en.pdf.

[670] While admitting that the Cameroon judiciary is corrupt, Justice Minister Amadou Ali tries to place the blame elsewhere: "la corruption existe parce qu'elle est entretenue par des corrupteurs, dont beaucoup se recrutent, malheureusement, dans le monde de l'entreprise ... Parce qu'ils veulent a tout prix gagner leurs procès, des chefs d'entreprises approchent des magistrats et leur font des offres alléchantes, les amenant ainsi a rendre des décisions qui, si elles arrangent leurs commanditaires, donnent de la justice camerounaise, l'image d'une justice inapte à soutenir le dévéloppement de l'entreprise et insécurisante pour les investissements." LE MESSAGER, no.

of the Republic has acknowledged that corruption exists in the judiciary system. In his 1999 New Year's Address to the Nation, after lamenting the scourge of corruption which has now spread to all sectors of Cameroonian society, he turned his attention next to "judicial and legal officers whose task is precisely to ensure respect for the rules governing our society." As regards this branch of government, the President observed that:

> "There are still many cases where justice is not rendered as it should. That is to say with dispatch and impartiality, in strict conformity with the laws and procedures in force. This should not be tolerated. Even though I would want to believe so, the majority of our judicial and legal officers are upright, the deviant practices observed may lay the institution open to suspicion ...."[671]

The picture of the judiciary in Cameroon painted herein above suggests that an action, whether collective or individual, to enforce the rights to development and to a healthy environment will yield little or no fruits. Perhaps an action may be brought against an oil MNC for violating the human right to a healthy environment in a U.S. court under the Alien Tort Claims Act (ATCA), which provides an opening for prosecution of behavior that violates international law. However, the practical and legal limits of applying the ATCA to MNCs, casts doubts on the viability of this option. This notwithstanding, the justiciability of economic and social rights is problematic.[672] The examination of the role of the legislature in assisting Cameroonians to enjoy the rights to development and to a healthy environment, indicates that Cameroonians cannot rely on the legislature. Equally, the Cameroonian judiciary system has been shown to be unreliable and unpredictable. Hence, it does not offer any viable mechanism for citizens to enforce their rights. The only other option which consists in bringing actions in the U.S. courts under the ATCA, appears to be doubtful. Thus, Cameroonians may have to look elsewhere for a solution to their problem of enforcing their rights to development and to a healthy environment.

1519/vendredi, 06 juin 2003, at 5

[671] Address by President Paul Biya, The Head of State's New Year Message to the Nation, (Dec. 31, 1999)

[672] Deval Desai, "Courting Legitimacy: Democratic Agency and the Justiciability of Economic and Social Rights", (2010), Interdisciplinary Journal of Human Rights Law.

9

JUSTICIABILITY OF THE RIGHTS TO A HEALTHY ENVIRONMENT AND TO DEVELOPMENT

9.0. Introduction

According to Collier J. and Lowe V.,[673] justiciability refers to the focusing of a disagreement or clash of interests into a concrete dispute, capable of resolution by a judicial process on the basis of the law. A dispute will therefore be justiciable if a specific disagreement exists and that disagreement is of a kind which can be resolved by the application of rules of law by judicial process. This chapter examines justiciability of the rights to development and to a healthy environment. If such rights are not justiciable, then even the most credible judiciary system will have nothing to offer in that respect. On the other hand, if such rights are justiciable, then focus will be on the credibility, predictability and reliability of the judiciary system in dealing with them. This chapter argues that economic and social rights, and consequently the right to development and the right to a healthy environment are justiciable rights. But, since the Cameroon Judiciary system has been portrayed to be unpredictable and unreliable, this chapter equally examines the possibility of instituting actions abroad. The chapter ends by arguing that although Cameroonians have the possibility of instituting actions abroad so as to enforce these rights, there are legal and practical limits on what foreign governments can do in this direction.

[673] The Settlement of Disputes in International Law: Institutions and Procedures, Oxford University Press, (1999) at p. 10.

9.1. Requirements for Justiciability

For the concept of justiciability to be invoked, certain rules must operate. They include the doctrine of locus standi, the exhaustion of domestic remedies, political questions and the lack of sufficient interest in the subject matter.

9.1.1. Locus Standi

This refers to the personal element in the adjudication of disputes. It implies that the litigant must have a legal interest in the subject matter of the dispute, which interest must be real and not merely illusory, and that substantial harm has been suffered. This doctrine was clearly articulated by Justice Brandeis in the following words:

> The court will not pass upon the validity of a statute upon complaint of one who fails to show that he is injured by its operations.... Among the many applications of this rule, none is more striking than the denial of the right to one who lacks a personal or property rights.[674]

The issue of locus standi was raised and discussed in the *Bakweri Lands Claims Committee – BLCC V. Cameroon*[675] where the BLCC filed a complaint under Articles 55, 56 and 58 of the African Charter of Human and Peoples' Rights concerning the violation of the land rights of the Bakweri people. In answer to the complaint, the State of Cameroon argued that the matter be thrown out on grounds inter alia that the BLCC had no locus standi to bring an action on behalf of Bakweri people. The Commission, however, ruled that the BLCC had the locus standi to file the complaint in view of the fact that the counsel and BLCC had been authorized by a resolution of an assembly of chiefs to do so.

---

[674] See Ashwander V. TVA, 297 U.S. 288 (1936).

[675] The African Commission on Human and Peoples Rights in Communication No. 260/2002. It should be noted that complainants were seeking a declaration from the Government of Cameroon that lands registered in the Imperial German land registers (Grundbuch), occupied by CDC since 1947, and defined as Private Property under Cameroon's 1974 Land Law belong to the Bakweri.

9.1.2. Exhaustion of Local Remedies

With respect to the admissibility of complaints in international law, the complainant, as a rule, has to exhaust all local remedies available to him before seeking adjudication by an international court or tribunal. This rule according to Brownlie[676] is justified by practical and political considerations and not by any logical necessity flowing from international law. Thus, where a complaint is brought against a State for transgressing the rights of her citizens, the said state ought to be given an opportunity by the complainant to provide redress under her own legal system. If the State is unable to provide the relief sought, then the complaint may then be brought before an international tribunal or court. In *BLCC V. Cameroon*,[677] a complaint was brought directly before the African Commission on Human and Peoples' Rights in disregard of the exhaustion of local remedies rule. The Commission threw the matter out on the ground that Cameroon had not been given the opportunity to provide local remedies. However, the exhaustion of local remedies rule would be said to have been satisfied if the proceedings are unduly and unreasonably delayed.[678] Where a case had been pending on appeal for over five years, it was held by the Commission that it was unduly delayed and consequently, the complainant will not be required to exhaust local remedies.[679]

9.1.3. Political Questions Doctrine

This doctrine limits the range of issues that the court can entertain. It frees the political branches from judicial review in respect of certain matters.[680] It is not just a question about the precise circumstances in which the courts act, but it represents a judgment that as to certain issues, the government will function best if the political branches operate without any judicial control at all.[681] In many cases, the political question doctrine is merely a confusing and unnecessary way to express the obvious point that the courts should not invent

[676] Principles of Public International Law, 6th Edition, Oxford University Press, (2003), at p. 473.

[677] See Communication No. 287/2004.

[678] Ibid.

[679] Ibid.

[680] Siegel, Jonathan, "A Theory of Justiciability", (1989), Texas Law Review, Vol. 86:73, at p. 74.

[681] Titanji Duga Ernest, "Justiciability of the Rights of Indigeneous Peoples in Municipal and International Law", Unpublished Ph. D thesis, University of Yaounde II SOA, July 2010, at p. 192- 3.

constraints on the political branches where the constitution does not impose any.[682] For a dispute to be justiciable, it must be susceptible of a decision on the basis of law. This means that the dispute must be a legal dispute, to which the court can apply the principle of law. Consequently, purely political questions cannot be justiciable.

9.1.4. Lack of Sufficient Interest in the Subject Matter

Where the claimant has no interest or no sufficient interest in the subject matter of the claim, the dispute will be inadmissible. A complainant may lack sufficient interest with respect to locus standi. In the *Barcelona Traction Case*,[683] Belgium's claim was thrown out on the ground that she lacked sufficient interest in the subject matter of the dispute. The fact that a majority of shareholders were Belgians, did not give Belgium the locus standi to bring an action on behalf of a company which was incorporated in Canada.

If the rights to a healthy environment and to development are to be enforced through adjudication, the complainant should first and foremost make sure that the complaint is justiciable on the basis of the foregoing discussion. Having highlighted the meaning of justiciability, it may now be necessary to examine the controversy surrounding this concept, so as to be able to determine whether Cameroonians can be able to enforce the rights mentioned herein above, by bringing actions before the courts.

9.2. The Justiciability Controversy.

The potential of Economic and Social Rights (ESR) as a tool to ensure the inherent dignity[684] of all has been, to use a popular phrase, "detained for questioning."[685] Over the last sixty years, debate has centered on arguments denying the justiciability and judicial enforcement of Economic and Social Rights. However, the former UN High Commissioner on Human Rights, Louise Arbour, recently stated that "it is now widely recognized that there

---

[682] Henkin, Louis, "Is there a Political Question Doctrine?" (1976), 85 Yale Law Journal, 597,622.

[683] Belgium v. Spain, Second Phase, ICJ Report, 3.

[684] International Covenant on Economic, Social and Cultural Rights (henceforth ICESCR), Preamble, 16 (December 1966).

[685] Deval Desai, "Courting Legitimacy :Democratic Agency and the Justiciability of Economic and Social Rights", (2010), Interdisciplinary Journal of Human Rights Law.

is nothing inherently non-justiciable about economic, social and cultural rights."[686] The enactment of an Optional Protocol on Economic, Social and Cultural Rights, detailing an international "communications procedure" for violations of ESR supports Ms Arbour's contention.[687] However, scholars, nation-states, and courts themselves still argue against the idea that ESR are justiciable rights capable of being adjudicated by the courts of law. Even where objections to ESR's justiciability are overcome, arguments are still made in favour of limiting the scope of judicial oversight, oft-times by the courts themselves.[688]

The assertion that an elected government only, and not the courts, has the absolute and exclusive legitimacy to decide on questions of resource allocation is a sham. Traditional arguments against the justiciability of ESR are rooted in the concept of *democratic deficit*; traditional arguments in favour of ESR are made in terms of a comparative analysis to civil and political rights (CPR). This is based in the concept of the indivisibility of rights. ESR are instruments providing for certain social outcomes.[689] To this extent, they are normative, and are rooted in the presumption of achieving human dignity through every individual's right to minimum levels of certain, interlinked goods, such as food, water, healthcare, education, healthy environment, good roads, and the like. These are to be provided through a combination of the state's direct action and the state putting in place conditions that enable each individual to gain access to the same. Because these social outcomes have some distributive implications, it follows that they impact the social order, and, further, as rights, they exist in law. Michelman asserted that:

> When a legal inquiry will identify ECS Rights as one of those norms to which anyone who aims to be law-abiding should, for that very reason, normally feel a substantial if not decisive pressure to adhere.

[686] High Commissioner backs work on mechanism to consider complaints of breaches of economic, social and cultural rights, United Nations Press Release, 16 July 2007, at www.unhchr.ch/huricane/huricane.nsf/view01/BAB7C795CD5D6F23C125731B004C4E7B? open document (accessed 28 October 2010).

[687] United Nations Department of Public Information, Third Committee Recommends General Assembly Adoption of Optional Protocol to International Convention on Economic, Social and Cultural Rights Press Release GA/SHC/3938 (18 Nov. 2008), www.un.org/News/Press/docs/2008/gashc3938.doc.htm (accessed 28 October 2010).

[688] cf supra note 679.

[689] Ibid.

> To get a norm into law is to produce a state of public affairs in which that sort of pressure can be expected to impinge on whoever is supposed to bear obligations attendant upon the norm.[690]

This argument suggests that there is an expectation upon all arms of the state that they will develop and execute policies in order that, or, more generally, to ensure that social outcomes desired by the citizenry are achieved. The fact that this obligation exists upon the legislative and executive branches is uncontroversial. However, the involvement of the judicial branch has led the intellectual debate onto a more rugged, contested terrain. Indeed, such a line of argumentation comes from those who are extremely positive about civil and political rights (CPR). Aryeh Neier, a notable "believer in very strong civil and political rights," posited in relation to ESR's justiciability as follows:

> ... ESR are unmanageable through the judicial process and that intrudes fundamentally into an area where the democratic process ought to prevail.... The purpose of the democratic process is essentially to deal with two questions: public safety and the development and allocation of a society's resources.... Economic and security matters ought to be questions of public debate. To withdraw either of them from the democratic process is to carve the heart out of that process.... A court is not the place where it is possible to engage in the necessary sort of negotiation and compromise.[691]

These arguments against justiciability lean on the issue of resource distribution and legitimacy and suggest that a court cannot and should not decide on issues of resource distribution because arguably, it is not set up to do so nor does it have the mandate to do so. This appears to be the dominant situation in Cameroon drawing from the fact that this research did not come across any cases in that light. To argue against justiciability is to presuppose that the court is an inappropriate forum to decide questions of public resource-allocation and people's material well-being, which in turn, is to presuppose that the moral and rational approach of a court is *deontological*, while that of the government is *utilitarian*. This implies that the government, with its utilitarian

---

[690] Frank I. Michelman, "Socio economic Rights in Constitutional Law: Explaining America Away" , (2008), 6 INT'L J. CONST. L. 663, 667.

[691] Aryeh Neier, "Social and Economic Rights: A Critique", (2006), 13 HUM. RTS. BRIEF 1, 1-2.

approach, is best placed to deal with public funds as they are limited, and thus a utility-maximizing approach is to be preferred. This traditional deontological/utilitarian distinction between the approaches of the court and legislature means that courts were inherently incapable of allocating resources; however, recent studies show that there is no inherent difference between the possible allocative logics of the court and legislature when dealing with ESR. The courts' decision making, in fact, takes into account a host of factors in the same way that the legislature's does, including popular demands, infrastructural issues, governmental priorities, resource allocation.[692] If the court is in fact capable of executing such an approach, objections to justiciability then fall into two categories: practical and normative. The former set of objections contends that the court lacks sufficient practical capacity to engage in questions of resource allocation. The latter set contends that the judiciary is not competent to rule on ESR matters as they involve budgetary allocation and the running of programmes, which only the legislature and executive are competent to carry out. The implication is that it would not be legitimate for the judiciary to carry out a costing exercise when democratically elected rulers should do so. In this view, the judiciary's role is at best one of oversight. This is the democratic deficit argument. If ESR were to be considered justiciable:

> ... courts would stray too far from their legitimate role in a constitutional democracy if they adjudicated these kinds of rights ... ESR are too vague, costly, and institutionally complex for the judiciary to implement. In order to enforce a housing guarantee in the face of government neglect, for example, courts might have to design housing programs, require money be spent to implement them, and perhaps even take over their administration. Thus, it is argued, that courts cannot enforce ESR without usurping the role of the legislative and/or administrative branches of government ... Yet, even those who argue for a robust judicial role in the enforcement of ESR admit that their full implementation threatens to strain judicial capacities and push boundaries of judicial legitimacy.[693]

---

[692] Varun Gauri & Daniel M. Brinks, Introduction: The Elements of Legalization and the Triangular Shape of Social and Economic Rights, in Varun Gauri & Daniel M. Brinks (eds.), Courting Social Justice 1, 5 (2008).

[693] Alana Klein, "Judging as Nudging: New Governance Approaches for the Enforcement of Constitutional Social and Economic Rights", (2008), 39 Colum. Hum. Rts. L. Rev. 351, 353-4.

Historically, it has been argued and traditionally accepted that socio-economic rights are non-justiciable.[694] Advocates of this position asserted that, while these rights have value as moral statements of a nation's ideals, they should not be viewed as a legal declaration of enforceable rights.[695] Adjudication of such rights requires an assessment of fundamental social values that can only be carried out legitimately by the political branches of government, and the proper enforcement of socio-economic rights requires significant government resources that can only be adequately assessed and balanced by the legislature. Judges and courts therefore, lack the political legitimacy and institutional competence to decide such matters. The argument goes on to assert that economic, social and cultural rights are "aspirational" or "abstract"; they cannot be the subject of either affirmative state obligation or immediate realization and enforcement.

This notwithstanding, if we go by the current UN doctrine which proclaims that all human rights are, "universal, indivisible, interdependent and interrelated,"[696] they must all be accorded equivalent enforcement mechanisms. The heart of this argument, however, lies in the contention that state compliance with economic, social, and cultural rights must be "justiciable", subject to the possibility of formal third-party adjudication, with remedies for findings of noncompliance. Also, both the Indian and South African courts have effectively rejected this non-justiciability argument.[697] To make economic and social rights resonate for the vast majority of the human population for whom these rights are critical, this thesis agrees with the South African Constitutional Court which adopts the "affordability"[698] argument by stating that:

> It is true that the inclusion of socio-economic rights may result in courts making orders that have direct implications for budgetary

[694] Eric C. Christiansen, "Adjudicating Non-Justiciable Rights: Socio-Economic Rights and the South African Constitutional Cour"t, (2007), Columbia Human Rights Law Review.

[695] Ibid.

[696] Vienna Declaration and Programme of Action, pt. I, para. 5, UN Doc. A/CONF.157/23 (1993), 32 ILM 1661 (1993) (adopted at the 1993 World Conference on Human Rights)

[697] See the remarks of former Indian Chief Justice Bhagwati on Public Interest Litigation (PIL) as a necessary tool to foster the enforcement of economic and social rights in the case of People's Union v. Union of India [1983] 1 S.C.R 456, 469.

[698] This argument provides that the enforcement of social and economic rights must be dependent on the capacity of a state to afford the cost entailed.

> matters. However, even when a court enforces civil and political rights such as equality, freedom of speech and the right to a fair trial, the order it makes will often have such implications. A court may require the provision of legal aid, or the extension of state beneficiaries of such benefits. In our view, it cannot be said that by including socio-economic rights within a bill of rights, a task is conferred upon them by a bill of rights that it can result in a breach of the separation of powers.[699]

Indeed, Shadrack Gutto[700] opined that the incorporation of justiciable rights in the Bill of Rights of a constitutional democracy that respects the Rule of Law, under conditions of social inequalities, "... means that such rights and processes of their justiciability are open to all - rich and poor, the advantaged and disadvantaged."[701] According to him, the rich and advantaged are entitled to use the rights to defend their position, while the poor and disadvantaged are entitled to do so in pursuit of their interests to enter the camp of the rich and advantaged and to improve their life conditions."[702] Although Gutto argues that the social actions of all social classes tend to "balance out", the more important issue is that social and economic rights are not obscure entitlements. Such rights can, indeed, be the subject of rights discourse and enforcement at the domestic level. The judgment of the South African court goes a considerable distance in clarifying what has traditionally been an extremely murky terrain.[703]

The African Charter on Human and Peoples Rights has been extolled,[704] particularly with respect to the recognition of economic, social, and

[699] Certification Judgment of the South African Constitutional Court, (10) BCLR P 77. See also Shadrack Gutto, "Beyond Justiciability: Challenges of Implementing/Enforcing Socio-Economic Rights in South Africa", (1998), 4 Buff. Hum. Rts. L. Rev. 79, 89-91.

[700] Shadrack Gutto, "Beyond Justiciability: Challenges of Implementing/Enforcing Socio-Economic Rights in South Africa", (1998), 4 Buff. Hum. Rts. L. Rev. 79, 89-91.

[701] Ibid. at p. 92.

[702] Ibid.

[703] This can also be illustrated by the Indian examples where the process of Social Action Litigation (SAL) has considerably expanded the parameters of the judicial enforcement of human rights. See P.N. Bhagwati, Liberty and Security of the Person in India, with a particular emphasis on Access to Courts, in Developing Human Rights Jurisprudence 203-216 (Commonwealth Secretariat/Inter-rights ed. 1998).

[704] Rose D'sa, "Human and Peoples' Rights: Distinctive Feaures of the African Charter", (1985), 29 J. Afr. Law 72, 72-81.

cultural rights.[705] In this connection, the Charter in its Preamble stipulates that it is "henceforth essential" to pay particular attention to the right to development.[706] In the same vein, it asserts that civil and political rights "cannot be dissociated" from economic, social and cultural rights in conception as well as in universality.[707] The preamble concludes, with an affirmation that "... the satisfaction of economic, social and cultural rights is a guarantee for the enjoyment of civil and political rights."[708] Thus, civil and political rights could therefore not be fully justiciable while social and economic rights are non-justiciable.

Some scholars have argued that all that the African Charter accomplishes is to place economic, social and cultural rights and group ("third generation") rights on the same footing as civil and political rights.[709] Therefore, the Charter has conceptually shifted the emphasis from the traditional focus on civil and political rights alone, to one including economic and social rights.

The justiciability of economic and social rights suggests that an action could be individual or collective. The institution of an individual action poses fewer difficulties than will the institution of a collective action. The institution of a collective action will raise issues of locus standi or standing to sue. An understanding of the issues involved here necessitates an examination of the concept of public law litigation.

9.2.1. Public Law Litigation.

The phrase "public law litigation" is used to refer to the practice of American lawyers seeking to achieve social change through adjudication.[710] The emergence of this kind of litigation in the United States of America is linked to the case of *Brown v. Board of Education of Topeka*.[711] In that case, the

---

[705] Nana K.A. Busia & Bibiane Mbaye, "Filing Communications on Economic and Social Rights under the African Charter on Human and Peoples' Rights (The Banjul Charter)", (1996), 3 E. Afr. J. Peace & Hum. Rts. 191, 191-193.

[706] See Preamble of the Charter. See also Jean-Marie Bernard, International Instruments Relating to Human Rights, (1997), 18 Hum. Rts. L. J. 79.

[707] Ibid.

[708] Ibid.

[709] See supra note 670 at p. 192.

[710] Chayes, A. "The role of the judge in Public Law Litigation", (1976) 89 Harvard Law Review 1281.

[711] (1954), 347 US 483.

U.S. Supreme Court declared unconstitutional state segregation of pupils on the basis of race. The procedural features of this case now form part of public law litigation. In that case, the defendant was a public institution; the claimants were a self-constituted group whose membership changed over time; relief was prospective, seeking to reform future action by government agents; and the judge played a major role.[712] These features clearly show the difference between public interest litigation and the ordinary classical litigation where there is a private bipolar dispute marked by individual participation and the imposition of retrospective relief involving a tight fit between right and remedy.[713]

Public Interest Litigation, which is synonymous with Public Interest Law, is therefore the process whereby organizations or individuals use litigation in the courts to enforce collective rights or to influence social change.[714] There is typically either a single plaintiff who seeks to create a precedent, or a class action of people "similarly situated" as described under the US Federal Rules of Civil Procedure. The class may act as a collective matter, but there is always a clearly identifiable plaintiff, or class of plaintiffs, with classic standing. What makes it public interest is that in a way—but only in a way—the success of the suit is more important to those prosecuting the case than the success of the particular plaintiff. A clear picture of the purpose of Public Interest Litigation was painted by the former Chief Justice of India, P.N Bhagwati in Peoples Union for Democratic Rights and Others in the following terms:[715]

> Public Interest Litigation as brought before the court is not for the purpose of enforcing the right of an individual against another as happens in the case of ordinary litigation, but is intended to promote and vindicate public interest which demands that violations of constitutional or legal rights of large numbers of people who are poor, ignorant or in a socially or economically backward position should not go unnoticed or unredressed.

[712] Herskoff, H " Public Interest Litigation: Selected Issues and Examples", (2000): Available at http://wwwl.worldbank.org/publicsector/legal/access.htm#public (last accessed on 30 October 2010).

[713] Fuller, L. "The Forms and Limits of Adjudication", (1978) 92 Harvard Law Review, 353.

[714] Odhiambo, C. R, The University of Nairobi Law Journal, Vol. 1, 2003, 256 – 266, at 256.

[715] All India Report, 1982 SC 1473.

Public Interest Litigation therefore is the lawyer's response to the violations of the right to development as indicated in the Declaration on the Right to Development, as well as the violation of the right to a healthy environment. It is a form of civil litigation which must be filed and prosecuted in a prescribed form. Such actions take the form of representative suits or class actions. Lord Shand in the case of Duke of *Bedford v. Ellis*[716] pointed out that:

> The rule has been framed and adopted for a useful and important object - the saving of the multiplication of actions with the attendant costs, in cases where one action would serve to determine the rights of persons in question with another party called a defendant. A series of different actions one after another by different plaintiffs as to be no longer necessary in cases where numerous persons have same interest in one cause or matter for, in such cases, one or more of such persons may sue on behalf of or for the benefit of all persons so interested.

The legal difficulties that must be overcome for one to successfully carry out a public interest litigation are the existence of a cause of action and the issue of locus standi.[717]

9.2.1.1. Cause of Action

It is a well settled and established rule of procedure that a court of law will not entertain an action which does not clearly outline a cause of action. In this connection, cause of action has been defined as:

> An act or excision of one party in violation of the legal right or rights of the other, and its essential elements are legal right of the plaintiff, correlative obligation of the defendant and act or omission of the defendant in violation of the said legal right.[718]

The Philippine Supreme Court in the case of *Oposa v. Factoran & Others,*[719] dealt with the issue of cause of action. It not only recognized that the Philippine

---

[716] 1901, AC 1.

[717] Titanji, D. E, Justiciability of the Rights of Indigenous Peoples in Municipal and International Law, Unpublished Ph.D thesis, University of Yaounde II SOA, July 2010, at 216 – 218.

[718] Madrona V. Rosal, 204 SCRA 1 [1991] (Philopmer).

[719] Reported in Judicial Decisions/National Decisions, Vol. 1, at p. 22 – 33.

constitution guarantees the right of citizens to a balanced, ecologically healthy environment, but also that the petitioners in the suit had a valid cause of action to claim under the head of inter-generational responsibility and justice for generations to come. This ruling implies that a court which is seized of a matter may extend its jurisdiction to cover causes of action which prima facie do not expose an immediate cause of action especially in relation to novel collective rights like the RTD and the right to a healthy environment.

9.2.1.2. Locus Standi

The issue which merits attention here is: who has the standing to sue in relation to class actions. All members of the class must have standing – or be deemed to have it. Capacity to sue is a matter of law and fact and not a mere matter of discretion. For one to have the standing to bring a public interest litigation suit, there must exist a special relationship between the plaintiff and the person sued. Such a relationship can be as general as one being a citizen of a country. On the other hand, there does need to be a similarity of circumstances among the members of the class. However, the issue of standing to sue, especially in relation to class actions may be extended to all interested persons, representatives of groups and also to non-governmental organizations. Khamoni J.[720] pointed out that:

> In law, each of the parties ... is a legal person just as each one of the parties in the Notice of Motion before me is. As such, each legal person is capable of suing and being sued in a court of law independently of all the rest ....

On the strength of the foregoing discussions, it is logical that economic and social rights so long as they are collective or group rights, could be enforced through adjudication either by an individual or group of individuals, and either in a domestic or international tribunal. The possibility of the success of such a claim in Cameroon is however slim owing to the weak and unreliable nature of the judiciary system and on the arduous task of satisfying the exhaustion of domestic remedies doctrine. This raises the issue of the possibility of instituting actions abroad.

---

[720] Kenyan case of R v. Minister for Information & Broadcasting & Ahmed Jibril ex Parte EATN.

9.3. Actions Against Oil MNCs in the U.S. for Violating Human Rights Abroad.

A handful of cases proceeding through U.S. federal courts have established the novel proposition that an MNC may be held directly liable for violating some norms of customary international law. These cases are significant because they raise the possibility of using international standards for tort claims against defendants acting in their private capacities, a category of defendants that, under Anglo-American tort principles, includes corporations. This approach uses domestic fora to hold private corporations directly liable for violating international law. Prof. Koh[721] described this as transnational public law litigation, signifying suits brought by individuals in the United States challenging violations of international law. Such litigation seeks redress for individual victims at the same time as articulating a norm of international law that can be applied to non-state violators of international law.[722] This gave rise to the ATCA, a statute that grants U.S. district courts, which are federal courts of first instance, the jurisdiction to hear claims arising from violations of "the law of nations."[723] The ATCA states simply and in its entirety that: "The district courts shall have original jurisdiction of any civil action by an alien for a tort only, committed in violation of the law of nations or a treaty of the United States."[724]

American courts, comfortable with the legal fiction that equates legal individuals (i.e., corporations) *mutatis mutandis* with natural individuals for purposes of civil liability, have expressed no conceptual difficulty using

---

[721] Harold H. Koh, Transnational Public Law Litigation, 100 Yale L.J. 2347, 2349 (1991). In essence, Professor Koh argues that American courts have always addressed international legal concerns, and as matters of policy and history are uniquely well-positioned to continue to do so, not least for their ability to use a number of limiting principles to assure that only meritorious cases are heard.

[722] Ibid.

[723] Alien's Action for Tort (also referred to as the Alien Tort Statute), 28 U.S.C. Sect. 1350 (1994).

[724] Despite several superficial changes to the ATCA's wording, no substantive changes have been made since the statute was enacted as part of the first Judiciary Act, ch. 20, Sect. 9, 1 Stat. 73, 77 (1789). See Anne-Marie Burley, The Alien Tort Statute and the Judiciary Act of 1789: A Badge of Honor, 83 Am. J. Int'l L. 81 (1989), for the ATCA's scope and history. See Anthony D'Amato, The Alien Tort Statute and the Founding of the Constitution, 82 Am. J. Int'l L. 62 (1988); Kenneth C. Randall, Federal Jurisdiction Over International Law Claims: Inquiries Into the Alien Tort Statute, 18 N.Y.U. J. Int'l L. & Pol. 1 (1985)]; Kenneth C. Randall, Further Inquiries into the Alien Tort Statute and a Recommendation, 18 N.Y.U. J. Int'l L. & Pol. 473 (1986), for an overview of different theories about the origins of the ATCA, and Anthony D'Amato, The Alien Tort Statute and the Founding of the Constitution, 82 Am. J. Int'l L. 62 (1988).

the ATCA against private legal entities. Cases brought under the ATCA have suggested that it is possible to maintain a claim against an MNC that has allegedly violated particular norms of international law. However, a number of political, jurisdictional and practical limitations, drawn from international and domestic sources, appear to limit the ATCA's applicability primarily to MNCs based in the U.S., or those MNCs that have significant contacts with the United States.

The statute, which was part of the first Judiciary Act of 1789, was rarely invoked for the first 190 years of its existence.[725] It achieved its iconic status as an instrument of punishing private individuals as human rights violators through the decision in the case of *Filartiga v. Pena-Irala*,[726] and gained new prominence in *Kadic v. Karadzic*.[727] In the absence of precedent, legislative background or Supreme Court[728] authority to establish uniformity, current cases against corporate defendants follow the basic ATCA adjudication laid out in these two cases. A successful claim under the ATCA must present three elements, namely, that an alien has standing to sue, for a tort, committed in violation of the law of nations.[729]

The cases of *Filartiga* and *Karadzic* created solid precedent[730] for applying international human rights norms to domestic adjudication, even where, as

[725]Judiciary Act ch. 20 § 9, 1 Stat. 73, 77 (1789). For an overview of the development of ATCA litigation, see Beth Stephens & Michael Ratner, International Human Rights Litigation in U.S. Courts (1996).

[726] Filartiga v. Pena-Irala, 630 F.2d 876 (2d Cir. 1980).

[727]Kadic v. Karadzic, 70 F.3d 232 (2d Cir. 1995).

[728]The Supreme Court has been taciturn about the ATCA, rejecting the opportunity to review important ATCA cases like Karadzic .

[729]See Kadic, 70 F.3d at 238, (citing Filartiga, 630 F.2d 876). See also Amerada Hess Shipping Corp. v. Argentine Republic, 830 F.2d 421, 425 (2d Cir. 1987).

[730]See note 111, infra. According to one source, an electronic search revealed that 84 cases mention Filartiga, while only one criticized it. Hari M. Osofsky, Note, Environmental Human Rights Under the Alien Tort Statute: Redress for Indigenous Victims of Multinational Corporations, 20 Suffolk Transnat'l L. Rev. 335 (1997) (allegations of corporate abuses in Indonesia and Ecuador) at 360. Among the more prominent decisions are Abebe-Jira v. Negewo, 72 F.3d 844 (11th Cir. 1996) (Nigerian police official who engaged in torture violated customary international law); In re Estate of Ferdinand Marcos Alien Rights Litigation, 25 F.3d 1467 (9th Cir. 1994) (former Phillippine dictator liable for ordering execution of civilians); Xuncax v. Gramajo, 886 F. Supp. 162 (D. Mass. 1995) (Guatemalan official liable for torture); Forti v. Suarez-Mason, 672 F. Supp. 1531 (N.D. Cal. 1987) (Argentinian official liable for torture in violation of international law). See Paul Hoffman, The Blank Stare Phenomenon: Proving Customary International Law in U.S. Courts, 25 Ga. J. Int'l & Comp. L. 181, 188 (1995), on the ATCA's success even before conservative judges.

was the case in *Karadzic*, the defendant is an individual acting in a private capacity.[731] This expansion of the range of international law to cover individual, non-state defendants sets the backdrop for the wave of lawsuits now targeting corporate defendants.

It is necessary to examine some cases where foreign plaintiffs have invoked the ATCA against private corporate defendants.

9.3.1. *The Case Against Unocal and Total*

A group of Burmese residents filed a lawsuit against Unocal in U.S. Federal court in 1996. The plaintiffs alleged that they had suffered human rights abuses such as forced labour, murder, rape and torture in the hands of the Burmese military during construction of a gas pipeline, and that Unocal was complicit in these abuses. Unocal and Burma's military government were in a consortium for the pipeline's construction. The parties reached an out-of-court settlement in which Unocal agreed to compensate the plaintiffs and provide funds for programmes in Burma to improve living conditions and protect the rights of people from the pipeline region. This settlement was accepted by the court, and the case was closed on 13 April 2005.

9.3.2. *The case against Coca-Cola*

The United Steelworkers Union and the International Labor Rights Fund sued the Coca-Cola Company and two of its Latin American bottlers – Bebidas y Alimentos and Panamerican Beverages, Inc. (Panamco) – in July 2001 in US federal court. The lawsuit was brought by the Colombian trade union Sinaltrainal and five individuals and survivors who alleged that the companies hired, contracted with or otherwise directed paramilitary security forces that murdered and tortured the leaders of Sinaltrainal (which represents workers at the bottlers' facilities). The defendant companies argued that the plaintiffs

[731] Alan Frederick Enslen, Note, Filartiga's Offspring: The Second Circuit Significantly Expands the Scope of the Alien Tort Claim Act with Its Decision in Kadic v. Karadzic, 48 A.L.A. L. Rev. 695 (1997) (the court's reasoning is explained in detail); David P. Kunstle, Note, Kadic v. Karadzic: Do Private Individuals Have Enforceable Rights and Obligations Under the Alien Tort Claims Act?, 6 Duke J. Comp. & Int'l L. 319 (1996). But see Justin Lu, Note, Jurisdiction Over Non-State Activity Under the Alien Tort Claim Act, 35 Colum. J. Transnat'l L. 531 (1997) (contrary argument that the Kadic decision was incorrect in extending liability to private, non-state actors).

failed to demonstrate complicity between the companies and the paramilitary security forces. In 2003, the court dismissed the case against Coca-Cola, but it allowed the case to proceed against the two bottlers. The following year the plaintiffs filed an amended complaint seeking to include Coca-Cola in the lawsuit due to its part ownership of Panamco through a 2003 acquisition. In September of 2006, the court dismissed the claims against the two Coca-Cola bottlers and rejected the plaintiffs' attempt to bring Coca-Cola back into the lawsuit. The court held that the plaintiffs' claims did not suffice to allege war crimes under international law, because the plaintiffs did not claim that the abuses occurred in the course of hostilities. It also held that plaintiffs' claims did not suffice to allege violations of other international human rights because the plaintiffs did not claim a sufficiently close relationship between the Colombian Government and the companies' alleged involvement in the abuses. In August 2009, the US Court of Appeals for the Eleventh Circuit affirmed the lower court's dismissal of the lawsuit.

9.3.3. The cases against Texaco/Chevron (re Ecuador)

In 1993, a group of Ecuadorian citizens of the Oriente region filed a class action lawsuit in US federal court against Texaco (*Aguinda v. Texaco*), and in 1994, a group of Peruvian citizens living downstream from the Oriente region also filed a class action lawsuit against Texaco in US Federal court (*Jota v. Texaco*). Both complaints alleged that between 1964 and 1992, Texaco's oil operations polluted the rainforests and rivers in Ecuador and Peru, resulting in environmental damage and damage to the health of those who live in the region. Both lawsuits were dismissed by the US Federal court in 2002, on grounds of forum non conveniens (i.e., the court stated that Ecuador was a more appropriate venue for litigating these claims). In connection with the dismissal, Texaco agreed that courts in Ecuador and/or Peru would have jurisdiction over the plaintiffs' claims.

In 2003, a class action lawsuit was brought against Texaco (acquired by Chevron in 2001) in Ecuador alleging severe environmental contamination of the land where Texaco conducted its oil operation activities. The claimants alleged that this contamination led to increased rates of cancer as well as other serious health problems for the residents of the region. Judicial inspections of the allegedly contaminated sites commenced in August 2004. In early 2008, an independent expert appointed by the court in Ecuador recommended to the court that Chevron should pay $7-16 billion in compensation for the pollution. This expert increased his estimate of damages to $27 billion in November 2008. In 2008, Chevron reportedly lobbied the US Government to end trade preferences with Ecuador over this lawsuit. Following allegations of judicial misconduct, the original trial judge withdrew himself from the case and a new judge was appointed. The new judge has indicated that a verdict is unlikely until some time in 2011. Following a successful petition in a U.S. court to receive unused footage from the documentary "Crude", Chevron filed a petition with the court in August 2010 seeking to dismiss the lawsuit based on the company's assertion that certain parts of this footage show alleged fraud on the part of the plaintiffs. In September 2010, the plaintiffs submitted a new assessment of damages for the claims stating that the cost would be between $90 and $113 billion. In December 2006, and again in September 2009, Chevron filed an international arbitration claim before the Permanent Court of Arbitration at The Hague, alleging that the Government of Ecuador violated an U.S-Ecuador bilateral investment treaty. Chevron claimed that the Government of Ecuador violated international law by unduly influencing the judiciary and thereby compromising the judiciary's independence. In March 2010, the arbitration panel ruled that Ecuador's government had violated the bilateral investment treaty and international law by delaying rulings on the commercial dispute currently pending in Ecuador's courts. The Government of Ecuador and the plaintiffs in the Ecuadorean lawsuit filed a lawsuit in US federal court seeking an injunction barring Chevron from proceeding with arbitration under the bilateral investment treaty. The parties argued that due process rights in Ecuador would be denied should Chevron proceed with its arbitration. In March 2010, the US court ruled that Chevron may pursue international arbitration in this case. The plaintiffs and Government of Ecuador appealed this ruling. In an effort to prove its case, Chevron sued in ten different US Federal courts to try to obtain discovery documents from various consultants.

9.3.4. Chevron lawsuit (re Nigeria)

In 1999, a group of Nigerians of the Niger Delta region, where Chevron engages in oil production activities, brought a lawsuit against Chevron in a US Federal court. The plaintiffs alleged that they suffered human rights violations, including torture and summary execution, at the hands of the Nigerian military and police acting in concert with Chevron to suppress the plaintiffs' protests against Chevron's environmental practices in the Niger

Delta. The claims against Chevron are based on two incidents. First, two members of the protesting group were shot by Nigerian military and police allegedly recruited by Chevron at its Parabe offshore platform. Second, two Nigerian villages, Opia and Ikenyan, were attacked by Nigerian soldiers using helicopters and boats allegedly leased and/or owned by Chevron, and these attacks allegedly caused the death and injury of a number of villagers. In March of 2007, a federal judge dismissed the federal racketeering claims against Chevron, but the judge declined to dismiss the remaining nine claims made by the plaintiffs. In August of 2007, a federal judge issued a series of decisions regarding Chevron's motions for summary judgment. The judge's orders narrowed the lawsuit, but the plaintiffs' central claims regarding Chevron's complicity in human rights violations were allowed to stand. On 1 December 2008, the Federal jury cleared Chevron of the charges in this case. In March 2009, the Federal judge denied the plaintiffs' request for a new trial, finding that the evidence presented at the trial supported the jury's verdict. The plaintiffs filed an appeal with the Ninth Circuit Court of Appeals in April 2009. The Court of Appeals heard the appeal in June 2010. In September 2010, the Court of Appeals issued a decision upholding the verdict of the trial court.

9.3.5. *Wiwa v. Shell*

In 1996, Royal Dutch/Shell was sued in US federal court by Ken Wiwa (son of the late Ogoni activist Ken Saro-Wiwa who was executed in 1995) and other members of the Movement for the Survival of the Ogoni People (MOSOP). MOSOP campaigned against the environmental damage caused by oil extraction in the Ogoni region of Nigeria and for increased autonomy for the Ogoni ethnic group. Ken Saro-Wiwa and other members of MOSOP were detained illegally in 1994, held incommunicado in military custody, then tried by a special court established by the military government using procedures in violation of international fair trial standards, convicted of murder and executed. The plaintiffs alleged that the Nigerian military government and security forces committed human rights violations, including torture and summary execution of MOSOP members, to suppress MOSOP's activities and that Royal Dutch/Shell was complicit in the commission of these abuses. The plaintiffs won several pre-trial rulings, including a motion by the defendants to dismiss the case.

In early June 2009, the parties announced that they had agreed to a settlement in the case for $15.5 million. The settlement provides compensation for the ten plaintiffs and covers a portion of the plaintiffs' legal costs. The settlement also established The Kiisi Trust, intended to benefit the Ogoni people, which will be governed by independent trustees. This trust is to fund initiatives in Ogoni such as education, women's programmes, adult literacy and small enterprise support.

9.3.6. *Kiobel v. Shell*

A related claim was filed by Esther Kiobel, the wife of Dr. Barinem Kiobel – an Ogoni activist who was executed at the same time as Ken Saro-Wiwa. The Kiobel lawsuit was filed against the same defendant companies as the Wiwa lawsuit. This lawsuit alleged Shell, through its Nigerian subsidiary Shell Petroleum Development Company of Nigeria (SPDC), provided transport to Nigerian troops, allowed company property to be used as staging areas for attacks against the Ogoni and provided food to the soldiers and paid them. The plaintiffs claimed the defendant companies were complicit in the commission of torture, extrajudicial killing and other violations, and were liable pursuant to the ATCA. In March 2008, the district court (Second Circuit) granted the defendants' motion to dismiss for lack of personal jurisdiction. On 16th November 2009, the plaintiffs' motion for reconsideration was granted asking the court to re-examine the issue of jurisdiction. The court said in the motion that a direct business relationship between the USA and SPDC must be established in order for ATCA to apply. On 21st June 2010, the district court ruled that the plaintiffs had not shown that this direct business relationship had existed, and the judge dismissed the suit against SPDC.[732] The plaintiffs appealed this ruling, and on 17th September 2010, a three-judge panel of the court of appeals issued a sweeping opinion addressing ATCA lawsuits involving corporate defendants.[733] The majority opinion affirmed lower court's dismissal of the lawsuit, and it also stated that ATCA could not be used to sue corporations for violations of international law. A separate opinion was written by the third judge from the appeals court panel, who concurred with the majority in judgment only. This judge vigorously disagreed with the majority's reasoning; he wrote that the majority's opinion dealt a "substantial blow to international law and its undertaking to protect fundamental human rights." On 14th October 2010, the plaintiffs filed a petition for a rehearing.

---

[732] Business and Human Rights Resource Center, Website, Last visited on November 10, 2010.
[733] Ibid.

9.3.7. Talisman lawsuit (re Sudan)

In 2001, the Presbyterian Church of Sudan, as well as a number of Sudanese individuals, filed a suit in US Federal court against Talisman Energy. They alleged the company's complicity in the Sudanese Government's human rights abuses against non-Muslim Sudanese living in the area of Talisman's oil concession in southern Sudan and that these abuses amounted to genocide. The plaintiffs alleged that the Sudanese Government was engaged in an armed campaign of ethnic cleansing against the non-Muslim Sudanese which included massive civilian displacement, extrajudicial killing of civilians, torture, rape and the burning of villages, churches and crops. The court granted Talisman's motion to dismiss on the 12th of September 2006, finding that the plaintiffs had failed to supply sufficient admissible evidence to permit the lawsuit to go to trial on the plaintiffs' claims.[734] In February of 2007, the plaintiffs appealed this dismissal to the US Court of Appeals for the Second Circuit. On 2 October 2009, the Court of Appeals ruled on this case, and it affirmed the lower court's dismissal of the lawsuit. The Court of Appeals also found that to determine liability under the Alien Tort Claims Act, the plaintiffs must show that the defendant "purposefully" aided and abetted a violation of international law.[735] On 15th April 2010, the plaintiffs filed a petition for *certiorari* with the Supreme Court asking the court to hear an appeal of the lower court's dismissal of the case. On 20th May 2010, Earth Rights International filed an amicus brief with the Supreme Court urging it to hear the appeal and overturn the dismissal of the case. In October 2010, the Supreme Court announced that it would not hear the appeal in this case.[736]

9.3.8. The Rio Tinto Lawsuit

Residents of the island of Bougainville in Papua New Guinea (PNG) filed a suit against Rio Tinto under the Alien Tort Claims Act in the US Federal court in 2000. The plaintiffs alleged that: Rio Tinto was complicit in war crimes and crimes against humanity committed by the PNG army during a secessionist conflict in Bougainville; environmental impacts from Rio Tinto's Panguna

---

[734] http//www.business-humanrights.org/categories/lawsuits/lawsuitsSelectedcases/TalismanlawsuitreSudan#news.

[735] Ibid.

[736] Ibid.

mine on Bougainville were alleged to have harmed the plaintiff's health in violation of international law; and Rio Tinto engaged in racial discrimination against its black workers at Panguna.

In 1988, residents from the Panguna region began protesting Rio Tinto's labour and hiring practices as well as the environmental harm caused by the mine; eventually these protests escalated and some became violent. The PNG Government responded to this uprising with an attack against civilians. A decade-long civil war followed (1989-99), in which Bougainville sought independence from PNG, and during which the plaintiffs alleged that Rio Tinto was complicit in war crimes and crimes against humanity by the PNG army. Rio Tinto sought dismissal of the case, which the district court granted in 2002.[737] Rio Tinto argued in the trial court that the case raised questions that are "nonjusticiable because they involve acts of the state and political questions, and because a ruling on them would breach standards of international comity. The trial court agreed, relying in part on a letter from the US State Department favouring dismissal. The plaintiffs subsequently appealed. In August of 2006, the US Court of Appeals overturned the dismissal; a three-judge panel of the US Court of Appeals rehearing the case confirmed the reversal of the lower court's dismissal in April 2007.[738] The US Court of Appeals, in August of 2007, granted Rio Tinto a rehearing *en banc* with a full panel of 11 judges. In December 2008, the Court of Appeals decided to remand the case back to the district court for the lower court to determine whether the plaintiffs were required to exhaust the remedies in their home country prior to filing the lawsuit in the US.[739] After another rehearing *en banc* before the Court of Appeals on 26th October 2010, the court referred the case to another judge to explore the possibility of mediation. One appeal court judge dissented from this order arguing that it was inappropriate for the court to consider mediation before it determines whether it has jurisdiction over the case.[740]

A cursory look at these cases indicates that foreign plaintiffs can cause U.S. courts to hold corporate violators of international law liable under the ATCA. However, the sweeping opinion of the court in the case of *Kiobel v. Shell* has put to question the strength of the ATCA in providing a remedy to foreign

---

[737] http//www.business-humanrights.org/categories/lawsuits/lawsuitsSelectedcases/RioTintolawsuitrePapuaNewGuinea#news.

[738] Ibid.

[739] Ibid.

[740] Ibid.

plaintiffs. The court stated in this case that the ATCA could not be used to sue corporations for the violation of international law. Perhaps the opinion of the court in this case was informed by the fact that there exists an array of practical and legal limits to the strength of U.S. courts in applying the ATCA.

9.4. Restrictions on the Role of the ATCA

The number of lawsuits brought against oil MNCs in the U.S. courts under the ATCA seem to give the impression that this is a viable solution to foreign litigants who are victims of human rights violations by oil multinational corporations. However, a number of restrictions exist on the extent to which it can play this role. Once a plaintiff manages to craft a complaint whose pleadings sufficiently allege a violation of the law of nations, the corporate defendant can array a number of defenses to challenge the court's jurisdiction or convince the court not to hear the case. All these defenses involve issues normally applicable to any dispute in federal courts, but the extraterritorial nature of ATCA claims, combined with the complications of the MNC form, further limit the applicability of the ATCA. The defenses to be considered here include the defense of personal jurisdiction and that of *forum non conveniens.*

9.4.1. Personal Jurisdiction

In order for federal courts to hear ATCA claims against MNCs, the courts must naturally first establish that they have personal jurisdiction over the defendant. In other words, the issue is one of jurisdiction to adjudicate, establishing a court's authority to hear claims against particular defendants.[741] The key impact of personal jurisdiction requirements for ATCA litigation is that it compels plaintiffs to target the parent body of MNCs , which is more likely to have contacts with the forum state, instead of the MNC subsidiary or affiliate whose actions directly involve the human rights abuse at issue in the case. This requirement is not particularly difficult to satisfy when the defendant

[741] Kenneth C. Randall, Federal Jurisdiction Over International Law Claims: Inquiries Into the Alien Tort Statute, (1985), 18 N.Y.U. J. Int'l L. & Pol. 1 [hereinafter Alien Tort Statute I]; Kenneth C. Randall, Further Inquiries into the Alien Tort Statute and a Recommendation, (1986), 18 N.Y.U. J. Int'l L. & Pol. 473 for an overview of different theories about the origins of the ATCA, and Anthony D'Amato, The Alien Tort Statute and the Founding of the Constitution, (1988), 82 Am. J. Int'l L. 62.

is an MNC headquartered in the U.S., but it can be more problematic in the case of MNCs based outside the United States. [742] Under the U.S. Federal law, asserting personal jurisdiction over an MNC requires either that the suit arises out of the defendant's contacts with the forum ("specific" personal jurisdiction), or that the defendant's contacts with the U.S state are substantial enough to allow jurisdiction even without a direct connection on the subject matter of the suit ("general" jurisdiction).[743]

In *Kiobel v. Shell*, in March 2008, the district court granted the defendants' motion to dismiss the case for lack of personal jurisdiction. On 16 November 2009, the plaintiffs' motion for reconsideration was granted asking the court to re-examine the issue of jurisdiction. The court said in the motion that a direct business relationship between the USA and SPDC must be established in order for ATCA to apply. On 21 June 2010, the district court ruled that the plaintiffs had not shown that this direct business relationship had existed, and the judge dismissed the suit against SPDC.

9.4.2. *The Doctrine of Forum Non Conveniens*

Aside from personal jurisdiction limiting ATCA jurisdiction, another very important practical consideration that might deter a court from hearing a case against a corporate defendant is the doctrine of *forum non conveniens*. This doctrine seeks to protect American courts from wasting their resources on fruitless or needlessly complicated efforts where the complication comes at least in part from the fact that the witnesses are elsewhere, and it can be used to deter victims of human rights abuse from receiving justice.[744]

The doctrine of *forum non conveniens* is a common law doctrine based on

---

[742] Saman Zia-Zarifi, Suing Multinational Corporations in the US for Violating International Law, (1999), Journal of International Law and Foreign Affairs.

[743] John Doe I v. Unocal Corp., 27 F. Supp. 1174, 1184 (C.D. Cal. 1998).

[744] See Daniel J. Dorward, The Forum Non Conveniens Doctrine and the Judicial Protection of Multinational Corporations from Forum Shopping Plaintiffs, 19 U. Pa. J. Int'l Envtl. L. 141 (1998). See also Randall, supra note 23, at 70-71. For contrasting views on the role of this doctrine, compare Cleveland, supra note 98, at 1576-77 (arguing that forum non conveniens has not been very important in ATCA cases and that the doctrine does not conflict with the goals of the ATCA), with Dorward, at 142 (arguing that U.S. courts should continue to develop the doctrine in order to curb international forum shopping and protect MNCs from the burden of defending foreign suits in the U.S.).

the convenience of both parties as well as the court.[745] If a court otherwise has jurisdiction over a lawsuit, it may nonetheless decline jurisdiction if it finds that it can be litigated more efficiently or fairly in another forum. To do so, the court must first determine that an alternate, adequate, forum exists.[746] If such a forum does exist, the court will engage in a balancing test: the court will weigh the plaintiff's choice of forum, private factors (such as ease of access to evidence), and public factors (such as the court's local interest in the case and the burden imposed on the court and community) to determine whether the court should dismiss the case from the plaintiff's chosen forum.[747]

It is likely that the key factor for *forum non conveniens* analyses will be the availability of an alternate, adequate forum. In the *Kiobel v. Shell*, for instance, District Judge Wood dismissed the suit on *forum non conveniens* grounds because she held that England (one of the two corporate headquarters of Shell) provided an alternative forum, despite plaintiffs' claim that they could not raise their claim under English law.[748] Judge Wood opined that the case could be brought in England, even if the likelihood of success was very low, or more accurately, even if the likelihood of failure was nearly certain.[749] This decision seems to draw a fine distinction between being unable to file a case altogether and being able to bring a suit knowing that it will fail under the controlling law, with only the former protecting plaintiffs' case from dismissal on grounds of *forum non conveniens*.

The comparative ease of showing that the U.S. is the forum conveniens for dealing with U.S. MNCs is highlighted by the Unocal litigation. There, the lack of an alternative forum was manifestly clear to the court, as Burma's military government did not provide the court with confidence about the adequacy of Burmese courts as alternate fora.[750] Nevertheless, the Unocal plaintiffs went to some lengths to avoid a dismissal on *forum non conveniens* grounds by

---

745 Piper Aircraft Co. v. Reyno, 454 U.S. 235 (1981).

746 The adequacy of the alternate forum is a matter of some debate. The Supreme Court has stated that:

Where the remedy offered by the other forum is clearly unsatisfactory, the other forum may not be an adequate alternative, and the initial requirement for dismissal, may not be satisfied. Thus, for example, dismissal would not be appropriate where the alternative forum does not permit litigation of the subject matter of the dispute.

747 See supra, note 663, at p. 20.

748 Ibid.

749 Ibid.

750 John Doe I v. Unocal, 963 F. Supp. at 886.

focusing their claim on events in the U.S., alleging that the corporate conduct they challenged (namely, provision of resources to the pipeline project and decision making regarding labour relations on the project) had occurred in the United States, in order to tip the balance of the court's forum non conveniens inquiry in their favour.[751] The court apparently had no problems in weighing this aggregate of factors to decide that it would not dismiss the case on the grounds of *forum non conveniens*.

The case of *Kiobel v. Shell* indicates the limits to ATCA litigation imposed by the forum non conveniens doctrine, namely, that the only cases almost certain to pass this hurdle are those which target a U.S. MNC whose violations occurred in a State with a manifestly unfair legal system. If the MNC is based in a country with a legal system that provides an alternate forum, or if the violations occurred in such a country, then U.S. courts are much more likely to protect their resources and send the case elsewhere. The countervailing factor in this consideration is the unique ability and mission of U.S. federal courts, as mandated by the First Congress, through the ATCA, to address violations of international law.

In fact, *forum non conveniens* and personal jurisdiction considerations which have placed limits on ATCA litigation serve a dual function. Firstly, they protect the resources of American courts and international law from over extensive American civil jurisdiction. While frustrating for human rights advocates, these limitations if judiciously applied, assure that only meritorious cases appear before American courts, and that these courts will not overstep their authority in rendering judgment. The New York district court dismissing the environmental claims against Texaco pointed out that:

> Plaintiffs' imaginative view of this Court's power must face the reality that United States district courts are courts of limited jurisdiction. While their power within those limits is substantial, it does not include a general writ to right the world's wrongs.[752]

In the same light, the federal court in New York, pointed out in the Filartiga case that:

> In the modern age, humanitarian and practical considerations have combined to lead the nations of the world to recognize that respect

[751] Ibid.

[752] Aguinda III, 945 F. Supp. at p. 628.

> for fundamental human rights is in their individual and collective interest.... Our holding today, giving effect to a jurisdictional provision enacted by our First Congress, is a small but important step in the fulfillment of the ageless dream to free all people from brutal violence.[753]

From the foregoing discussion, litigation under the ATCA appears at first blush to offer a welcome relief to Cameroonians contemplating an action against an oil company considered to be violating their human rights. However, the limits to ATCA litigation, together with the sweeping opinion of the court in the case of *Kiobel v. Shell* (that ATCA could not be used to sue corporations for violations of international law), makes the future of this option very bleak.

[753] Filartiga, 630 F.2d at p. 890.

10

RECOMMENDATIONS AND CONCLUSION

10.1. Recommendations

Before making any recommendations, it is important to highlight a success story in the management of the oil industry.

10.1.1. The Norwegian Experience

Norway is a leading oil producer in Europe and the third largest oil exporter in the world.[754] It has proven oil reserves of 10.2 billion barrels.[755] The manner in which Norway has managed its abundant natural resources has raised questions about the existence of a resource curse and has generated discussions on how to handle oil wealth.[756] The Norwegian experience may be very instructive on how to approach natural resource development, leading to the utilization of oil wealth for the benefit of the citizens.

[754] Daphne Eviatar, Petrol Peril: Why Iraq's Oil Wealth May Do More Harm than Good, The Boston Globe, Apr. 13, 2003, available at http:// www.boston.com/news/packages/iraq/globe_stories/041303_ideas2.htm (last accessed on Nov. 11, 2010).

[755] Norway, Energy Information Administration, Country Analysis Briefs available at http:// www.eia.doe.gov/emeu/cabs/norway.html (last accessed on Nov. 11, 2010).

[756] See, e.g., Gavin Wright & Jesse Czelusta, Exorcizing the Resource Curse: Minerals as a Knowledge Industry, Past and Present (Stanford Univ. Econ. Dep't, Working Paper No. 02008, 2002), available at http://www-econ.stanford.edu/faculty/workp/swp02008.pdf (last accessed on 13 Nov., 2010).

Norway became a net exporter of oil in 1976.[757] Its windfall was not at the level of many oil-exporting countries, but this increase still had an effect on the country's economy and polity.[758] Norway's initial reaction to the receipt of revenues from petroleum export, shared some similarities with the experience of other resource-rich countries. Because of steps taken by policy makers in response to increased oil revenues, spending increased, the public sector expanded, and consumption boomed.[759] However, unlike most other oil producers, Norway had adequate institutions at the time oil revenues started flowing.[760] It had the advantage of a vibrant civil service that promoted merit and attracted the best talents in society.[761] Corruption was not a fact of life in the country.[762] The rule of law prevailed; democratic institutions were well-developed, and the people participated actively in determining their destiny.[763] After oil's entrance, Norway did not allow corruption to creep in nor did its political leaders embark on the construction of white elephant projects.[764]

Over time, Norway established a petroleum fund.[765] With the fund in place, oil wealth was stored instead of being used to replace tax revenue.[766]

Another factor that worked to Norway's advantage was the country's cultural homogeneity,[767] which leaves less room for fighting between ethnic groups.[768] Conversely, where there is cultural heterogeneity, as in Cameroon, there is a higher tendency for rival groups to compete for rents and push the country towards a resource curse.[769]

---

757 See, e.g., Terry Lynn Karl, The Paradox of Plenty: Oil Booms and Petro-States 202 (1997), (citing Venezuela's and Iran's decreased reliance on domestic tax revenue as immunizing government officials from accountability to the public).

758 Ibid. at pp. 214-15.

759 Ibid., at pp. 213 – 214.

760 See James A. Robinson et al., Political Foundations of the Resource Curse (Center for Economic Policy and Research, Discussion Paper Series No. 3422, 2002), available at http://ideas.repec.org/p/cpr/ceprdp/3422.html (last accessed on Nov. 11, 2010).

761 Ibid. supra, note 747.

762 Ibid., at p. 217.

763 Ibid.

764 Ibid., at p. 219.

765 Ibid., at p. 220.

766 Ibid.

767 Ibid., at p. 216.

768 See Roland Hodler, The Curse of Natural Resources in Fractionalized Countries 2 (2004), available at http:// www.diw.de/english/produkte/veranstaltungen/epcs/papers/docs/Paper-132.pdf (last accessed on Nov. 11, 2010).

769 Ibid., at 2, 13.

Armed with these auspicious conditions, favourable factors, and carefully designed policies, Norway was able to stave off the harmful rentier behaviour that has been a regular staple in other countries that experienced booms from their resources.[770]

The central lesson that Norway's experience provides a country like Cameroon is that structures matters. The influence of effective institutions is not insignificant. Where appropriate institutions are in place, a state has considerably good prospects of managing the commencement of oil development and greater capacity to handle booms that occur thereafter.[771]

It is, however, a difficult task to compare Cameroon and Norway. Nevertheless, there are two broad lessons that Cameroon can learn from Norway in order to avert, mitigate, or reverse the curse associated with oil resources. These lessons are first, to check rent-seeking through strong institutions and social norms[772] and second, to spend properly oil revenues.[773]

This work proposes the implementation of the concept of trust funds which will handle community development activities. In this connection, it may be necessary to present a general discussion on the concept of Trust and then highlight the trust-like instrument which is used in Chad, as an example which Cameroon can emulate.

---

[770] Ibid., supra, note 751, at p. 219.

[771] Ibid., at 220. Karl further notes:

In Norway, where state capacity is high, such institutions counteracted the temptation to accelerate development, defused potentially divisive political issues through the use of routine procedures, developed clear policy alternatives, corrected mistaken policy decisions, and controlled the spread of rent-seeking behavior.

[772] Before beginning the exportation of oil, Norway already had strong institutions and good social norms. A well-entrenched norm of equality, for instance, may have helped Norway obviate the fractional fights and predatory behavior that characterize other oil exporters, thereby ensuring that its resources constitute a blessing rather than a curse. See Erling Róed Larsen, Escaping the Resource Curse and the Dutch Disease? When and Why Norway Caught Up With and Forged Ahead of Its Neighbors 22 (Statistics Norway Research Dep't, Discussion Paper No. 377, 2004), available at http://www.ssb.no/publikasjoner/DP/pdf/dp377.pdf (last accessed on Nov. 11, 2010).

[773] An ever-present characteristic of states dependant on externally generated rents is unwise spending on white elephant projects instead of investing adequately in the people and infrastructure. While countries like Cameroon waste resources on industrial projects that serve only to benefit corrupt politicians, Norway made huge investments in its citizens. See Erling Róed Larsen, Escaping the Resource Curse and the Dutch Disease? When and Why Norway Caught Up With and Forged Ahead of Its Neighbors 22 (Statistics Norway Research Dep't, Discussion Paper No. 377, 2004), available at http://www.ssb.no/publikasjoner/DP/pdf/dp377.pdf

10.1.2. The Concept of Trust Funds

A trust is an arrangement in law in which legal ownership of an asset, is transferred to a trustee, who becomes responsible for managing the asset for the benefit of another person or persons, as the beneficiaries.[774] Keeton defines a trust in the following words:

> A trust is the relationship which arises wherever a person (called the trustee) is compelled in equity to hold property, whether real or personal, and whether by legal or equitable title, for the benefit of some persons (of whom he may be one and who are termed beneficiaries) or for some object permitted by law, in such a way that the real benefit of the property accrues, not to the trustees, but to the beneficiaries or other objects of the trust.[775]

In the case of oil trust funds, the revenue, or a part thereof, derived from oil exploration and production constitutes the trust assets which a board of trustees is empowered to manage for the benefit of the general population. This concept emerged as a result of deficiencies in the legal mechanisms, instituted for the management of property.[776] Thus, the inadequacies attendant to oil revenue management in Cameroon make this a particularly attractive concept. Lately, trust funds have been attracting attention in academic and policy circles, as pragmatic tools for addressing the unfortunate predicament, generally manifesting in countries blessed with natural resources, especially oil.[777] Stephen Krasner pointed out that:

> Oil has been a curse for the developing countries in which it has been located leading to less democracy and lower rates of growth. Oil concentrates resources in the hands of the state. The road to wealth and power for any ambitious individual leads through the offices of the central government, not through individual

---

[774] Marianne Guerin-McManus, Conservation Trust Funds, 20 UCLA J. Envtl. L. & Pol'y 1, 3 (2001).

[775] L.A. Sheridan & George W. Keeton, The Law of Trusts 5 (Professional Books Ltd. eds., 11th ed. 1983)

[776] See Guerin-McManus, supra note 768, at p. 5.

[777] Stephen Krasner, Troubled Societies, Outlaw States, and Gradations of Sovereignty 41 (July 20, 2002), available at www.sas.upenn.edu/brownecip/200304%20Papers/Krasner%20paper.pdf.

> enterprise or productive economic activity. Oil wealth makes it possible for the state to buy off dissenters, and to build military machines that can be used to repress those who cannot be bought off. Only a few political entities, such as Alaska and Norway, have been able to use oil wealth wisely. Domestic governance in oil rich developing countries could be enhanced by creating oil trusts. The board of directors of such trusts would be composed of national and non-national actors. For instance, national directors could be appointed by the country's parliament or head of state and non-national figures by the World Bank. All oil revenues would be paid into an escrow account in a foreign bank. All transfers from the account would have to be approved by the board of directors of the trust. There might be commitment to using these revenues for specific activities such as health care and education. The trust would monitor the use of the funds after they had been transferred to the national government.[778]

Utilizing trust funds to manage public properties, including natural resources, is not an entirely new phenomenon, nor is the creation of a trust wholly dependent on the mismanagement of resources.[779] A trust fund can be used to accomplish a variety of objectives including the conservation of natural resources,[780] the protection of the environment,[781] and the development of communities.[782] This thesis proposes the creation of trust fund not only because of mismanagement in the oil industry, but also firstly, for the conservation of oil which is an exhaustable resource ; secondly for the protection of the environment so as to enhance an enjoyment of the right to a

[778] Id. The proposal described by Krasner bears significant resemblance to the oil management and monitoring arrangement under the Chad-Cameroon Pipeline Project. See generally Save the Children, Lifting the Resource Curse: Extractive Industry, Children and Governance 11 (2003) (describing the Chad Oil Pipeline Project's revenue management arrangement as an oil trust fund).

[779] Tito et al. v. Waddel et al. (No. 2) [1977] 3 All ER 129 (a dispute over whether the Crown was the trustee of the funds collected from phosphate sale royalties for the inhabitants of an island colony in the Western Pacific).

[780] Guerin-McManus, supra note 768, at p. 8.

[781] Peter H. Sand, Trusts for the Earth: New International Financial Mechanisms for Sustainable Growth, in Sustainable Development and International Law 167-70 (W. Lang ed., 1995).

[782] Kyle W. Danish, International Environmental Law and The "Bottom-Up" Approach: A Review of The Desertification Convention, 3 Ind. J. Global Leg. Stud. 133, 169 n.162 (1995).

healthy environment ; and thirdly for the development of communities so as to enhance an enjoyment of the right to development.

It is important to emphasize that the trust institution is not the exclusive preserve of Western legal systems.[783] African societies have been able to devise trust-like institutions to address particular needs, such as the management of family or communal property.[784] In Amodu Tijani v. Secretary of Southern Nigeria,[785] Viscount Haldane points out that:

> The notion of individual ownership is quite foreign to native ideas. Land belongs to the community, the village or the family, never to the individual. All the members of the community, village, or family have an equal right to the land, but in every case the Chief or Headman of the community or village, or head of the family, has charge of the land, and in a loose mode of speech, is sometimes called the owner. He is, to some extent, in the position of a trustee and as such holds the land for the use of the community or family.[786]

In *Ozomah v. Ozomah*,[787] the court held that the head of the family, who took over the management of a brother's property at his death, was the trustee of the property, where the deceased kinsman died without a son who was sui juris.[788] The trustee is therefore accountable to the 'cestui que trust' until the beneficiary-son comes of age and demands return of the property.

Another justification for the trustee analogy in relation to the position of the head of the family was presented by Graham-Paul J., in *Balogun v. Balogun*,[789] on the grounds that:

> The family head is in charge and control of the family property; he collects the revenue of the family property; he has to make certain disbursements out of the family revenue for family purposes, upkeep of the family property, funeral, marriage and baptism ceremonial expenses of the members of the family often involving

[783] J.O. Fabunmi, Equity and Trusts in Nigeria 144 (1986).

[784] T.O. Elias, Nigerian Land Law 78 (4th ed. 1971).

[785] 2 A.C. 399 (1921).

[786] Ibid. at 404.

[787] M.N.L.R. 88 (1965/66) (mentioned in J.D. Bakibinga, Law of Trusts in Nigeria 5 (1989)).

[788] Ibid.

[789] 2. W.A.C.A. 290 (1935).

the entertainment of strangers, litigations on behalf of the family, maintenance of indigent members of the family, and education of children.[790]

It is important to indicate that under English law, legal ownership of the trust property resides in the trustee, but under Cameroon customary law, the person in the position of trustee is not the owner; the property belongs to the family or community as a whole. Nevertheless, the trustee's duty of management of common property for the general benefit is analogous to that of the English concept of trust. Hence, considering that the essence of the proposed trust funds is the proper management of communal assets by those holding a fiduciary position, it could be submitted that our customary version of trust fits properly.

An example of a trust fund or trust-like arrangement introduced in an African country to ensure the proper management of oil revenue, is the Revenue Management Plan established for the people of Chad under the Chad-Cameroon pipeline project.[791] In addition to recommending this trust-like arrangement for Cameroon, some institution-specific recommendations are also necessary.

10.1.3. Recommendations to the Legislature.

Through their lawmaking functions, legislators can support the passage of laws or other instruments that create an enabling environment for sustainable and accountable management of oil and minerals. For example, recommendations made by the Norwegian Parliament helped determine the appropriate management systems, when large offshore oil and gas deposits were discovered in the late 1960s. The Norwegian legislature continues to play a central role in overseeing management of the extractive industries. The legislatures in a number of countries are improving their ability to fulfill their responsibilities by strengthening committee systems, research and analysis capacity, and rules of procedures. South Africa's National Assembly Research Unit produces briefs for use in reviewing executive branch budget proposals.

[790] Ibid. at p. 299.

[791] The World Bank and IFC Chad-Cameroon: Petroleum Development and Pipeline Project, Project Appraisal Document, Apr. 13, available at http://www-wds.worldbank.org/servlet/WDS_IBank_Servlet?pcont=details&eid=000094946_ 00102111244720.

Nigeria's National Assembly has established a Budget and Research Office to improve its ability to engage the executive, more substantively on budget and public expenditure issues. Consequently, the Cameroon Legislature is called upon to:

- Take advantage of international interest and support for increased transparency and accountability in the management of extractive industries to develop more specialized knowledge of the extractive industry, and become more engaged in management and oversight issues.
- Seek prominent representation on multi-stakeholder bodies, such as local EITI committees, that provide a forum for addressing accountability and management challenges posed by extractive industry activities. Legislators who participate in such groups, should provide regular updates to their colleagues and constituents.
- Develop contacts with international organizations, local advocacy groups and the private sector (which may have developed access to information, normally withheld or not made readily available by governments) to increase the understanding of areas of concern and any policy recommendations made by advocacy groups. Improved cooperation and coordination between civil society, the private sector and legislatures can help transform recommendations into laws and reinforce the legislature's responsibility to represent citizens.
- Establish contact with peers from other resource-rich countries, who confront similar challenges or have played a role in addressing them. The Southern Africa Development Community Parliamentary Forum (SADC-PF), the Global Organization of Parliamentarians Against Corruption (GOPAC) and the Commonwealth Parliamentary Association, are examples of organizations that regularly bring legislators together to share information, best practices and lessons learned on a variety of policy issues.
- Make better use of existing legislative resources to influence policy and conduct oversight activities from standing committees that deal directly with the extractive industry to finance and budget committees that have an impact on revenue management.

Improved utilization of existing resources and even the most limited oversight powers over the short term, can help legislators to build a stronger case for increased resources – whether financial, human or technical – from the medium to long term.

10.2. Conclusion

The issue of Corporate Human Rights violations today is a front page news item in the business world. The debate is no longer, whether human rights issues should be an integral part of the law of the global economy, but how to ensure that the global economy complies with corporate human rights laws. The issue is all the more important in Cameroon today because of the expanding nature of the economy. Recent developments in Cameroon's oil industry bring to sharper focus, the raison d'etre for incorporating human rights issues in the industry's activities. The number of oil companies vying for permits or licences to explore and exploit petroleum, on-shore and off-shore in Cameroon as well as in the Gulf of Guinea, together with the recently constructed Chad-Cameroon pipeline project, are enough reasons to worry about corporate human rights violations. The oil companies involved in these operations have a very high potential to violate the human rights of Cameroonians. The state of the art is that these rights are actually being violated. There exist both domestic and international regulations, as well as private codes of conduct, which provide benchmarks for best practices by corporate entities engaged in the oil industry.

The research gap that this research sets out to fill relates to the reason why in spite of the presence of laws providing benchmarks for best practices, Cameroonians have not witnessed an enhancement in the enjoyment of their human rights to development and to a healthy environment. In an attempt at providing a solution to this problem, this research, based on the Principle of Permanent Sovereignty over Natural Resources, first of all established that oil exploited from Cameroon belongs to Cameroonians with the government being only a trustee who is supposed to manage the revenue for the benefit of the citizenry. The right to development and the right to a healthy environment have been established to be inalienable human rights of Cameroonians which need to be promoted and fulfilled. The research therefore identifies the factors which account for the resource curse in Cameroon to include: regulation (laws), the Social Responsibility of oil multinationals and the state, the enforcement (monitoring) of regulations, Independent legislature, and transparency in the management of the oil industry. Based on the libertarian theory, this thesis has argued that if Cameroonians are involved in the management of the oil industry, they will also derive benefits there from. The role of the legislature has been examined, pointing out that since it seems to be the lapdog of the executive, Cameroonians can not count much on it. The role of the judiciary in enhancing the enjoyment of the rights to development and to a healthy environment, has also been examined with the conclusion that Cameroon has a weak judiciary system wherein the justiciability of human rights is problematic. Hence, the judiciary is wanting in relation to the protection, promotion and fulfillment of the said rights. Equally, the mechanisms for the management of oil revenue have been examined, with keen attention to Cameroon's commitment to the EITI initiative. In this conection, greater commitment to its principles has been recomended.

There is a need for greater monitoring and oversight of the industry. This entails a vibrant and independent legislature, which will propose more effective laws, challenge oil contracts and conventions, with clauses which supersede national laws and require transparency in the management of the oil industry. There is equally a need for an effective judiciary. If comprehensive laws are put in place and the executive and oil companies forced to align with them, then local communities and Cameroonians in general will enjoy the right to development and live in a healthy environment.

If the Cameroon government intends to empower her citizenry and by so doing, achieve sustainable development, then this research work must be given close attention. If that is done, we may succeed in avoiding the kind of sad situations occurring in the oil-rich delta region of Nigeria which seems to be presenting the same characteristic as the Rio del Rey basin, one of Cameroon's three oil fields.

BIBLIOGRAPHY

BOOKS

1. Abram Chayes, *The New Sovereignty: Compliance with International Regulatory Agreements*, Cambridge: Harvard University Press, 1995.
2. AFRODAD, *The contribution of Oil to Debt and Under-Development in Africa: The Case of the Chad-Cameroon Oil Pipeline Project*, 2007.
3. Andrew Clapham, *The Human Rights Obligations of Non- State Actors*, Oxford University Press, 2006.
4. Brierly, L. J : *The Basis of Obligation in International Law*, (1958), Oxford Clarendon Press.
5. Brownlie I., *Principles of Public International Law*, 4th ed. 1990.
6. Burke M. E., *Corporate Community Relations: The Principle of the Neighbour of Choice*, London: Quorum Books, 1999.
7. Collier J. and Lowe V., *The Settlement of Disputes in International Law: Institutions and Procedures*, Oxford University Press, (1999)
8. David Hunter et al., *International Environmental Law and Policy*, (3d ed. 2007)
9. Etikerentse G., *Nigerian Petroleum Law*, MacMillan Publishers, 1985.
10. Francois A., Nah T. F., Simon T.T., *The Law Governing Commercial Companies in the OHADA Zone (A Comparative Study with Ghanian and Nigerian Laws)*, Juriscope, 2010.
11. Frans Viljoen, *International Human Rights Law in Africa*, Oxford University Press.(2007).
12. Global Rights, The Justiciability of Economic, Social, and Cultural Rights in the USA, 2004
13. Jack Donnelly, *Universal Human Rights Theory and Practice*, NY: Cornell University Press, 2004.
14. Lauterpacht, G, *Private Law Sources and Analogies of International Law*, Archon Books, 1970.
15. Mencham K., Ulrich B., Harinder M., and Milan C., *Lifting the Oil Curse: Improving Petroleum Revenue Management in Sub-Saharan Africa*, IMF Washington DC, 2004.
16. Michel Kounou, *Petrole et Pauvrete au Sud du Sahara*, Edition Cle, 2006.
17. Oliver A. Houck, *Environmental Human Rights*, The Tulane Centre for International Human Rights and International Criminal Law, (2010).
18. Paul Sieghart, *The International Law of Human Rights*, The Clarendon Press: Oxford University Press, 1983.

19. Philip Alston and Mary Robinson, *Human Rights and Development: Towards Mutual Reinforcement*, Oxford University Press, 2005.
20. Philip Alston, *Non-state Actors and Human Rights*, Oxford University Press, 2005
21. Rachel Murray, (2004).*Human Rights in Africa: From the OAU to the AU*, Cambridge University Press, 2004.
22. Rene Provost,(2005). *International Human Rights and Humanitarian Law*, Cambridge University Press, 2005.
23. Rodulf Traub-Merz and Douglas Tates, *Oil Policy in the Gulf Of Guinea: Security and Conflict, Economic Growth, and Social Development*, Friedrich Ebert Stiftung (FES), 2004.
24. S. James Anaya, *Indigenous People in International law*, Oxford University Press 2nd Edition, 2004.
25. Shari B, & Barrie H, *Transparency and accountability in Africa's Extractive Industry: The Role of the Legislature*, NDI, 2007
26. Sornarajah, *The International Law on Foreign Investment*, Cambridge University Press, Cambridge, 2004
27. Starmer and Christou, edited by Beattie, Christou, Raymond and Starmer, *Human Rights Manual and Source Book for Africa*, British Institute of International Comparative Law, 2005.
28. Subrata Roy Chowdbury, *The Right to Development in International Law*, Martinus Nijhoff Publishers, 2001.
29. Thomas M. Frank, *Fairness in International Law and Institutions*, Oxford: Clarendon Press,1989.
30. United Nations, *Human Rights, A compilation of International Instruments*, NewYork and Geneva, Vol. I., 2002.
31. Uwafiokun Idemudia, *Community Perceptions and Expectations: Reinventing the Wheels of Corporate Social Responsibility Practices in the Nigerian Oil Industry*, Business and Society Review, Blackwell Publishing, 2007.

ARTICLES, MONOGRAPHS AND EXTRACTS FROM COLLECTIVE WORKS

1. Abram Chayes, "Public Law Litigation and the Burger Court", (1982), *96 Harvard Law Review, 4*
2. Addo Michael, "Human Rights and Transnational Corporations", (1999), *Kluwer Law International.*
3. Alana Klein, "Judging as Nudging: New Governance Approaches for the Enforcement of Constitutional Social and Economic Rights", (2008), *39 Colum. Hum. Rts. L. Rev. 351.*
4. Alexander Kiss, "The Peoples' Right to Self Determination", (1986), *7 Human Rights Law Journal, 165.*
5. Alexandros Zervos, "Linking Natural Resource Exploitation and Primary Health Care in Developing Countries", (2006), *11 UCLA Journal of International Law and Foreign Affairs, 227.*
6. Alice Farmer, "Towards a Meaningful Rebirth of Economic Self-Determination:

Human Rights Realization in Resource Rich Countries", (2006), *39 New York University Journal of International Law and Politics, 417.*

7. Alison Lindsay Shinsato, "Increasing the Accountability of Transnational Corporations for Environmental Harm: The Petroleum Industry in Nigeria", (2005), *4 Northwestern University Journal of International Human Rights.*
8. Ambrose O.O. Ekpu, "Environmental impact of Oil on Water: A Comparative Overview of the Law in the United States and Nigeria", (1995), *24 Denver Journal of International Law and Policy.*
9. Andreanna M. Truelove, "Oil, Diamond and Sunlight: Fostering Human Rights Through Transparency in Revenue from Natural Resources", (2003), *35 Georgetown Journal of International Law, 207*
10. Andrew Clapham and Scott Jerbi, "Categories of Corporate Complicity in Human Rights Abuses", (2001), *24 Hastings International and Comparative Law Review.*
11. Andrew T.F. Lang, "Re-Thinking Trade and Human Rights", (2007), *15 Tulane Journal of International and Comparative Law, 335.*
12. Angela, M. B, "The Emerging Custom of Human Rights-Based Development: A model Agreement for Successful Exploitation of Lake Albert's Oil Reserves", (2009), *32 Boston College International and Comparative Law Review.*
13. Anthony D'Amato, "The Alien Tort Statute and the Founding of the Constitution", (1988), *82 Am. J. Int'l L. 62.*
14. Antoinette Baroni, "Human Rights, Corporate Responsibility – A dialogue", (2000), *(eds) Stuart Rees and Shelley Wright, Australian Journal of Human Rights, Plato Press, Sydney.*
15. Antony Anghie, "'The Heart of My Home'": Colonialism, Environmental Damage, and the Nauru Case", (1993), *34 Harvard International Law Journal, 445.*
16. Anupam Chander & Madhavi Sunder, "The Romance of the Public Domain", (2004), *92 California Law Review, 1331.*
17. Arjun Sengupta, "The Human Right to Development", (2004), *Oxford Development Studies, vol. 32.*
18. Aryeh Neier, "Social and Economic Rights: A Critique", (2006), *13 Human Rights Brief 1.*
19. Audrey Koecher, "Corporate Accountability for Environmental Human Rights Abuse in Developing Nations: Making the Case for Punitive Damages Under the Alien Tort Claims Act", (2007), *27 Journal of Transnational Law and Policy.*
20. Balakrishnan, R. "Corruption, Legitimacy and Human Rights: The dialectic of the Relationship", (1999), *Connecticut Journal of International Law.*
21. Barbara A. Frey, "The Legal and Ethical Responsibilities of Transnational Corporations in the Protection of International Human Rights", (1997), *6 Minnesota Journal of Global Trade, 153.*
22. Beddard Ralph, "Duties of Individuals under International and Regional Human Rights Instruments", (1999), *Human Rights Quarterly, No. 1.*
23. Bede, O.N, "Human Rights and the International Natural Resource Industry. MNCs and the BTC Pipeline Project: Any Hope for Human Rights and Sustainable Development?", (2004), *OGEL, Vol.2, Issue 4.*

24. Ben Sebree, "Oil, Gas and Energy Resources Law", (2009), *72 Texas Bar Journal, 678.*
25. Benedict Kingsbury, "Indigenous Peoples in International Law: A Constructivist Approach to the Asian Controversy", (1998), *92 American Journal of International Law,414.*
26. Berry St. John & Craig Wyman, "Restoration of Oil Field Sites", (1999), *American Bar Association.*
27. Beverly M. Barrett, (1993), "Oil and Gas: Roye Reality v. Watson: Are Royalties owed on All Take-Or-Pay Settlements in Oklahoma?", (1993), *46 Oklahoma Law Review.*
28. Bodansky D., "Protecting the Marine Environment From Vessel-Source Pollution: UNCLOS III and Beyond", (1991), *18 ECOLOGY L.Q. 719.*
29. Boehm A., "Corporate Social Responsibility : a contemporary perspective of community and corporate leaders", (2002), *2 Business and Society Review, 107.*
30. Brownlie, "The Rights of Peoples in Modern International Law", (1985), *9 BULL. AUSTL. SOC'Y LEGAL PHIL. 104.*
31. Carl Bruch, Elana Roffman, Eugene Kim, "Legislative Representation and the Environment in African Constitutions", (2003), *21 Pace Environmental Law Review, 119.*
32. Carlos J. Moreno, "Oil and Gas Exploitation and Production in the Gulf of Guinea: Can the New Gulf be Green?", (2009), *31 Houston Journal of International Law, 419.*
33. Caroline Dommen, "Claiming Environmental Rights: Some Possibilities Offered by the United Nations' Human Rights Mechanisms", (1998), *11 Georgetown International Environmental Law Review.*
34. Caroline Kaeb, "Emerging Issues of Human Rights Responsibility in the Extractive and Manufacturing Industries: Patterns and Liability Risks", (2008), *6 Northwestern University Journal of International Human Rights.*
35. Chayes A. "The Role of the Judge in Public Law Litigation", (2005), *89 Harvard Law Review, 1281.*
36. Christen Broecker, "Better the Devil You Know: Home State Approaches to Transnational Corporate Accountability", (2008), *41 New York University Journal of International Law and Politics, 159.*
37. Christine Bader, "Business and Human Rights: Corporate Recognition and Responsibility", (2008), *China Rights Forum, No. 1.*
38. Christopher C. Joyner, "Biodiversity in the Marine Environment: Resource Implications for the Law of the SEA", (1995), *28 Vanderbilt Journal of Transnational Law.*
39. Christopher M. Larkins, (1996), "Judicial Independence and Democratization: A Theoretical and Conceptual Analysis", (1996), *44 American Journal of Comparative Law, 605.*
40. Christopher M. Ryan, "Discerning the Compliance Calculus: Why States Comply with International Investment Law", (2009), *38 Georgia Journal of International and Comparative Law, 63.*

41. Christopher N. Camponovo, "Dispute Settlement and the OECD Multilateral Agreement on Investment", (1996), *1 UCLA Journal of International Law and Foreign Affairs.*
42. Christopher N. Camponovo, Maria B. Pica, and Bennett Freeman, "A New Approach to Corporate Responsibility: The Voluntary Principles on Security and Human Rights", (2001), *24 Hastings International and Comparative Law Review, 423.*
43. Claire Moore Dickerson, "How do Norms and Empathy Affect Corporation Law and Corporate Behaviour? Human Rights: The Emerging Norm of Corporate Social Responsibility", (2001), *Tulane Law Journal, Vol. 76.*
44. Claire Moore Dickerson, "Cultural and Trans-Border Effects: Northern Individualism Meets Third Generation Human Rights", (2002), *54 Rutgers Law Review.*
45. Claire Moore Dickerson, "Ozymandias as Community Project: Managerial/ Corporate Social Responsibility and the failure of Transparency", (2003), *35 Connecticut Law Review.*
46. Claire Moore Dickerson, "Harmonizing Business Laws in Africa: OHADA Calls the Tune", (2005), *44 Columbia Journal of Transnational Law, 17*
47. Claudio Grossman and Daniel D. Bradlow, "Are We Being Propelled Towards a People Centered Transnational Legal Order?", (1993), *9 American University Journal of International Law and Policy.*
48. Craig Scott, "Translating Torture into Transnational Tort: Conceptual Divides in the Debate on Corporate Accountability for Human Rights Harm", (2001), *Hart Publishing.*
49. Cristina Baez, (1999), "Multinational Enterprises and Human Rights", (1999), *8 University of Miami International and Comparative Law Review.*
50. Cynthia A. Williams, "Civil Society Initiatives and 'Soft Law' in the Oil and Gas Industry", (2004), *36 New York University Journal of International Law and Politics.*
51. Dana L. Clark, "The World Bank and Human Rights: The Need for Greater Accountability", (2002), *15 Harvard Human Rights Journal, 205.*
52. Daniel A. Farber and Philip P. Frickey, "Foreword: Positive Political Theory in the Nineties", (1992), *80 Georgetown Law Journal, 457*
53. Daniel Aguirre, "Multinational Corporations and the Realisation of Economic, Social and Cultural Rights", (2004), *35 California Western International Law Journal, 53.*
54. Daniel C. Turack, "The African Charter on Human and Peoples' Rights: Some Preliminary Thoughts", (1984), *17 Akron Law Review, 379.*
55. Daniel J. Dorward, "The Forum Non Conveniens Doctrine and the Judicial Protection of Multinational Corporations from Forum Shopping Plaintiffs", (1998), *19 U. Pa. J. Int'l Envtl. L. 141.*
56. Daniel J.H. Greenwood, "Democracy and Delaware: The Mysterious Race to the Bottom/Top", (2005), *23 Yale Law and Policy Review, 381.*
57. Daniel Kopec and Philip Peterson, "Crude Legislation: Liability and Compensation under the Oil Pollution Act of 1990", (1992), *23 Rutgers Law Journal.*

58. David D. Caron and Pieter H. F. Bekker, "Land and Maritime Boundary Between Cameroon and Nigeria (Cameroon v. Nigeria; Equatorial Guinea Intervening)", (2003), *97 American Journal of International Law, 387*
59. David J. Halperin, "Human Rights and Natural Resources", (1968), *9 Wm. & Mary L. Rev. 770.*
60. David Kinley and Junko Tadaki, "From Talk to Walk: The Emergence of Human Rights Responsibilities for Corporations at International Law", (2004), *44 Virginia Journal of International Law, 931.*
61. David Marcus, "The Normative Development of Socio-Economic Rights Through Supranational Adjudication", (2006), *42 Stanford Journal of International Law, 53.*
62. David N. Fagan, "Achieving Restitution: The Potential Unjust Claim of Indigenous Peoples Against Multinational Corporations", (2001), *76 New York University Law Review.*
63. David Scheffer, "The Growing Relevance and Enforceability of Corporate Human Rights Responsibility", (2008), *6 Northwestern University Journal of International Human Rights, 218.*
64. Deval Desai, "Courting Legitimacy: Democratic Agency and the Justiciability of Economic and Social Rights", (2010), *4 Interdisciplinary Journal of Human Rights Law, 29.*
65. Dieterich J, "The Gulf of Guinea and the Global Oil Market: Supply and Demand", (2004), *Traub-Merz and Yates, No. 5, 28*
66. Dinah Shelton, "Human Rights, Environmental Rights, and the Right to the Environment", (1991), *28 Standfort Journal of International Law, 103.*
67. Dinah Shelton, "International Decisions: Decision Regarding Communication 155/96 (Social and Economic Rights Action Center/Center for Economic and Social Rights v. Nigeria)", (2002), *96 Am. J. Int'l L. 937.*
68. Dinah Shelton, "What Happened at Rio to Human Rights?", (1992), 3 Y.B. Int'l Envtl. L. 75.
69. Douglas Sanders, "Collective Rights", (1991), *13 Human Rights Quarterly, 368.*
70. Douglass Cassel, "Corporate Initiatives: A second Human Rights Revolution", (1996*), 19 Fordham International Law Journal.*
71. Douglass Cassel, "Corporate Aiding and Abetting of Human Rights Violations: Confusion in the Courts", (2007), *6 NW U. J INT'L Human Rights 218.*
72. Dowling J. and Pfeffer J., "Organisational Legitimacy: Social Value and Organisational Behaviour", (1975), *18 Pacific Sociological Review.*
73. E.S Nwauche, (2007), "A Bill of Rights as the Basis of a Common Law in a Pluralist Nigeria", (2007), *African Journal of Legal Theory, Vol. 1*
74. Edwin Mujih, "The Regulation of Multinational Corporations operating in Developing Countries: A Case Study of the Chad-Cameroon Pipeline Project", (2004), *Social Responsibility International Journal.*
75. EI-Obaid Ahmed EI-Obaid and Kwadwo Appiagyei-Atua, "Human Rights in Africa – A New Perspective on Linking the Past to the Present", (1996), *41 McGill Law Journal, 819.*
76. Emeka Duruigbo, "Multinational Corporations and Compliance with

International Regulations Relating to the Petroleum Industry", (2001), *7 Annual Survey of International and Comparative Law, 101.*
77. Emeka Duruigbo, "Managing Oil Revenue for Socio-Economic Development in Nigeria: The Case for Community-Based Trust Funds", (2004), *30 North Carolina Journal of International Law and Commercial Regulation, 121.*
78. Emeka Duruigbo, "The World Bank, Multinational Oil Corporations, and the Resource Curse in Africa", (2005), *26 University of Pennsylvania Journal of International Economic Law.*
79. Emeka Duruigbo, "Permanent Sovereignty and Peoples' Ownership of Natural Resources in International Law", (2006*), 38 George Washington International Law Review.*
80. Emeka Duruigbo, "Corporate Accountability and Liability for International Human Rights Abuses: Recent Changes and Recurring Challenges", (2007), *6 NW U. J INT'L Human Rights 218.*
81. Emeka Duruigbo, "The Global Energy Challenge and Nigeria's Emergence as a Major Gas Power: Promise, Peril or Paradox of Plenty", (2009), *21 Georgetown International Environmental Law Review, 395*
82. Emeka Duruigbo, "The Global Energy Challenge and Nigeria's Emergence as a Major Gas Power: Promise, Peril or Paradox of Plenty?", (2009), *21 Georgetown International Environmental Law Review, 395*
83. Emmy B. Simmons, "Linking Trade and Sustainable Development: Key Note Address", (2003), *18 American University International Law Review, 1271.*
84. Enyinna S. Nwauche, "Ethnicity, Human Rights and Constitutionalism in Africa", Ed. George M. Wachira, (2008), *6 Minn. J. Global Trade.*
85. Eric C. Christiansen, "Adjudicating Non-Justiciable Rights: Socio-Economic Rights and the South African Constitutional Court", (2007), *38 Columbia Human Rights Law Review.*
86. Eric C. Christiansen, "Adjudicating Non-Justiciable Rights: Socio-Economic Rights and the South African Constitutional Court", (2007), *Columbia Human Rights Law Review.*
87. Eric Engle, "Extraterritorial Corporate Criminal Liability: A remedy for Human Rights Violations?", (2006), *20 Saint John's Journal of Legal Commentary.*
88. Francis Nguendi Ikome, "Conflict in the Niger Delta of Nigeria: Issues and Dynamics", (2005), *Institute for Global Dialogue, Issue No. 44.*
89. Frank I. Michelman, "Socioeconomic Rights in Constitutional Law: Explaining America Away", *(2008), 6 INT'L J. CONST. L. 663.*
90. Frederick Tung, "Before Competition: Origins of the Internal Affairs Doctrine", (2006), *32 Journal of Corporation Law, 33.*
91. Frey Barbara, (1997), "The Legal and Ethical Responsibilities of Transnational Corporations in the Protection of International Human Rights", (1997), *6 Minnesota Journal of Global Trade.*
92. Fuller, L. "The Forms and Limits of Adjudication", (1978), *92 Harvard Law Review, 353.*
93. Genoveva Hernandez Uriz, "To Lend or not to Lend: Oil, Human Rights and the

World Bank's Internal Contradictions", (2001), *14 Harvard Human Rights Journal.*
94. Genoveva Hernandez Uriz, "The Application of the World Bank Standard to the Oil Industry: Can the World Bank Group Promote Corporate Responsibility?", (2002), *28 Brooklyn Journal of International Law.*
95. George Kell, Corporate Citizenship: Defining the New Responsibilities, (2000), Chatham House.
96. Greta Gainer, "Nationalization: The Dichotomy Between Western and Third World Perspectives in International Law", (1983), *26 Howard Law Journal, 1547.*
97. Gunther Handl, "Controlling Implementation of and Compliance with International Environmental Commitments: The Rocky Road from Rio", (1994), *5 Colorado Journal of International Environmental Law and Policy, 305*
98. Hari M. Osofsky, "Learning from Environmental Justice: A New Model for International Environmental Rights", (2005), *24 Stan. Envtl. L.J. 71.*
99. Harold Hongju Koh, "Why Do Nations Obey International Law", (1997), *106 Yale Law Journal, 2599.*
100. Harry A. Inman, (1989), "Harnessing International Law to Restrain and Recapture Indigenous Spoliations", (1989), *83 American Journal of International Law, 56.*
101. Henkin, Louis, "Is there a Political Question Doctrine?" (1976), *85 Yale Law Journal.*
102. Hilmy Ismail, "Forum Non Conveniens, United States Multinational Corporations, and Personal Injuries in the Third World: Your Place or Mine?", (1991), *11 Boston College Third World Law Journal, 249.*
103. Ibibia Lucky Worika, "Deprivation, Desspoliation and Destitution: Whither Environment and Human Rights in Nigeria's Niger Delta?", (2001), *Journal of International and Comparative Law.*
104. Ibrahim F. I. Shihata, "Implementation, Enforcement, and Compliance with International Environmental Agreements- Practical Suggestions in Light with World Bank's Experience", (1996), *9 Georgetown International Environmental Law Review, 37.*
105. Idris M. Diaz, "Human Rights, Multinational Business and International Financial Institutions", (1994), *88 American Society of International Law Proceedings, 271.*
106. Iris Halpern, "Tracing the Contours of Transnational Corporations' Human Rights Obligations in the Twenty-First Century", (2008), *14 Buffalo Human Rights Law Review, 129.*
107. Isabella D. Bunn, "The Right to Development: Implications for International Economic Law", (2000), *15 American University International Law Review, 1425*
108. Iveta Hodkova, "Is There A Right to a Healthy Environment in the International Legal Order?", (1991*), 7 Connecticut Journal of International Law, 65.*
109. James C. Owens, "Government failure in Sub-Sahara Africa: The International Community's Option", (2003), *43 Virginia Journal of International Law, 1003*
110. James N. Hyde, "Permanent Sovereignty over Natural Wealth and Resources", (1956), *50 Am. J. Int'l L. 854.*
111. James T. McClymonds, "The Human Right to a Healthy Environment: An International Legal Perspective", (1992), *37 New York Law School Law Review, 583.*

112. Jamie Mayerfeld, "The Democratic Legitimacy of International Human Rights Law", (2009), *19 Indiana International and Comparative Law Review, 49*
113. Jan Wouters & Leen Chanet, " Corporate Human Rights Responsibility: A European Perspective", (2007), *6 NW U. J INT'L Human Rights 218.*
114. Jason Lloyd, "Let There Be Justice: A Thomistic Assessment of Utilitarianism and Libertarianism", (2003), *8 Texas Review of Law and Politics, 229.*
115. Jay G. Martin and Ann L. MacNaughton, "Sustainable Development: Impacts of Current Trends on Oil and Gas Development", (2004*), 24 Journal of Land, Resources and Environmental Law, 257.*
116. Jean Paillusseau, "Entreprise, Societe, actionnaire, salaries, quell rapports?", (1999), *Recueil Dalloz.*
117. Jenkins H., "Corporate Social Responsibility and the Mining Industry: Conflicts and Constructs", (2004), *11 Corporate Social Responsibility and Environmental Management Journal 1.*
118. Jennifer A. Downs, "Note, A Healthy and Ecologically Balanced Environment: An Argument for a Third Generation Right", (1993), *3 Duke Journal of Comparative & International Law, 351.*
119. John Hare, "Port State Control: Strong Medicine to Cure a Sick Industry", *(1997), 26 GA. J. INT'L & COMP. L. 571.*
120. John Lee, "The Underlying Legal Theory to Support a Well-Defined Human Right to a Healthy Environment as a Principle of Customary International law", (2000), *25 Columbia Journal of Environmental Law, 283.*
121. Jonathan I. Charney, "The Marine Environment and the United Nations Convention on the Law of the Sea", (1994), *28 International Lawyer, 879.*
122. Jonathan R. Siegel, "A Theory of Justiciability", (2007), *86 Texas Law Review.*
123. Jonathan Wolff, "Libertarianism, Utility, and Economic Competition", (2006), *92 Virginia Law Review, 1605.*
124. Joshua P. Eaton, "The Nigerian Tragedy, Environmental Regulation of Transnational Corporations, and the Human Right to a Healthy Environment", (1997), *15 Boston University International Law Journal, 261*
125. Judith Kimerling, "Indigenous Peoples, Transnational Corporations and Sustainable Development in Amazonia", (2002), *27 Columbia Journal of Environmental Law.*
126. Judith Kimerling, "Rights, Responsibilities and Realities: Environmental Protection Law in Ecuador's Amazon Oil Fields", (1995), *2 Sw. J.L. & Trade Am. 293.*
127. Julia Swanson, "The Emergence of New Rights in the African Charter", (1991), *12 New York Law School Journal of International and Comparative Law, 307.*
128. Juliette, B, "Multinational Corporations, Social Responsibility and Conflict", (2002), *Journal of International Affairs, vol.55, No.2*
129. Justice Albie Sachs, "Social and Economic Rights: Can they be made Justiciable", (2000), *53 SMU Law Review, 1381.*
130. K. Horta, 'The Chad-Cameroon Oil and Pipeline Plans for Environmental Monitoring: Multilayered Conflict of Interest', in S. A. Bronkhorst (ed.), *Liability*

for Environmental Damage and the World Bank's Chad-Cameroon Oil and Pipeline Project, Netherlands Committee for IUCN, The Hague, July 2000

131. Kaniye S.A. Ebeku, "Biodiversity Conversation in Nigeria: An Appraisal of the Legal Regime in Relation to the Niger Delta Area of the Country", (2004), *16 Journal of Environmental Law.*
132. Karin Mickelson, (1998), "Carrots, Sticks or Stepping Stones: Differing Perspectives on Compliance with International Law", *in* TRILATERAL PERSPECTIVES ON INTERNATIONAL LEGAL ISSUES: FROM THEORY INTO PRACTICE (1998), *35 ,Thomas J. Schoenbaum, et al. eds.*
133. Karol N. Gess, "Permanent Sovereignty Over Natural Resources: An Analytical Review of the United Nations Declaration and Its Genesis", (1964), *13 ICLQ 398.*
134. Kathleen Morris, "The Emergence of Customary International Law Recognising Corporate Liability for Violations of International Human Rights and Environmental Law" (2008), *11 Gonzaga Journal of International Law 4*
135. Keba M'Baye, "Le Droit au Developpement Comme un Droit de L'Homme", (1972), *5 Revue des Droits de L'Homme, 503.*
136. Kenneth A. Shepsle, "Congress is a 'They,' not an 'it': Legislative Intent as Oxymoron", (1992), *12 International Review of Law and Economics, 239.*
137. Kenneth C. Randall, "Federal Jurisdiction Over International Law Claims: Inquiries Into the Alien Tort Statute", (1985), *18 N.Y.U. J. Int'l L. & Pol. 1*
138. Koriambanya S. A Carew, (2002), "David and Goliath: Giving the Indigenous People of the Niger Delta a Smooth Pebble- Environmental Law, Human Rights and Re-Defining the Value of Life", (2002), 7 Drake Journal of Agricultural Law 493.
139. Lachs, "Development and General Trends of International Law in Our Times", (1980), *169 RECUEIL DES COURS 2.*
140. Larisa Wick, (2003), "Human Rights Violations in Nigeria: Corporate Malpractice and State Acquiescence in the Oil Producing Deltas of Nigeria", (2003), *12 Michigan State Journal of International Law, 63*
141. Larry Alexander and Maimon Schwarzschild, "The Uncertain Relationship Between Libertarianism and Utilitarianism", (2000), *19 QLR, 657.*
142. Li-ann Thio, "Battling Balkanization: Regional Approaches Toward Minority Protection Beyond Europe", 43 Harvard International Law Journal, 409, (2002)
143. Lorne S. Clark, "International Law and Natural Resources", (1977), *4 Syracuse Journal of International Law and Commerce, 377.*
144. Louis B. Sohn, "The New International Law: Protecting the Rights of Individuals Rather than States", (1982), *32 American University Law Review, 1.*
145. Luis E. Cuervo, "OPEC From Myth to Reality", (2008), *30 Houston Journal of International Law, 433.*
146. Lynn Berat, "Defending the Right to a Healthy Environment: Toward a Crime of Genocide in International Law", (1993), *11 B.U. Int'l L.J. 327.*
147. Makau wa Mutua, "The Banjul Charter and the African Cultural Fingerprint: An Evaluation of the Language of Duties", (1995), *35 Virginia Journal of International Law, 339.*

148. Mark J. Kadish, "Article 36 of the Vienna Convention on Consular Relations: A Search for the Right to Consul", (1997), *18 Michigan Journal of International Law, 565.*
149. Matthew Bennett, "Two Branches on the Same Tree: Libertarian Perspectives of a Small Town Market", (2001), *12 Journal of Contemporary Legal Issues, 3.*
150. Matthew H. Kramer and Hillel Steiner, "Theories of Rights: Is There a Third Way", (2007), *27 Oxford Journal of Legal Studies, 281.*
151. Melissa Robbins, "Powerful States, Customary Law and the Erosion of Human Rights Through Regional Enforcement", (2005), *35 Cal. W. Int'l L.J. 295.*
152. Meron Theodore, "State Responsibility for Violation Human Rights", (1989), *American Society of International Law, Proceedings of 83rd Annual Meeting.*
153. Michael Anderson, "Transnational Corporations and Environmental Damage: Is Tort Law the Answer?", (2002), *41 Washburn Law Journal, 399*
154. Michael J. Dennis, David P. Stewart, "Justiciability of Economic, Social, and Economic Rights: Should the Be an International Complaints Mechanism to Adjudicate the Right to Food, Water, Housing, and Health?", (2004), *98 American Journal of International Law, 462*
155. Michael S. Straubel, "Textualism, Contextualism and the Scientific Method in Treaty Interpretation: How Do We Find the Shared Intent of the Parties?" (1994), *23 Wayne Law Review, 111.*
156. Micheal W. Reisman, "Institutions and Practice for the Restoration and Maintaining Public Order", (1995), *6 Duke Journal of Comparative and International Law, 175.*
157. Moderator Thomas M. McDonnell, "Human Rights and Non-State Actors", (1999), *11 Pace International Law Review, 205.*
158. Muchlinsk Peter, "Human Rights and Multinationals: Is there a problem?", (2001), *77 International Affairs, No. 1.*
159. Nana K. A. Busia & Bibiana Mbaye, "Filing Communications on Economic and Social Rights under the African Charter on Human and Peoples' Rights (The Banjul Charter)", (1996), *3 East African Journal of Peace and Human Rights, 191.*
160. Nasi J., S. Nasi, N. Phillips and S. Zyglidopoulos, "The evolution of corporate responsiveness: an exploratory study of Finnish and Canadian forestry companies," (2003), *3 Business and Society Review 36.*
161. Ndiva Kofele-Kale, "Patrimonicide: The International Economic Crime of Indigenous Spoliation", (1995), *28 Vanderbilt Journal of Transnational Law, 45.*
162. Ndiva Kofele-Kale, (2000), "The Right to a Corruption-Free Society as an Individual and Collective Human Right: Elevating Official Corruption to a Crime Under International Law", (2000), *34 International Law Journal. 149.*
163. Neil A. F. Popovic, "In Pursuit of Environmental Human Rights: Commentary on the Draft Declaration of Principles on Human Rights and the Environment", (1996), *27 Columbia Human Rights Law Review, 487.*
164. Nsongurua J. Udombana, "Towards the African Court on Human and Peoples' Rights: Better Late than Never", (2000), *3 Yale Human Rights and Development Law Journal, 45.*

165. Nsongurua J. Udombana, "Between Promise and Performance: Revisiting States' Obligations Under the African Human Rights Charter", (2004), *40 Stan. J. Int'l L. 105.*
166. Nwobike J.C and Wokocha R.A, "Privileging Investor Rights over Public Interest: The Human Rights Implications of the Chad/Cameroon Convention of Establishment ", (2006), *Centre for African Legal Studies.*
167. O'Keefe P.J., "The United Nations and Permanent Sovereignty Over Natural Resources", (1974), *8 Journal of World Trade Law, 239.*
168. Oben P. M., "A Survey of Environmental Management System initiatives in Industries along the Atlantic coast of Cameroon", (2006), *International Journal of Sustainable Business.*
169. Oloka-Onyango J, "Reinforcing Marginalized Rights in an Age of Globalization: International Mechanisms, Non-State Actors, and the Struggle for Peoples' Rights in Africa", (2003), *18 American University International Law Review, 851.*
170. Oloka-Onyango J., (2000), "Human Rights and Sustainable Development in Contemporary Africa: A New Dawn, or Retreating Horizons", (2000), *6 Buffalo Human Rights Law Review, 39.*
171. Oscar Omar Salazar-Duran, "A Human Rights Approach to Corporate Accountability and Environmental Litigation", (2009), *43 University of San FRANCISCO Law Review, 733.*
172. Patrick Macklem, "Indigenous Rights and Multinational Corporations at International Law", (2001), *24 Hastings International and Comparative Law Review, 475*
173. Patrick Macklem, (2008), "Indigenous Recognition in International Law: Theoretical Observations", (2008), *30 Michigan Journal of International Law.*
174. Paul Hoffman, "The Blank Stare Phenomenon: Proving Customary International Law in U.S. Courts", (1995), *25 Ga. J. Int'l & Comp. L. 181, 188.*
175. Pemmaraju Sreenivasa Rao, "Multiple International Judicial Forums: A Reflection of the Growing Strength of International Law or Its Fragmentation?", (2004), *25 Michigan Journal of International Law, 929.*
176. Peter Eigen, (2007), "Fighting Corruption in a Global Economy: Transparency Initiatives in the Oil and Gas Industry", (2007), *29 Houston Journal of International Law, 327.*
177. Peter J. Spiro, (1997), "New Players on the International Stage", (1997), *2 Hofstra Law and Policy Symposium, 19.*
178. Peter Jones, "Human Rights, Group Rights and Peoples' Rights", (1999), *21 Human Rights Quarterly, 80.*
179. Peter Vallentyne, "Left Libertarianism and Private Discrimination", (2006), *43 San Diego Law Review, 981.*
180. Philip Alston, "The Shortcomings of a "Garfield the Cat" Approach to the Right to Development", (1985), *15 California West International Law Journal, 510.*
181. Philip M. Nichols, "Corruption in the World Trade Organisation: Discerning the Limits of the World Trade Organisation's Authority", (1996), *28 New York University Journal of International Law and Politics, 105.*

182. Philip M. Nichols, "GATT Doctrine", (1996), *36 Virginia Journal of International Law, 379.*
183. R. Shep Melnick, "Statutory Reconstruction: The Politics of Eskridge's Interpretation" (1995), *84 Georgetown Law Journal, 91*
184. Raidza Torres, "The Rights of Indigenous Populations: The Emerging International Norm", (1991), *16 Yale Journal of International Law, 127.*
185. Randy E. Barnett and Douglas B. Rasmussen, "The Right to Liberty in a Good Society", (2001), *69 Fordham Law Review, 1603.*
186. Reisman W. Michael, "Sovereignty and Human Rights in Contemporary International Law", (1990), *84 American Journal of International Law, 866.*
187. Richard Desgagne, "Integrating Environmental Values into the European Convention on Human Rights", (1995), *89 American Journal of International Law, 263*
188. Richard Gittleman, "The African Charter on Human and Peoples' Rights: A Legal Analysis", (1982), *22 Virginia Journal of International Law, 667.*
189. Richard N. Kiwanuka, (1988), "The Meaning of 'Peoples' in the Charter on Human and Peoples' Rights", (1988), *82 American Journal of International Law, 80.*
190. Robert Dufresne, "The Opacity of Oil: Oil Corporations, Internal Violence, and International Law", (2004), *36 New York University Journal of International Law and Politics.*
191. Roscoe E. Hill, "Legal Validity and Legal Obligation", (1970), *80 Yale Law Journal, 47.*
192. Rudolf Dolzer, "Permanent Sovereignty over Natural Resources and Economic Decolonization", (1986), *7 Human Rights Law Journal, 217.*
193. Ruth Gordon, " Racing U.S. Foreign Policy", (2003), *17 Nat'l Black L.J. 1*
194. S. Leubuscher, 'Obligations and possible Liabilities resulting from the COTCO Convention of Establishment', in S. A. Bronkhorst (ed.), *Liability for Environmental Damage and the World Bank's Chad-Cameroon Oil and Pipeline Project*, Netherlands Committee for IUCN, The Hague, July 2000
195. Saman Zia-Zarifi, "Suing Multinational Corporations in the US for Violating International Law", (1999), *4 UCLA Journal of International Law and Foreign Affairs, 81.*
196. Samuel K.B. Asante, "The Concept of Stability of Contractual Relations in the Transnational Investment Process", in Legal Aspects of the New International Economic Order 234, 234-(1980), *35 Kamal Hossain ed.*
197. Seth P. S., "Dimensions of Corporate Social Responsibility: An Analytical Framework," (1975), *3 California Management Review 17.*
198. Shadrack B. O. Gutto, (1998), "Beyond Justiciability: Challenges of Implementing/Enforcing Socio-Economic Rights in South Africa", (1998), *4 Buffalo Human Rights Law Review.*
199. Siegel, Jonathan, "A Theory of Justiciability", (1999), *Texas Law Review, Vol. 86*
200. Sinclair M.B.W. , "Legislative Intent: Fact or Fabrication?", (1997), *41 New York Law School Law Review, 1329*
201. Smith M. B. E, (1973), "Is There a Prima Facie Obligation to Obey the Law?", *82 Yale Law Journal, 950.*
202. Sol Picciotto, "Rights, Responsibilities and Regulation of International Business", (2003), *42 Columbia Journal of Transnational Law, 131.*

203. Stephen M. Schwebel, 'The Story of the U.N.'s Declaration on Permanent Sovereignty over Natural Resources", (1963), *49 A.B.A.J. 463.*
204. Stephen McCaffrey, "Liability for Environmental Damage and the World Bank's Chad-Cameroon Oil and Pipeline Project", (2001), *14 Transnational Lawyer, 73.*
205. Stephen P. Marks, "Emerging Human Rights: A New Generation for the 1980's?", (1981), *33 RUTGERS Law Review 435.*
206. Stephen Marks, "The Human Right To Development: Between Rhetoric and Reality", (2004), *17 Harvard Human Rights Journal, 137.*
207. Steven P. Croley, "Libertarianism as Critical Theory", (1996), *1 Michigan Law and Policy Review, 179.*
208. Steven R. Ratner, "Corporations and Human Rights: A Theory of Legal Responsibility" (2001), *11 Yale Law Journal.*
209. Suchman M. C., "Managing Legitimacy: Strategic and Institutional Approaches," (1995), *4 Academy of Management Review 3.*
210. Sumudu Atapattu, "The Right to a Healthy Life or the Right to Die Polluted?: The Emergence of a Human Right to a Healthy Environment Under International Law", (2002), *16 Tulane Environmental Law Journal.*
211. Tawny Aine Bridgeford, "Imputing Human Rights Obligations on Multinational Corporations: The Ninth Circuit Strikes Again in Judicial Activism" (2003), *18 American University International Law Review, 1009.*
212. Terry Collingsworth, "The Key Human Rights Challenge: Developing Enforcement Mechanisms", (2002), *15 Harvard Human Rights Journal.*
213. Theo van Boven, "The Relations Between Peoples' Rights and Human Rights in the African Charter", (1986), *7 Human Rights Law Journal, 183.*
214. Thomas A. Campbell, "The Public Trust, What's its Worth?", (1994), *34 Natural Resource Journal, 73.*
215. Tibor R. Machan, "Considerations of the Libertarian Alternative", (1979), *2 Harvard Journal of Law and Policy, 103.*
216. Troy Rule, "Using 'Norms' to Change International Law: UN Human Rights Laws Sneaking Through the Back Door?", (2004), *5 Chicago Journal of International Law, 325.*
217. U. O. Umozurike, "The African Charter on Human and Peoples' Rights", (1983), *77 American Journal of International Law, 902.*
218. Viljam Engstrom, "Who is Responsible for Corporate Human Rights Violations?", (2002), *Abo Akademi University, Institute for Human Rights.*
219. Virally, "Panorama du droit international contemporain: Cours général de droit international public", (1983), *183 RECUEIL DES COURS 9.*
220. Waddock A. S. and Boyle M., "The Dynamics of Change in Corporate Community Relations", (1995), *37 California Management Review.*
221. William W. Enders, "The oil Pollution Act of 1990: The Financial Responsibility Requirement- Questioning Congressional Intent and the Management Service Interpretation of 'Offshore Facility'", (1995), *23 Virginia Environmental Law Journal.*

THESIS

1. Dieudonne Alemagi, Towards a Comprehensive Strategy for the Effective and efficient Management of Industrial Pollution Along the Atlantic Coast of Cameroon, Faculty of Environmental Science and Process Engineering of the Brandenburg University of Technology Cottbus, Ph.D Thesis, 2006
2. Lorenzo Cotula, Property rights, negotiating power and foreign investment: An international and comparative law study on Africa, University of Edinburgh – School of Law, PhD Thesis, 2009.
3. Mesenbet Assefa Tadeg, The Right to Development as a Normative Framework for the Human Rights Obligations of International Financial Institutions, Faculty of Law, University of Pretoria, LL.M Thesis, 2008.
4. Titanji Duga Ernest, "Justiciability of the Rights of Indigeneous Peoples in Municipal and International Law", Unpublished Ph. D thesis, University of Yaounde II SOA, July 2010

WORKING PAPERS, REPORTS, PRESENTATIONS AND MANUALS

1. Albert G. Zeufack, Governance and Oil Revenue in Cameroon, GDN Tenth Annual Conference, 'Natural Resources and Development', February 1 – 5, 2009, Kuwait.
2. Amnesty International, 'Contracting Out of Human Rights: The Chad-Cameroon Pipeline Project', September 2005.
3. Anna E. Gouwenberg, 2009, The Legal Implications of the Right to Development, Grotious Centre for International Legal Studies-Leiden University.
4. Brown, Halina Szejnwald, Martin de Jong, and Teodorina Lessidrenska. 2007. "The Rise of the Global Reporting Initiative (GRI) as a case of Institutional Entrepreneurship." Corporate Social Responsibility. Working Paper No. 36. Cambridge,MA: John F. Kennedy School of Government, Harvard University.
5. Eye On EITI, Civil Society Perspectives and Recommendations on the EITI, Publish What You Pay, 2006
6. Felix Kirchmeier, 2006, The Right to Development – Where do we Stand? Occassional Paper Published by Friedrch Erbert Stiftung.
7. Feyide M.O. , 2007, "Oil in World Politics", Proceedings of 1986 Public Lecture at University of Lagos.
8. Fitzgerald E.V.K., 'Regulating Large International Firms', UNRISD Programme on Technology, Business and society, Paper No. 5, November 2001
9. Greg Muttitt, 2005, Production Sharing Agreements: Privatisation by Another Name? Paper presented to the General Union of Oil Employees' Conference on Privatisation, Basrah, Iraq
10. INTERNATIONAL MONETARY FUND, 2007. Guide on Resource Revenue Transparency
11. Jenkins R., 'Corporate Code of Conduct: Self Regulation in a Global Economy', UNRISD Programme on Technology, Business and Society. Paper No. 2. April 2001.

12. Joseph Kiarie Mwaura, (2008). " Corporate Human Rights Norms and the Clog Limited Liability Within Corporate Groups: Towards an International Convention", Human Rights Program at Harvard Law School Working Paper.
13. K. Mate, Communities, Civil Society Organisations and the Management of Mineral Wealth, Mining, Mineral and Sustainable Development, International Institute for the Environment and Development, World Business Council for Sustainable Development, No. 16 (2002)
14. Kirsten Bindemann, 1999, Production Sharing Contracts: An Economic Analysis, Oxford Institute for Energy Studies.
15. O.S. Olusi, "Nigerian Oil Industry and the Environment", Proceedings of the 1981 International seminar, Lagos, Nigeria, NNPC 1981
16. Stephane Cosse, 2006, Strengthening Transparency in the Oil Sector in Cameroon: Why Does it Matter? IMF Policy Discussion Paper.
17. The Gulf of Guinea Citizens Network A Regional Advocacy Project

INTERNET SOURCES

1. www.wbes.org
2. http://www.law.northwestern.edu/journal/jhr/r6/n2/1
3. http://www.worldbank.org/faudd/English/0696/article/08069.htm
4. http://www.gasandoil.com/ogel/samples/frearticles/articles32.htm
5. http://www.tufts.edu,stories/091603oilcurse.htm
6. http://www.thefrontiertelegraph.com/content/oil_oil_in_our_land.html
7. www.waado.org/environment
8. http://www.unilorin.edu.ng/unilorin/publications
9. http://www.imf.org/external/np/sec/2000/pn0062.htm
10. http:// www.hrw.org/press/2000/06/ang0622.htm
11. http:// www.transparency.org/working_papers/cockcroft/cockcroft.html
12. http://africanpress.wordpress.com/2008/04/12/cameroon-signs-oil-production-sharing-contract
13. http://www.oilvoice.com/n/Perenco_Signs_ProductionSharing_Contract_in_Cameroon/db5
14. http://www.oas.org/juridico/English/treaties/a-52.html
15. www.cidh.org/annualrep/2004eng/Belize.12053eng.htm
16. http:// www.unep.org/Documents.
17. http://www.rigzone.com/news/article.asp?a_id
18. http://www.kosmosenergy.com
19. http://www.kosmosenergy.com/cameroon.html
20. http:// www.undp.org/humandev
21. http://www.postnewsline.com/2005/07/limbe_industrial.html
22. http:// www.dfid.gov.uk/pubs/files/eitidraftreportstatement.pdf
23. http://www1.umn.edu/humanrts/africa/comcases/155-96.html
24. www.eitransparency.org
25. www.worldbank.org/wbi/governance
26. www.snh.cm

27. www.spm.gov.cm
28. http://www.globalwitness.org/reports/show.php/en.0043.html
29. http:// www.publishwhatyoupay.org
30. at http:// www.chevrontexaco.com/cr_report/social_issues/ethics/revenue_transparency.asp
31. http://www.globalwitness.org/press_ releases/display2.php?id=217.
32. http:// www.dfid.gov.uk/pubs/files/eitidraftreportstatement.pdf
33. http://www.g8.fr/evian/extras/506.pdf
34. http://edennewspaper.net/index.php?
35. http://www.dfid.gov.uk/news/news/files/eiti_draft_report_isis.htmtop
36. http://www.hrw.org/wr2k2/pdf/business.pdf.
37. http:// www.dfid.gov.uk/News/News/files/eiti_guide_b.pdf
38. http://www.eiticameroon.org
39. www.amnesty.org.uk
40. http:// www.globalreporting.org/about/brief.asp
41. http www.globalreporting.org
42. http:// www.globalreporting.org/guidelines/
43. http:// www.exxonmobil.com/corporate
44. http://www.iied.org/mmsd/mmsd_pdfs/marshall_corruption.pdf
45. http://www.edf.org/pubs/reports/c_chadcam
46. www.worldbank.org/pics/pidcm51059.txt
47. www.edf.org/pubs/Reports/chadcam.html.
48. http://www.worldbank.org/afr/ccproj/project/pro_overview.htm
49. www.unhchr.ch/huricane/huricane.nsf/view01/BAB7C795CD5D6F23C125731B004C4E7B?
50. www.un.org/News/Press/docs/2008/gashc3938.doc.htm
51. http://wwwl.worldbank.org/publicsector/legal/access.htm#public
52. http://www.state.gov/r/pa/ei/bgn/26431.htm.
53. http://www.state.gov/g/drl/rls/hrrpt/1999/231.htm.
54. http://www.transparency.org/content/download/1566/8095/file/barometer2003.en.pdf

NEWS PAPERS

Asong Ndifor, 'Criminal Law: A Conflict of Systems', THE HERALD, June 16-17 2003

LE MESSAGER, no. 1519/vendredi, 06 juin 2003.

Michael Peel, 'Oil Curse' Stalks Africa's Newest Petro-State, Financial Times, January 27, 2005.

Milton Friedman, The Social Responsibility of Business is to Increase its Profit, N. Y. Times Magazine, September 13, 1970.

THE POST, No. 0495, August 11, 2003 (Cameroon)